Navigating Global Environmental Sustainability

Navigating Global Environmental Sustainability

Enriching Well-Being in the Wake of the Great Recession

Bret L. Billet

LEXINGTON BOOKS
Lanham • Boulder • New York • London

Published by Lexington Books
An imprint of The Rowman & Littlefield Publishing Group, Inc.
4501 Forbes Boulevard, Suite 200, Lanham, Maryland 20706
www.rowman.com

86-90 Paul Street, London EC2A 4NE

British Library Cataloguing in Publication Information Available

Library of Congress Cataloging-in-Publication Data

Names: Billet, Bret L. (Bret Lee), author.
Title: Navigating global environmental sustainability : enriching well-being in the wake of the great recession / Bret L. Billet.
Description: Lanham, Maryland : Lexington Books, 2023. | Includes bibliographical references and index. | Summary: "The impact of the 2007-2009 Great Recession on the consumption of vital environmental services is evaluated via the testing of two ecological theories, Ecological Modernization and Ecological Unequal Exchange. The incorporation of Aristotelean well-being, a large number of cases, and multiple country subsets, contribute to a rich and robust analysis"-- Provided by publisher.
Identifiers: LCCN 2023017411 (print) | LCCN 2023017412 (ebook) | ISBN 9781498579575 (cloth) | ISBN 9781498579582 (epub)
Subjects: LCSH: Sustainability--Economic aspects. | Global Financial Crisis, 2008-2009--Environmental aspects.
Classification: LCC HC79.E5 B547 2023 (print) | LCC HC79.E5 (ebook) | DDC 338.9/27--dc23/eng/20230626
LC record available at https://lccn.loc.gov/2023017411
LC ebook record available at https://lccn.loc.gov/2023017412

For My Family
Paula, Brandon, Brittany, Gemma, Baltar, and Tinker
I Love You Intensely, Without Reservation, One and All

Contents

Acknowledgments

The year was 1974, the global population had just surpassed a *meager four billion*, and I had started to travel to destinations previously only imagined. While these new cultures provided unlimited fascinations to contemplate, I have always given priority to exploring how the community/country respects and nurtures its children and the environment, for these are typically decent markers in understanding additional facets of the greater culture. These fascinations have been, in part, borne out of the Lakota precept that Earth *must* be treated well *because it is simply on loan to us* by our children. That children and the environment are interdependent, that the future well-being of each is premised on that of the other, is certainly a debatable proposition albeit one that many consider largely indisputable.

Fast forward to June 21, 2011. The United Nations General Assembly, acting on the recommendation of the Security Council, unanimously appointed Ban Ki-moon to a second term as secretary-general. Exactly three months later, Ban would deliver the "We the Peoples" address to the Sixty-Sixth General Assembly. While notable for several reasons, the speech was perhaps highlighted by Ban's call for "Sustainable Development Goals" as a reflective continuation of the Millennium Development Goals, which would conclude in 2015. This appeal aligned with what Ban envisioned to be the most critical of his "five imperatives . . . five generational opportunities to shape the world of tomorrow": *sustainable development.* Inter alia, Ban stated that sustainable development requires such interdependent goals as "saving our planet, lifting people out of poverty, advancing economic growth . . . [and] sustainable energy for all." The idea that these considerations are not mutually exclusive was far from unique; they certainly gave credence to the argument for the interdependence of children and the environment. Ban bolstered the importance of achieving these goals by reminding members that the following month would see a child born who would symbolically denote a world population of *seven billion.*

Fast forward again. As I sit writing in 2023, world population has recently surpassed *eight billion*, double what it was when I first started traveling the globe, taking account of children and the environment that they have lent to their parents. There is no denying the positive advances vis-à-vis the global environment that have occurred during these past fifty years. My summary estimation, however, is that this time has been considerably more favorable to the goals of advancing economic growth and nonsustainable energy supplies, with significantly less regard for posterity and the environmental assets that children will have lent to their parents. For reasons that will be clear in the coming pages, this competing preoccupation with nonsustainable energy supplies and economic growth should not be surprising, as it is constantly reflected in our behaviors. A simple example will suffice. With every new year comes a bevy of toasts for the future: "here's to prosperity," "to friendship," "to personal health," "to financial success," "to happiness," "to the future of our children," and so forth. What is never present, however, is a toast in recognition of a globally sustainable environment that can provide for our needs. Even when *The Sustainable Development Goals Report 2022* cast grave doubt as to successful completion of the goals by 2030 and stated that "an urgent rescue effort for the SDGs" is needed, there is still no recognition of our interdependence.

I would like to acknowledge the past, present, and future of the global sustainable environment. Please forgive our repeated lapses in being good stewards of your gifts, our crippling demands in advancing excessive economic growth, our continual opposition to productive adaptation, and our obstinate ignorance of our interdependence. Here's to you, the global sustainable environment!

More conventionally, I would like to acknowledge those who have provided me with constructive feedback, encouragement, and/or patience as I composed. My sincere thanks to Victoria "Rose" Dietz for her quality feedback on the first two chapters. I am also greatly indebted to Dr. Gregory Fulkerson for his review and thoughtful commentary on the whole of the manuscript. The final product has been improved immensely due to their efforts. My spouse, Paula, participated in several discussions that facilitated increased clarity of my thoughts and encouraged me to think about alternatives and to remember that life doesn't exclusively revolve around my writing. Similarly, I am forever indebted to her and the rest of my immediate family for their encouragement, for being desperately patient with me, and for understanding my need to create. I am also indebted to many of my students in my Environmental Politics and Policy course over the years who provided an astute insight, a spark for a fiery idea, or a level of passion for the environment that rejuvenated my own enthusiasm. It was at these times that I knew my learning had a positive effect on theirs. Finally, I am greatly appreciative of the team at Lexington Books, including Joseph Parry and Anna Debiec, for their invaluable guidance throughout the process. As usual, however, any errors of omission and/or commission rest entirely with me. To all my family, friends, and colleagues, Godspeed.

List of Acronyms

AAAD	Average of Annual Aggregated Data
AFYPG	Average Five-Year Percentage Growth
BASIC	Brazil, South Africa, India, China
BNA	Basic Needs Approach
CA	Capabilities Approach
CFC	Chlorofluorocarbon
CO_2	Carbon Dioxide
CORE	Core country subset
CWE	Capitalist World Economy
EE-MRIO	Environmentally Extended Multiregional Input–Output
EF	Ecological Footprint
EGP	Economic Growth Paradigm
EIT	Ecological Iron Triangle
EKC	Environmental Kuznets Curve
EM	Ecological Modernization
EUE	Ecological Unequal Exchange
FDI	Foreign Direct Investment
GCC	Global Climate Change
GDP	Gross Domestic Product
GDPPC	Gross Domestic Product per capita
GHG	Greenhouse Gases
GNI	Gross National Income
GSE	Global Sustainable Environment
GWP	Global Warming Potential
ha	hectares
HCFC	Hydrochlorofluorocarbon
HDI	Human Development Index
HEP	Human Exemptionalist Paradigm
HFC	Hydrofluorocarbon

IBRD	International Bank for Reconstruction and Development
IEF	Index of Economic Freedom
IFI	International Financial Institutions
IMF	International Monetary Fund
ISI	Import Substitution Industrialization
kg	kilogram
LDC	Least Developed Country subset
LIFDC	Low-Income Food Dependent Country subset
LLDC	Landlocked Developing Country subset
MDG	Millennium Development Goals
MNC	Multinational Corporation
mt	metric tons
NDC	Nationally Determined Contributions
NEP	New Ecological Paradigm
NIEO	New International Economic Order
ODA	Official Development Assistance
ODS	Ozone-Depleting Substances
OECD	Organisation for Economic Co-Operation and Development
OPEC	Organization of the Petroleum Exporting Countries
PCSE	Panel Corrected Standard Errors
PDI	Participatory Democracy Index
PERI	Periphery country subset
PPP	Purchasing Power Parity
PQLI	Physical Quality of Life Index
SAP	Structural Adjustment Policy/Program
SDG	Sustainable Development Goals
SEMI	Semiperiphery country subset
SIDS	Small Island Developing States subset
SITC	Standard International Trade Classification
t	tons
TOP	Treadmill of Production
UN	United Nations
UNDP	United Nations Development Programme
UNECLA	United Nations Economic Commission for Latin America
UNEP	United Nations Environment Programme
UNFAO	United Nations Food and Agriculture Organization
UNFCCC	United Nations Framework Convention on Climate Change
UN-OHRLLS	United Nations Office of the High Representative for the LDCs, LLDCs and SIDS
US	United States

V-Dem	Varieties of Democracy Index
VES	Vital Environmental Services
WORLD	World country set

List of Figures

List of Tables

Chapter 1

The Historical Emergence of the Global Sustainable Environment

The importance that the environment holds for the earth's inhabitants is beyond question. Simply put, it provides the foundational nourishment that sustains the human condition and its associated growth, development, and overall well-being. This perfunctory, all too casual observation, however, has been markedly absent throughout the vast majority of human existence. Unabashedly, perhaps even callously, we simply took the importance of the global sustainable environment (GSE) for granted. The epiphany that there would one day emerge an environmental crisis with the potential of catastrophic implications was an unimaginable proposition. Indeed, the human condition was well into the twentieth century before *substantial* (i.e., meaningful) recognition as to the importance of the GSE and to the deleterious impact of unabated economic growth and development would be realized by even the most ardent nonenvironmentalists.

The historical reality is that the GSE has always been under threat, whether by *anthropogenic* or *naturogenic* causes. Recent evidence from Qesem Cave, east of Tel Aviv, Israel, suggests that Homo sapiens may have habitually utilized fire for their meaningful needs during the late Middle Pleistocene to around four hundred thousand years ago (Roebroeks and Villa, 2011, p. 5211). Roebroeks and Villa (2011) likewise maintain that the *intentional* use of fire would come much later:

> It is only much later, with the Neandertals and their contemporaries elsewhere in the Old World, that fire became an integral part of the technological repertoire of the human lineage. From the late Middle Pleistocene of Europe onward and in the Late Pleistocene of Europe and South Africa, the evidence indicates that Neandertals and (early) modern humans used fire not only for warmth, cooking, or extending the length of day but also as an important component of technology for the production of new materials, including adhesives for the hafting of stone artifacts. (p. 5212)

Similarly, substantial evidence from Wonderwerk Cave, west of Johannesburg, South Africa, suggests that Homo erectus likewise habitually utilized fire approximately one million years ago (Berna et al., 2012, pp. E1217–E1218). While no one realistically envisions either of these hominins sitting around a fire, whether intentionally started or not, contemplating the effect of their carbon emissions on the environment, the fact remains that these anthropogenic forces impacted, albeit perhaps not meaningfully, existent biocapacity and the GSE.

It is also the case that naturogenic forces have routinely threatened the GSE. For example, the aforementioned habitual use of fire was in large part a function of lightning strikes. Natural disasters, such as the Antioch earthquake in 115 CE, not only took the lives of approximately 250,000 but also resulted in a tsunami that left depositional swamp-like conditions along Mediterranean coastal areas such as Beirut. Moreover, the Antioch earthquake in 526 CE not only resulted in more than 250,000 lives lost but also resulted in the fiery destruction of most remaining structures.

In sum, although environmentalism as a well-defined social movement became prominent only in the twentieth century, it is fallacious to believe that the GSE was not being threatened thousands of years earlier. Indeed, environmental concerns existed long before the introduction of a formidable mid-twentieth-century environmental movement (Grove, 2002, p. 50). Throughout history, preservationists and conservationists as well as casual observers of environmental conditions have pointed to more acute, specific environmental issues plaguing humankind, albeit perhaps on a more isolated basis. Indeed, these more specific, idiosyncratic episodes coincided with several *historical causal factors* that accompanied economic growth and development and increased well-being. Taken in their totality, these historical factors concurrently served to produce the most gradual of shifts in societal attitudes, leading to the twentieth-century zeitgeist of sustainable environmentalism.

Related closely to the neo-Malthusian and Human Ecology schools of thought is the first historical causal factor, the *exponential growth of population*. Figure 1.1 illustrates that the pattern of population growth through approximately 1700 was relatively linear, growing from approximately 170 million in year 1 to 610 million in 1700. During this period, the average century population growth rate averaged 8 percent, while zero population growth was actually the norm between 100 CE and 500 CE. This linear growth is consistent with the tracking of population estimates backward through antiquity and especially through the period of prehistory when population did not even double, moving from four million to seven million, over a period of six thousand years (10,000–4,000 BCE)! Admittedly, numerous events took place during both of these extended periods that greatly impacted (i.e., checked) population growth. For example, nearly two million lives were lost

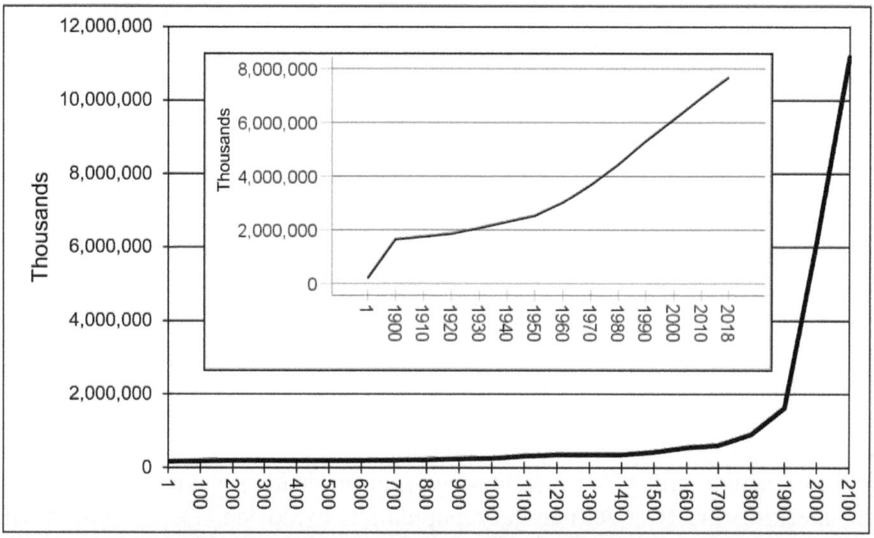

Figure 1.1. Population Growth by Century, 1–2100, and by Decade, 1900–2018

in the three Punic Wars (264–146 BCE), while a similar number perished in the Jewish-Roman Wars (66–136 CE). The Three Kingdoms War (184–280 CE) witnessed the death of some forty million Chinese (roughly one-fifth of the world population at the time) from direct warfare or the mass starvation left in its wake. A near similar number of Chinese (approximately thirty-six million) perished when General An Lushan rebelled against the Tang dynasty in the eighth century. Moreover, the Mongol Conquests (1206–1368) resulted in forty million deaths.

Beyond the toll of war, the role of infectious disease also played a critical role in keeping population growth in linear check. For example, the first two iterations of plague combined, the Plague of Justinian (sixth century) and the "Black Death" (fourteenth century), resulted in an estimated 150 million deaths (Tikhomirov, 1999, p. 12). Likewise, the population of Mexico declined nearly 90 percent in the sixteenth century, when the 1520 smallpox outbreak, coupled with two suspected salmonella outbreaks (resulting in paratyphoid) in 1545–1548 and 1576–1578, resulted in approximately twenty-five million deaths.

From 1700 onward, however, the pattern of population growth became relatively exponential in nature. While it took 1,804 years (one could argue 11,804 years) for global population to reach *one* billion, it has taken considerably fewer years to add each additional billion. For example, *two* billion was reached 123 years later, in 1927, while *three* billion became a reality 33 years later, in 1960. Successive one billion increases in population occurred in 1974, 1987, 1999, and 2011. The United Nations (UN) reports that global population reached eight billion in late 2022 and maintains that subsequent one billion increases in population will take longer to occur—in 2037, 2055, and 2088, respectively. In sum, while it took 11,804 years to reach one billion, it will have taken only 219 years to increase global population *sevenfold* (UN, 2019)!

The inset table in figure 1.1 provides a more detailed assessment of the twentieth- and early twenty-first-century population explosion, comparing the growth during this time to population growth from year 1 to 1900. Even during periods of exponential growth, factors such as war can place an effective check on population growth, albeit much more limited in historical comparative perspective due to a considerably larger global population. The vast majority of population growth in the twentieth century occurred in the post-WWII period concurrent with an increasing focus on development and the GSE. Obviously, both the loss of life during WWI (twenty-one million deaths) and WWII (eighty-five million deaths) played a major role in checking the twentieth-century population explosion. Less well-known wars such as the Chinese Civil War (1927–1949) and the Russian Civil War (1917–1922) cannot be ignored, given the loss of twelve million and nine million lives, respectively. Moreover, infectious disease also helped to limit the exponential nature of population growth in the early twentieth century. For example, the worldwide Spanish flu epidemic of 1918–1920 resulted in an estimated seventy-five million deaths.

Even during periods of linear growth, population-growth structure and related externalities have always negatively impacted the GSE. Periods of exponential growth, *typically* not characterized by detrimental wars and infectious diseases, have only served to exacerbate the population problem. The point remains that *the crisis has always been looming; exponential population growth has just dramatically accelerated the inevitable crisis*.

The implementation of both *empire* (circa 1450–1648) *and state imperialism* (1648–1914) also led to increasing pressure on the GSE in two significant ways. More than anything else, the raison d'être of classical imperialism was the economic motive. The enlargement of imperial power, and associated status, was predicated on exploiting mineral resources and raw materials in distant lands. In concert with imperialism, the economic philosophy of mercantilism dictated that the search for and acquisition of precious commodities, particularly gold and silver, were of paramount importance. While others also embraced mercantilism, the Spanish and British were spectacularly involved in the process of environmental usurpation and exploitation during this period. The Spanish primarily exploited gold in the Caribbean prior to 1510 and silver in present-day northern Mexico and Peru in the sixteenth century, while British operations primarily concerned themselves with extracting wealth from present-day Canada and the United States (US). Perhaps most illustrative of this orientation was King Ferdinand of Spain, when in 1511 he instructed "new world" explorers to acquire gold at any cost. While remarkable, Spanish successes paled in comparison to the Portuguese extraction of gold deposits in the Minas Gerais area of Brazil during the early eighteenth century (Minas Gerais, 2019).

Beyond mineral extraction, empire and state imperialism promoted environmental deterioration via the intentional movement (i.e., resettlement) of domestic populations to facilitate the colonization of yet unchartered territories. Although a relatively small-scale example, the Portuguese discovery and occupation of the island of Madeira illustrates the extent to which environmental destruction occurred during the colonization process. The accidental discovery of Madeira initiated the *Portuguese Age of Discovery* and led Prince Henry, under the guidance of his father, King João I, to instruct the colonizing forces to clear the land of the dense forest in order to promote settlements and crops. Several years later the clearing of forests would facilitate a rather lucrative sugar cane enterprise. Common lore suggests that the clearing of the ancient subtropical rainforest, *laurisilva*, was so extensive that destructive fires spanned a period of seven years (Madeira, 2017).

The advent of *large-scale industrialization* also fueled the increasingly rapid decline of the GSE. Inter alia, the European industrial revolution of the eighteenth and nineteenth centuries was tied to population growth, or rather growth among the more educated in society, and the accumulated wealth of European powers due to their colonies. Moreover, one may also argue that the *Age of Enlightenment* played a significant role in the expansion of European industrialization, as the importance of scientific reason increased while cultural attitudes that served to impede progress in the workplace lessened. The movement away from an agriculture-based economy to one rooted more in manufacturing enterprises also gave rise to a *second-order effect* as the rural population increasingly migrated to urban settings in order to obtain jobs and higher wages. This increase in rural migration, however, also placed increasing system stress on an already fragile urban environment.

The subsequent *technology-based industrial revolution* of the mid-nineteenth and early twentieth centuries continued to have a demonstrably negative impact on the GSE as well. Most notable at this time was the increasing use of external combustion, such as with steam-powered devices, and the introduction of the internal combustion engine. The latter served to profoundly increase the release of carbon dioxide (CO_2), and greenhouse gases (GHG) in general, into the atmosphere, as even the most efficient devices could not combust (i.e., burn) all of the carbon contained in the carbon-based fuels. Moreover, the combustion process also produced sulfur oxide, leading to increased concerns regarding acid rain. Figure 1.2 illustrates the exponential growth in global CO_2 emissions during the European industrial revolution and

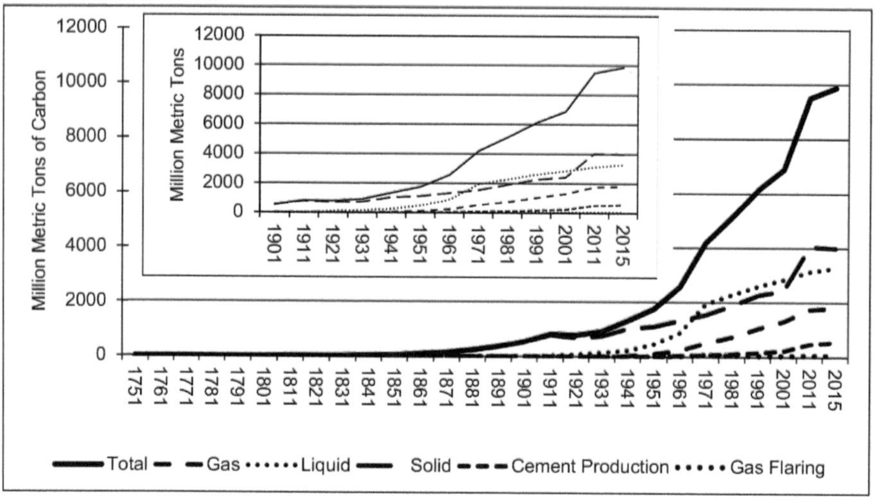

Figure 1.2. Global CO_2 Emissions by Source, 1751–2015

beyond. It is not coincidence that the *takeoff* in exponential CO_2 growth precisely mirrors the *takeoff* of global exponential population growth depicted in figure 1.1. Moreover, figure 1.2 indicates that the primary source of CO_2 emissions was solid fuel, followed closely by liquid fuel and gas fuel as the internal combustion engine became more prominent. Finally, the production of nitrogen oxide and ozone also spurred a generalized decline in the quality of the GSE.

While certainly not the only historical causal factors responsible, those aforementioned did serve to guide populations toward the idea that threats to the GSE were certainly worthy of increased attention. Moreover, it was also becoming clear that the environmental impact of the quest for greater economic growth and development and advances in well-being was growing quite large. For example, the volume of pollution caused by increasing urban populations and the industrial revolution in mid-nineteenth-century Great Britain was phenomenal when compared to environmental quality a century earlier. So bad were the overfishing and industrial dumping into rivers that various interests, representing conservationists, fishers, and industrialists, found themselves arguing on behalf of their respective "rights." As stated in MacLeod (1968) these stakeholders included

> the upper proprietors, usually sportsmen, anglers, and rod fishermen, who were most interested in protecting the spawning salmon; the lower proprietors, whose nets gathered the largest share of river salmon, but who were less interested in replenishing salmon stocks; the tidal fishermen, who enjoyed a common-law right to the tidal and estuary waters, and who were commercially inclined to

> catch salmon before they entered the fresh water; the mill owners, whose dams blocked the streams, and who were uninterested in salmon; and the riverside factory owners, to whom rivers had become convenient sewers for industrial wastes. (p. 116)

The net effect of their respective efforts was a series of "Salmon Acts" beginning in 1861 and culminating in the Salmon and Freshwater Fisheries Consolidation Act of 1880.

Similarly, the various nineteenth-century British Alkali Acts were a response to the increasing air pollution caused by heavy industry, particularly alkali producers. These Acts culminated in a relatively effective Alkali, &c. Works Regulation Act of 1906. The earlier iterations of the 1906 Act, similar to various iterations of the Salmon Acts, were significantly flawed as they did not provide an effective remedy in the eyes of conservationists or environmentalists (MacLeod, 1968). The following passage from *The British Medical Journal* regarding the implementation of the 1881 Alkali, &c. Works Regulation Act illustrates the initial lack of invasiveness in regulating emissions.

> It provides for the regulation of alkali, sulphuric acid, chemical manure, gas-liquor, nitric acid, sulphate and muriate of ammonia, and chlorine works. The owners of such works are to use the best practicable means for preventing the discharge of noxious and offensive gases from them, and they are to be under the supervision at all reasonable times of the inspectors appointed by the Local Government Board. (Alkali and Works Regulation Act, 1882, p. 24)

The Acts were far from effective laws. However, their passage indicates the extent to which society at that point in time viewed the juxtaposition between the GSE and economic growth and development as important. Moreover, these initiatives provided a path for further action in support of the GSE in Great Britain and in other countries that were also experiencing the environmental ills of their respective industrial revolutions.

The modern age of environmentalism in the US is predicated on over two hundred years of conservationist activity that led to the *establishment of governmental directives* and *private sector initiatives*. Perhaps the most notable of the latter was the establishment, by noted naturalist/preservationist John Muir and others, of the Sierra Club in 1892. Premised on the notion that the Sierra Nevada was a naturalist area in need of preservation, Muir was able to convince the state of California to cede this territory to the federal government under the auspices of establishing a federally protected Yosemite National Park. The successes of the Sierra Club were complimented by emerging environmentalist organizations such as the National Audubon

Society, the Wilderness Society, Save the Redwoods League, and the Izaak Walton League.

The involvement of government was also instrumental in the ongoing environmentalist movement in the US. The 1905 establishment of the US Forest Service, under the direction of the US Department of Agriculture, suggested to environmentalists that the government was both sympathetic and responsive to their arguments. Likewise, the provision for a National Park Service via passage of the 1916 National Park Service Organic Act, under the direction of the Department of the Interior, confirmed for many that the government shared in the public's resurgent interest in the GSE and believed this interest to be long lived.

The reemergence of a mid-twentieth-century iteration of the Survivalism discourse also served to produce a formidable foundational basis for change. Arguably, the early 1970s were the defining period for international environmentalism, as several governmental and intergovernmental agencies issued proclamations voicing support for greater environmental oversight in the concurrent quest for economic growth and development and advancement of well-being. Born out of John McConnell's 1968 vision of celebrating justice and the environment, the idea of *Earth Day* was born. Presented at the 1969 UNESCO conference in San Francisco titled "Man and His Environment," it was first celebrated on the vernal equinox in 1970 (McConnell, 2011). The concept was to spread globally as U Thant, then secretary-general of the United Nations, endorsed the idea by signing a proclamation on February 26, 1971. Subsequently, on March 21, 1971, U Thant helped celebrate the first UN-recognized *International Earth Day* at the UN headquarters in New York City. Upon the ringing of the Peace Bell, U Thant stated,

> Mankind's eternal aspirations for good instead of evil, for peace instead of war, have reached worldwide dimensions during this century. At long last the concept of EARTH DAY, of world patriotism and of the family of man, have come into being. May there only be peaceful and cheerful EARTH DAYS to come for our beautiful space ship Earth as it continues to spin and circle in frigid space with its warm and fragile cargo of animate life. (Lawrence and McConnell, 1999)

The first UN Conference on the Human Environment in Stockholm, Sweden, June 5–16, 1972, quickly followed in the steps of the first International Earth Day celebration. The conference delegates recommended the establishment of a permanent body to oversee various dimensions of the GSE. A vision of U Thant's in 1968, the General Assembly subsequently established, in 1972, the United Nations Environment Programme (UNEP). The UNEP provided the structural mechanism for a variety of international conferences and notable conventions such as the 1973 Convention on the International

Trade of Endangered Species, the 1979 Bonn Convention, the 1985 Vienna Convention, the 1987 Montreal Protocol, the 1989 Basel Convention, the 1992 Earth Summit (held in Rio de Janeiro), the 1997 general Assembly Special Session on the Environment (Earth Summit + 5), Conference of the Parties 3 (COP3–Kyoto), the 2002 World Summit on Sustainable Development (Rio + 10), the 2012 UN Conference on Sustainable Development (Rio + 20), and the 2015 COP21 meeting in Paris. These successful events are further evidence of the importance that national governments and international organizations are attaching to the GSE agenda. This realization, although waning periodically, has been a relative constant in the decades following Rio.

AN INCOMPATIBLE TROIKA? DEVELOPMENT, WELL-BEING, AND THE GSE

History has routinely considered *well-being* to be, in part, a function of advances in development. This is understandable as development, generally speaking, provides a continual foundational basis for work (i.e., income and wealth). Moreover, accumulated wealth provides the necessary resources with which to significantly improve the everyday lives of ourselves and others. Classical development economists maintain that liberal economic philosophy—and its manifest economic system, capitalism—provides the greatest opportunity for individuals to maximize income/wealth and thus provide a more enriching livelihood (i.e., well-being) (Mill, 2004; Ricardo, 2015: Smith, 2007). Regarded by many subsequent economists as a romantic tale at best and a development nightmare at worst, capitalism in its many subtle variations implements the purist of structural mechanisms—the free market—to stimulate the positive development of all countries regardless of their current development status.

Somewhat problematic is the frequently made assumption that "development" and "well-being" are synonymous concepts—that acquiring one automatically results in the acquisition of the other. This assumption often flows from another typical historical belief that development itself flows exclusively from economic growth—a concept for whose acquisition classical development economists clamored. However, while economic considerations are a vital piece of the development puzzle, they are only a small part of the picture of well-being, for the latter is considerably more expansive in both conceptual and practical terms.

The well-being of an individual, state, and the international system is inter alia a function of their levels of economic growth and development. However, "well-being" is more far-reaching than just the economic realm, for it also includes a plethora of what are primarily noneconomic indicators, such as personal freedoms, respect for the dignity of others (i.e., human rights), and quality of the GSE.

The quality of the GSE, as will be seen in chapter 2, is of considerable importance to the *perceived well-being* of individuals and countries. However, the data indicate that this perception varies greatly, depending on the environmental issue, the status of economic and energy development, perceptions of how well the economy is performing, and whether evaluating Organisation for Economic Co-Operation and Development (OECD) countries or non-OECD countries. The data in chapter 3 indicate that more than perceptions is important in gauging well-being. Whether the *production/consumption of vital environmental services* (*VES*) is sustainable is of key importance not only to current levels of well-being but to future levels as well.

This brief insight into development, well-being, and the GSE should suffice to illustrate that these are not mutually exclusive concerns. Changes in any one of these concerns will necessarily result, whether intentionally or otherwise, in altering levels associated with the other two. Posited earlier is the existence of an ever-increasing population that is exacting consistently increasing demands on the GSE. Given that these demands will likely continue largely unabated into the foreseeable future, the question of how to effectively manage the interaction of these related concerns becomes crucial for posterity.

A CONCEPTUAL INQUIRY INTO DEVELOPMENT AS WELL-BEING, AND THE GSE IN THE POST–GREAT RECESSION, 2010–2017

The primary purpose of this study is to evaluate the comparative utility of two economic-based environmental theories, Ecological Modernization (EM) theory and Ecological Unequal Exchange (EUE) theory, as they relate to the broader context of "development"—*well-being* and the GSE in the post–Great Recession period. It is fair to say that much of the literature regarding these two competing theories comes from the field of environmental sociology.[1] Both, however, are born of principles associated with various post-WWII theories of economic development and the political climate associated with each.

A second purpose relates to updating what we know about both the *subjective* and *objective* aspects of the GSE. We can all quickly conjure a response to how individuals perceive of the GSE and its relatedness to economic and energy concerns, but it is important to provide periodic updates to ensure the integrity of past patterns of behaviors. This is no less important when looking at objective data reflecting the historical and present consumption of VES.

Chapter 2 provides an intrusive look at US public opinion concerning the juxtaposition of economic and energy concerns with those related to the GSE and more specific aspects of the latter. The concepts of *psychological distance* and the *issue-attention cycle* are presented to lend greater explanation for the historical trends. Chapter 2 also includes comparative data for developed and developing countries regarding the importance of global warming. Chapter 3 begins with a warning about regarding data as "objective." Following this is a delineation of country subsets used in presenting the data on historical trends (i.e., patterns) pertaining to the consumption of VES. Cropland services, grazing services, forest services, fisheries and aquaculture services, and CO_2 emissions data are presented, in lustra, for 1961–2016.

This study also seeks to provide greater clarity with respect to the usage of several related concepts including but not limited to economic growth, development, the GSE, and well-being. There often exist certain ill-informed assumptions born out of the perceived relationship of these and other relevant concepts that have served to limit investigation into the explanatory efficacy of EM and EUE theory. Chapter 4 begins with an exposition of the meaning of "development" and argues that the Aristotelian concept of *eudaimonia* (i.e., well-being) enriches and helps to clarify the modern-day understanding of the characteristics of development. Concept differentiation, such as that of economic growth versus development, is offered in the context of historical economic philosophies. The second half of chapter 4 briefly chronicles the politicization of theories of development from modernization to postdevelopment and from classical development economics to neoclassical economics and the overt manifestation of the latter: neoliberalism. It provides a foundational understanding for the political and economic orientations from which EM and EUE theory arose.

A further objective of this study is the construction of a framework that allows a holistic comparative assessment of the potential explanatory utility of both EM and EUE theories in the immediate aftermath of the Great Recession of 2007–2009. The literature offers a plethora of models that utilize a variety of variable measures to this end while leaving sidelined a more holistic understanding regarding the historical development and intellectual roots of each theory. Chapter 5 fills this void by the emergence of EM and EUE as they grew out of the debate shadow of the Human Exemptionalist Paradigm (HEP) and the New Ecological Paradigm (NEP). While the HEP/NEP debate is significant in and of itself, the primary focus is on the evolution of EM and EUE theories. Facilitating the dissemination of information is a comparative framework that presents their historical and intellectual roots, a summary of their beliefs, and the predominant methods of inquiry utilized in the research pertaining to each theory. Finally, a brief overview of apparent irreconcilable differences and tacit parallels provides the basis for the argument that while they are "competing" environmental theories, EM and EUE taken together better inform our theoretical understanding as to the relationship between development, well-being, and the GSE in the post–Great Recession period.

A final objective relates to facilitating greater comparative understanding with respect to the explanatory utility of EM and EUE theories. The literature utilizes a goodly number of measures for the environment-related dependent variable, such as carbon emissions, deforestation, and environmental impact indexes, among others, to the point that it is largely futile to speak of meaningful comparisons of EM and EUE theories. Moreover, the impact of this on policy formulation pertaining to the development/well-being nexus in a post–global recession period, in the service of more effectively elevating the *well-being* of individuals and countries alike, is self-evident. To this end, chapter 6 provides the methodological particulars and issues pertaining to the analysis. In so doing, the existing literatures are incorporated to illustrate the extreme variation in areas such as variable conceptualization, measurement, case inclusion, and the like. The analysis provides some alternative measurements for established variables and includes a larger number of cases than most studies to date. Chapter 7 continues with a formal examination and evaluation of the empirical results pertaining to the explanatory utility of EM and EUE theory. The evaluation of the theories with respect to more select subsets of countries, both developed and developing, is incorporated. Finally, the conclusion offers concluding remarks and suggestions for further research.

NOTES

1. Alternative theories and schools of thought seeking to explain the relationship between different aspects of "development" and GSE certainly exist, including such ideas as Treadmill of Production, Treadmill of Destruction, and Human Ecology, to name a few. The current focus on EM and EUE theory should not be interpreted to mean that these alternative theories cannot contribute to understanding the relationship between "development" and the consumption of VES in the post–Great Recession period more effectively.

PART I

The Global Sustainable Environment

Chapter 2

Subjective Perceptions

A LONGITUDINAL EXAMINATION OF US PUBLIC OPINION

The perceived importance of the GSE in the twenty-first century, the general topic to which this chapter is devoted, has been elevated in part due to the foundational successes that earlier environmentalist generations have achieved. The importance of these subjective perceptions speaks to the EM hypothesis that a more "civil society" (i.e., democratic-oriented) can positively influence governments to protect the GSE. However, there at times remains great inconsistency regarding just how important the GSE is to societal members when juxtaposed with economic growth and development and human well-being concerns. The data in figure 2.1 illustrates that there are fundamental structural differences in how the US public perceives the importance of the GSE, especially when presented in relation to "economic-oriented" issues.[1] The Gallup Organization has routinely polled the US public about their sentiments regarding the prioritization of the environment and economic growth.[2] Annual data, 2001–2018, strongly indicate that current economic performance and public opinion regarding this perceived dichotomous choice are highly correlated.

In 2000, 70 percent of the public prioritized the environment over the economy. However, the 2001 recession led to a considerable narrowing of the margin by 2003–2004, when the difference in prioritization was but five percentage points (47 percent–42 percent and 49 percent–44 percent, respectively). As the economy started to improve (i.e., come out of the recession), however, prioritization of the environment became more pronounced, culminating in 55 percent of respondents opting for it in 2007. The emergence of the "Great Recession" of 2007–2009, however, subsequently led to a near perfect reversal of the 2007 results, as 2009 saw 51 percent prioritize the

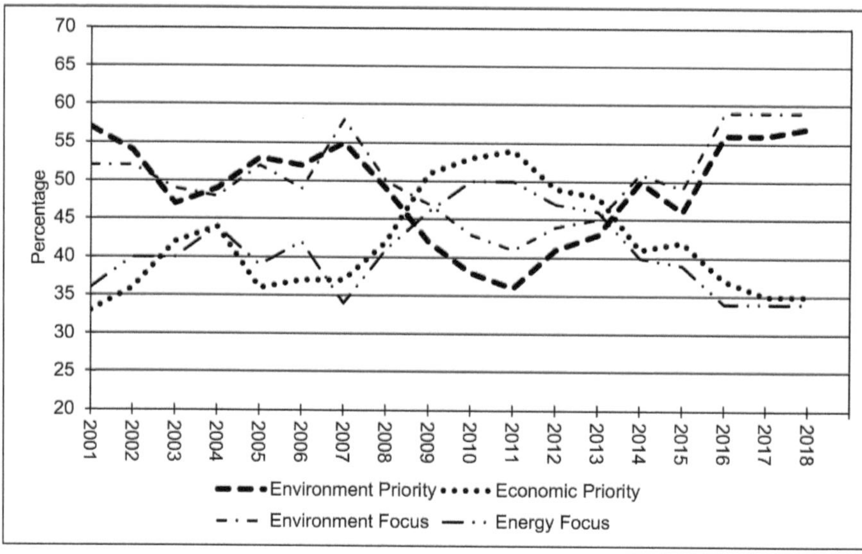

Figure 2.1. Percentage Overlay of Environment vs. Economic Priority and Environment vs. Energy Focus, 2001–2018

economy over the environment. As the effects of the recession "unofficially" continued into 2010–2011, so, too, did the percentage of the public that prioritized the economy (53 percent and 54 percent, respectively). Concurrently, prioritization of the environment dropped to a ten-year low at 38 percent and 36 percent, respectively.

Since 2015, when the US unemployment rate fell back to the pre-recession rate of 5 percent, greater economic recovery has once again translated into greater prioritization of the environment. The 2015–2018 period saw average support for the environment increase to nearly 54 percent, while average support for the economy dipped to 37 percent. The obvious conclusion drawn from this longitudinal data is that the US public is relatively more supportive of the environment only when economic times are good and are more than willing to discount the importance of the GSE during periods of economic decline. A statistically significant correlation of the annual aggregate data further tells the story: *the public views economic growth and environmental protection as incompatible* ($r(19) = -0.982$, $p < 0.001$). Moreover, *deeper economic troubles only bolster this conclusion*, as a statistically significant correlation exists between annual unemployment rates and the public prioritization of economic growth ($r(19) = 0.846$, $p < 0.001$).

Figure 2.1 also provides polling data on US public opinion regarding the need to focus on "protecting the environment" as opposed to "prioritizing energy development," a specific aspect of economic growth.[3] These polling data virtually mirror the general pattern revealed by the public when they are asked about prioritizing economic growth in general. Conceptually, they appear to link energy development to overall economic growth and development and consequently are just as likely to promote the development of energy supplies over environmental protection during an economic downturn. Moreover, these two alternatives are also perceived as significantly incompatible, statistically speaking ($r(18) = -0.958$, $p < 0.001$).

Figure 2.2 overlays the earlier reported data on environmental versus economic prioritization with US public opinion as to whether the environment is improving or worsening.[4] The 2000–2018 data indicate that the priority the public assigns to environmental protection versus economic growth is highly associated with the overall perception as to how well the environment is performing. Generally speaking, perceptions of an environment that is "improving" are statistically significant and negatively related to the need to prioritize environmental protection ($r(18) = -0.535$, $p < 0.05$), whereas perceptions of an environment that is "worsening" are statistically significant and positively related to prioritization ($r(18) = 0.652$, $p < 0.05$). The strength of this perceived association, however, appears less than when economic growth and energy development are juxtaposed with the environment.

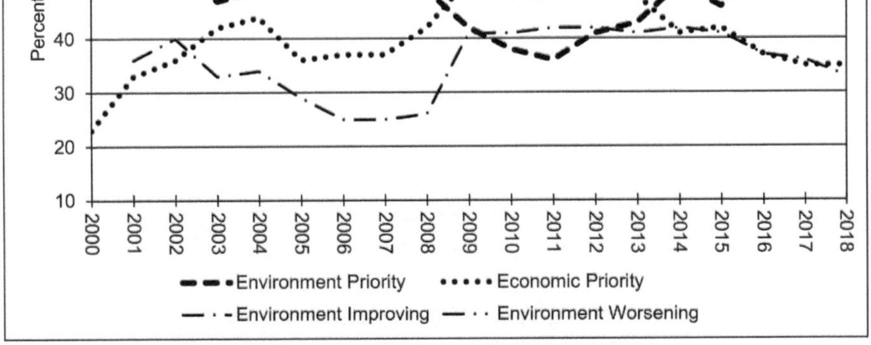

Figure 2.2. Percentage Overlay of Environment vs. Economic Priority and Environment Improving vs. Worsening, 2000–2018

THE PERCEIVED IMPORTANCE OF ENVIRONMENTAL ISSUE-AREAS

While the aforementioned documents perceptions regarding the perceived tradeoff between the economy and the environment in general terms, it does not provide more substantive detail as to the importance the US public attaches to specific issue-areas related to the GSE. The importance of the latter is obvious when considering the impact of public opinion on policymaking, implementation, and evaluation of specific aspects of the GSE such as air, water, toxic and hazardous wastes, and plant and animal species protection, among others.

Figure 2.3 provides a breakdown of annual Gallup polling data derived from asking to what extent people *worry a great deal* about specific environmental issues.[5] It is instructive to note that in only three of the seven major environmental issue-areas reported in figure 2.3, the annual Gallup poll on the environment has shown that a majority of the public "worried a great deal" about the issue. Over the 2001–2018 period, respondents consistently worried the most about pollution of drinking water. The average of annual aggregated data (AAAD) over this period showed that 56 percent worried a

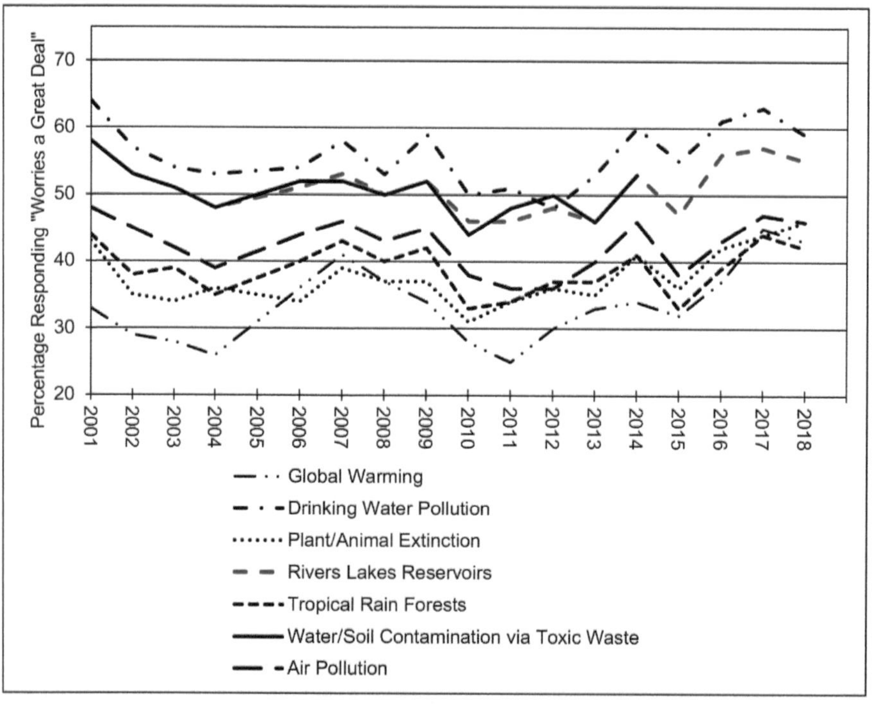

Figure 2.3. Public Perception of Vital Environmental Issues, 2001–2018

great deal about pollution of drinking water. While 64 percent of respondents in 2001 said that they worried a great deal about pollution of drinking water, this concern dipped to 59 percent in 2018. Only in 2012, however, did the percentage of the public worrying a great deal dip below a majority (48 percent).

The polluting of rivers, lakes, and reservoirs is also a specific environmental issue that, on annual average, a majority of respondents (51.2 percent) during the 2001–2018 period worried about greatly. While 58 percent of respondents in 2001 said that they "worry a great deal" about this issue, the concern dropped slightly to 55 percent in 2018. Moreover, public opinion dropped as low as 46 percent in both 2010 and 2011. The AAAD of the Gallup poll on the contamination of soil and water by toxic waste during the 2001–2014 period also shows that a majority (50.5 percent) stated that they "worry a great deal" about this particular issue. While 58 percent of respondents did so in 2001, the number dropped to 53 percent in 2014, the last year that Gallup incorporated the question in their annual environment survey. Similar to the pollution of rivers, lakes, and reservoirs, the lowest percentage response (44 percent) took place in the March 2010 poll administered just a few short weeks *before* the BP Deepwater Horizon disaster.

Concern over air pollution has consistently ranked lower than the three aforementioned environmental issue-areas. Gallup polling from the period 2001–2018 indicates that the issue reached its pinnacle in 2001 when 48 percent of those polled stated that they worried a great deal about the issue. The AAAD during this period was 42.5 percent, considerably lower than the more observable issues related to water. "Worry" about air pollution reached its lowest level (36 percent) in the 2011 and 2012 polls but rebounded to a near high of 46 percent by 2018.

Relatively speaking, public opinion during 2001–2018 worried the least about the loss of tropical rainforests, the extinction of plant and animal species, and global warming (i.e., climate change). The percentage of those worried a great deal about the loss of tropical rainforests never exceeded 44 percent (recorded in both 2001 and 2017). While 33 percent was the lowest value during this time (in both 2013 and 2015), US public opinion in 2018 showed that 42 percent were worried a great deal, higher than the AAAD (38.9 percent). The numbers pertaining to the extinction of plant and animal species were quite similar to the rainforest data. The recorded low (31 percent) in 2010 was, again, just a few short weeks *before* the BP Deepwater Horizon disaster. While 43 percent were worried a great deal in 2001, this number actually increased to a high of 46 percent in 2018. It is interesting that of the environmental issues in figure 2.3, the extinction of plant and animal species is the only one recording an increase in "worry" during 2001–2018. The AAAD (37.7 percent) was comparable to that of the rainforest data.

Perhaps most distressing for the GSE are the polling data pertaining to global warming. Arguably the most contentious of the environmental issue-areas in figure 2.3, it is also the most volatile in terms of the annual changes in the percentage of the public that worry a great deal about it. While the AAAD was 33.6 percent, the low (25 percent in 2011) contrasts significantly with the high (45 percent in 2017). A ten percentage point difference between 2001 and 2008 (33 percent to 43 percent) further indicates that a good deal of volatility with respect to worry about the issue exists.

The 2001–2018 polling data disclose that specific environmental issue-areas, such as the pollution of drinking water, are both significantly and consistently more worrisome for the public than are others, especially global warming. As has already been noted, understanding why these differences in public opinion exist is important to the policymaking, implementation, and evaluation process of sustainable environmental policies. Politically speaking, the policymaking apparatus is said to respond to the interest articulation and aggregation of concerns (i.e., public opinion as to what environmental issues need to be effectively addressed) (Downs, 1972; Key, 1961; Kirkwood and Hubrecht, 2001). Arguably, the differences presently noted among environmental issue-areas are easily explained by “psychological distance” and “issue-attention cycles.”

Psychological distance in construal-level theory (Liberman and Trope, 1998; Trope and Liberman, 2010) involves the extent to which events and/or issues are perceived as “distant” to the experience of an individual. In its totality, psychological distance involves the assessment of temporal, spatial, social, and hypothetical (i.e., certainty) “proximity” of personal experience to the event/issue being considered. Generally speaking, the closer the assessment of these proximity types are to the personal experience of the individual, the greater the level of perceived threat by that event. One corollary is that greater concern (i.e., whether one worries a great deal about an issue) is the result of the perception of greater perceived threat to the individual. Consequently, more psychologically distant events are those perceived to be farther from personal experience and not producing the same level of concern.

Psychological distance lends considerable explanation for the differences in public opinion regarding the seven environmental issue-areas in figure 2.3. For example, those issues where public opinion is greatest (i.e., where people worry a great deal) are issues pertaining to highly tangible events that are relatively “closer” to the physical experience of the individual. Pollution of drinking water, the polluting of rivers, lakes, and reservoirs, and the contamination of water/soil by toxic wastes are environmental issue-areas that are in close temporal, spatial, and social proximity to the everyday experience of the public. Moreover, events such as the Flint, Michigan, contamination of drinking water, the BP Deepwater Horizon disaster, and the Elk River,

West Virginia, chemical spill reinforce the perception that the psychological distance of the public regarding these specific threats to the GSE is quite small. One can surmise that the general perception is that these environmental events can happen at any time, to any population, with potentially great harm and even greater certainty that harm to the individual will most definitely materialize.

Public opinion about air pollution, conversely, does not fully meet the four dimensions of psychological distance. In the minds of many, air pollution is something that happens to other populations that are predisposed to lower air quality due to differences in a variety of factors, including population density, energy production, energy intensive manufacturing locations, and others. In essence, air pollution may be of great concern to members of the US public who reside in Los Angeles, Phoenix, or Hilo. However, other members of the public, who reside in less affected locales such as Seneca Falls, College Station, or Enid, may neither deem air pollution to be an immediate threat with great potential harm nor feel certain that the threat will materialize sooner rather than later and produce great personal harm.[6]

The psychological distance of the US public with respect to the loss of tropical rainforests, the extinction of plant and animal species, and global warming is overwhelmingly great, especially in comparison to the aforementioned water and air issues. Frankly, these concerns are substantially outside the personal experience of most of the US public. After all, the only *tropical* rainforest in the US is El Yunque National Forest in Puerto Rico. Moreover, while *temperate* rainforests exist in the US, they are largely located in the Pacific Northwest (e.g., Hoh Rain Forest in Washington) and even more the case in Alaska (e.g., Tongass National Forest and Chugach National Forest). Simply put, these environmental treasures are largely outside of the personal experience of most of the US public, exist in the tropics, are unlikely to cause direct personal harm, and are certainly not going to become a prevalent issue any time soon in the US.

The extinction of plant and animal species is a somewhat different calculation with respect to psychological distance. Although in decline, the existence of plant and animal species in the US is as diverse and numerous as the rainforests are not. The problem with the assessment of psychological distance, though, is in the knowledge base of the public when evaluating the importance of plant and animal species. Research has shown that media reporting significantly impacts the level of public concern for specific environmental issues (Brulle et al., 2012). Further research finds that the ability of the public to correctly identify animals on the endangered list is dependent upon the "exposure" given to the animal by the media and in movies, advertisements, and other outlets. For example, while the public correctly identifies gorillas and orangutans as endangered, they misidentify chimpanzees due to the prevalence of chimpanzees in movies (Ross et al., 2008, 2011). The net effect of this research is that the public perceives no problem with the population of the animal species illuminated by the aforementioned media sources. In essence, there is no “certainty” that a problem exists, that the public will somehow be harmed by the problem if it does exist, and that temporal immediacy is present. In short, the psychological distance with respect to the issue is maximized due to media “misrepresentation,” resulting in considerably less public concern (i.e., worry) about the issue.

As stated earlier, the findings for the global warming poll question during 2001–2018 were quite volatile over time. At first glance, it appears that US public opinion is unexplainable, with remarkable shifts often occurring. The work of Downs (1972), however, can provide valuable insight into why this public opinion volatility with respect to “worry” about global warming is so variable.

Downs (1972) proposed what he surmised to be a systematic construct that he labeled the *issue-attention cycle*. He argued that every issue proceeds through a five-stage process that enables one to comprehend the reasons more fully for the ascendance and decline of the issue at hand. In the *pre-problem* stage, the issue exists but lies mostly dormant, as only experts and related interest groups understand the gravity of the situation. The transition to the *alarmed discovery and euphoric enthusiasm* stage is precipitated by the occurrence of a significant event that is subsequently followed by great confidence among the public that the problem can be solved. The third stage, *realizing the cost of significant progress*, reflects increased understanding that cost involves both monetary resources and a restructuring of societal behaviors. The *gradual decline of intense public interest* results from increasing individual awareness of the high personal cost coupled with the low likelihood of positive change. It is during this fourth stage that individuals may feel threatened by the problem, discouraged, and/or bored with the issue and instead focus their attention on an alternative issue that is entering stage 2. The salience of the original issue greatly decreases in the *post-problem* stage but may periodically reemerge into the limelight of future public discourse. As Downs (1972) states,

> Any major problem that once was elevated to national prominence may sporadically recapture public interest; or important aspects of it may become attached to some other problem that subsequently dominates center stage. Therefore, problems that have gone through the cycle almost always receive a higher average level of attention, public effort, and general concern than those still in the pre-discovery stage. (p. 41)

Given this conceptual understanding of the *issue-attention cycle*, it is argued here that public opinion on global warming prior to 1990 exemplified Downs (1972) pre-problem stage, as most of the knowledge regarding global warming was contained within the scientific community and not widely disseminated among the public. Reports, such as that issued by the US National Academy of Sciences in 1979 (Climate Research Board, 1979) were largely consumed by relevant scientists and policymakers. Moreover, significant conferences and protocols, such as the 1985 Villach Conference and the 1987 Montreal Protocol, set the stage for catapulting global warming into the consciousness of the US public. The transition to stage 2 was facilitated by several fortuitous events surrounding the severe drought of 1988 (i.e., the "significant" triggering event) and the dramatic increase of media focus on the causes of the heat wave. Highly publicized pictures and stories of crop failure were concentrated in media presentations to the public. Ungar (1992) frames these events and the manner by which they represented a series of significant events that would impact public opinion:

> What rendered 1988 so extraordinary was concatenating physical impacts felt by the person in the street. North America suffered record-breaking heat, dangerous air pollution levels over cities, and a crop-destroying drought that reduced the US grain harvest to below consumption for the first time. In March, NASA reported the ozone layer had begun to thin globally. By the week of June 24, in the midst of Senate hearings on global warming, the agricultural department claimed half the counties in the country were suffering drought and half the grain crop was lost (Pearce, 1989, p. 1). Storms' frequency and intensity increased, and hurricane Gilbert was termed a "super hurricane." Forest fires were the worst of the century and gained particular prominence with the fire in Yellowstone National Park. . . . In June, stories about the weather and climate change moved up from the back pages of the "science section" of newspapers and magazines to the news section; by July, these events frequently took the lead on network news broadcasts and became cover stories and lead articles in print media. (p. 490)

This increased attention on global warming soon dissipated, however, as global warming skeptics utilized the media to attack the economics of regulations designed to significantly reduce global warming. From 1989 to 1992 the now defunct George Marshall Institute played a vital role in conveying to the public that government regulations dealing with global warming would be extraordinarily burdensome to the US economy. This dip into stage 3 of the issue-attention cycle was soon followed by a precipitous transition into stage 4, as the media began to increase its relative focus on the economic recession, the fall of communism, and the Persian Gulf War. Whereas 35 percent of the US public "worried a great deal" about global warming in 1991, that figure declined to 24 percent by October 1997. In essence, the issue-attention cycle had run its initial course. The issue, however, would soon become reemergent, as the signing of the Kyoto Protocol in December 1997 once again elevated the importance and threat of global warming. Indeed, the percentage of the US public who said they "worry a great deal" about the issue increased to 40 percent by 2000.

The volatility in public opinion during the 2001–2018 period reflects episodes where significant events triggered the reemergence of global warming as a significant worry for the public. In effect, the issue laid dormant until a "significant" triggering event served to thrust the issue back into its stage two media limelight. However, the 2001 economic recession would subsequently displace the re-emergence of global warming as a critical issue. By 2004, only 26 percent of the US public were now "worried a great deal" about global warming. Subsequent increases in 2006–2007 (36 percent and 41 percent, respectively) were in part due to the release of two epic films dealing with climatic disaster and global warming. *The Day after Tomorrow* was released in the US in May 2004, two months *after* the completion of the 2004 Gallup environment survey. Perhaps more noteworthy was the January 2006 Sundance Film Festival premiere of Al Gore's *An Inconvenient Truth* (released in May 2006). Brulle et al. (2012) state that the public should assign increasing legitimacy and issue salience to global warming due to Vice President Gore having received an Academy Award and the Nobel Peace Prize for his efforts (p. 175).

The increasing worry (41 percent) noted in the 2007 Gallup poll would be short lived as once again the salience of global warming would take a back seat to another, more pressing media concern. The 2007–2008 financial crisis, the 2008–2009 subprime mortgage crisis, and the associated Great Recession of the period would displace the media focus on global warming. The percentage of those "worried a great deal" about the issue would fall over the 2007–2011 period from 41 percent to 25 percent. Just as they did in 1988, extreme weather conditions throughout the US, coupled with the decreasing impact of the economic recession, would soon lead to a resurgent interest in global warming by both the media and US public. Severe weather events in 2011 ranged from a record 753 tornadoes in April to the most impactful one-year drought in Texas history. The latter alone resulted in the direct loss of nearly $10 billion worth of crops, livestock, and timber. Moreover, Hurricane Irene resulted in record flooding in the Northeast while record heat and wildfires were noted throughout the Southwest (Freedman, 2011). The continuous media reporting on the total destruction caused by these extreme weather events was front and center in the minds of the US public. Consequently, it comes as no great surprise that the 2011–2014 period would show a consistent increase (from 25 percent to 34 percent) in public "worry" about global warming. Moreover, the US was emerging from the wrath of the Great Recession.

The 2017–2018 uptick in "worry" about global warming was due to a confluence of events. The perceived failing of the 2015 Paris Agreement, due to both non-US participation and a relatively weak structure for determining country goals, and a US government dominated by a healthy number of Republican Party "global warming deniers and skeptics" are perhaps the two most important events leading to the increases in "worry" recorded in the 2017 and 2018 polls. In sum, all of the aforementioned volatility, the upswings and downswings in the extent to which the US public "worries a great deal" about global warming, are explainable when applying the "issue-attention cycle" posited by Downs (1972).

OECD AND NON-OECD COUNTRY PERCEPTIONS OF GSE IMPORTANCE

Public opinion, with respect to the importance that the GSE holds for developing countries, is more difficult to gauge due to the limitations in issue-area coverage, data availability/collection, and the fact that polling in developing countries presents a unique set of circumstances/concerns that may significantly impede the process.[7] Nevertheless, one can still acquire a reasonable picture of how both developed and developing countries perceive specific environmental issues. Table 2.1 provides 2013 and 2017 polling data from the Pew Research Center for nineteen OECD and fifteen non-OECD countries concerning their perceptions as to the seriousness of global warming for their respective countries.[8]

The data in table 2.1 demonstrate, inter alia, that on average, OECD countries considered global climate change (GCC) significantly more of a "major threat" to their respective countries in 2017 than in 2013 (65.2 percent vs. 58.1 percent). While Greece, Hungary, Japan, South Korea, and Poland recorded decreases between 2013 and 2017, it is noteworthy that five OECD countries recorded at least a one-third increase in the percentage of the population considering GCC a "major threat" to their country (UK 50 percent, US 40 percent, Spain 39.1 percent, Mexico 38.5 percent, and France 33.3 percent). The absolute percentage among OECD countries is also important, as it shows considerable variation among these five countries. While 72 percent in the UK, France, and Mexico regarded GCC as a "major threat," a considerably higher percentage of Spaniards (89 percent) and lower percentage (56 percent) of US respondents did. When considering the population that perceived GCC a "major or minor threat" to their country, the general conclusion noted above is again warranted, as the average percentage increased from

Table 2.1. Percentage of Respondents in OECD and Non-OECD Countries Stating that Global Warming Is a "Major Threat" or "Major or Minor Threat" Combined, 2013–2017

OECD	*Spring 2013*	*Spring 2017*	***Non-OECD***	*Spring 2013*	*Spring 2017*
Australia	52 (86)	58 (87)	Argentina	71 (84)	76 (86)
Canada	54 (88)	60 (88)	Brazil	76 (91)	67 (82)
Chile	68 (88)	86 (92)	Ghana	51 (78)	49 (70)
France	54 (87)	72 (92)	India	53 (78)**	47 (69)
Germany	56 (93)	63 (93)	Indonesia	59 (86)	56 (80)
Greece	87 (96)	79 (93)	Jordan	35 (77)	40 (74)
Hungary	66 (92)*	59 (92)	Kenya	57 (85)	76 (87)
Israel	30 (78)	38 (78)	Lebanon	74 (97)	58 (91)
Italy	64 (91)	65 (90)	Nigeria	41 (73)	43 (71)
Japan	72 (93)	67 (93)	Philippines	66 (92)	65 (85)
Korea	85 (94)	79 (96)	Russia	46 (80)	35 (78)
Mexico	52 (78)	72 (89)	Senegal	58 (74)	56 (73)
Netherlands	56 (90)*	64 (93)	South Africa	48 (74)	59 (79)
Poland	45 (82)	42 (79)	Tunisia	62 (76)	44 (60)
Spain	64 (90)	89 (96)	Venezuela	53 (72)	55 (76)
Sweden	64 (95)*	64 (96)			
Turkey	47 (74)	53 (78)			
UK	48 (83)	72 (89)			
US	40 (77)	56 (82)			
Average	58.1 (87.1)	65.2 (89.3)	**Average**	56.7 (81.1)	55.1 (77.4)
	High Income (n=17)	UM OECD (n=3)	UM Non-OECD (n=7)	Lower Middle (n=6)	Low Income (n=1)
2013	57.9 (88.2)	55.0 (81.3)	59.9 (72.3)	54.7 (80.2)	57.0 (85.0)
2017	66.5 (89.2)	61.3 (86.3)	57.0 (78.3)	52.7 (74.7)	76.0 (87.0)

* Spring 2016 data

** Winter 2013/2014 data

Source: Pew Research Center. (2017, August). *Globally, people point to ISIS and climate change as leading security threats.* http://www.pewglobal.org/2017/08/01/globally-people-point-to-isis-and-climate-change-as-leading-security-threats

87.1 percent to 89.3 percent between 2013 and 2017. Even though Greece, Italy, and Poland recorded decreases in 2017, it should be noted that both Greece and Italy still registered over 90 percent of those polled believing that GCC is either a "major or minor threat" to their country.

The data in table 2.1 also demonstrate that on average, non-OECD countries considered GCC marginally less of a "major threat" to their respective countries in 2017 than in 2013 (56.7 percent vs. 55.1 percent). In contrast to this general finding, five non-OECD countries (Argentina, Jordan, Nigeria, South Africa, and Venezuela) recorded marginal increases in 2017, while

Kenya saw a significant 33.3 percent increase in the percentage considering GCC a "major threat" to their country. When considering the population that regarded GCC a "major or minor threat" to their country, the general conclusion noted earlier is again merited, as the average percentage decreased from 81.1 percent to 77.4 percent between 2013 and 2017. Noteworthy are Brazil, Indonesia, Lebanon, the Philippines, and Russia, who experienced decreases between 2013 and 2017 but whose values were still greater than the average of the fifteen non-OECD countries. Lebanon is exceptional, as 91 percent polled believed GCC to be a "major or minor threat" to their country in 2017.

A few summary statements about the data in table 2.1 are in order. First, it is clear that both OECD and non-OECD countries, on average, viewed GCC as a "major threat" to their countries in both 2013 and 2017. This is especially the case for OECD countries in 2017, as they registered a 10.1 percentage point difference when compared to non-OECD countries (65.2 percent to 55.1 percent). Second, when considering GCC as a "major or minor threat" to their countries, a qualified majority of at least 75 percent in both OECD and non-OECD countries was recorded in both 2013 and 2017. Moreover, the six-point difference between OECD and non-OECD countries nearly doubled (11.9 percentage point difference) in 2017, as OECD countries experienced an increase while non-OECD countries recorded a decrease. Third, there is a good deal of variability in the scores. For example, the range of scores for OECD countries that consider GCC a "major threat" to their country is 57 percentage points in 2013 (30 percent–87 percent) and 51 percentage points in 2017 (38 percent–89 percent). Although less than in OECD countries, there is still a 41 percentage point range (35 percent–76 percent) for non-OECD countries in both 2013 and 2017 for the "major threat" category. When looking at the combined "major or minor threat" categories, the ranges, although expected to be smaller, still represent a good deal of variability. OECD countries reveal a 22 percentage point (74 percent–96 percent) and 18 percentage point (78 percent–96 percent) range for 2013 and 2017, respectively. Non-OECD countries registered a 25 percentage point (72 percent–97 percent) and 31 percentage point (60 percent–91 percent) range for 2013 and 2017, respectively. Fourth, the variability issue appears related to the fact that there is a good deal of difference in the economic development levels within and between both OECD and non-OECD countries. Utilizing the World Bank classification of countries for 2013, one finds that all the OECD countries in table 2.1 are categorized as "high income" except for Hungary, Mexico, and Poland, which are classified as "upper middle income." The list of non-OECD countries is considerably more diverse with respect to economic development. While Russia is categorized as "high income" in 2013, seven countries on the list (Argentina, Brazil, Jordan, Lebanon, South Africa, Tunisia, and Venezuela) are "upper middle income," six (Ghana, India,

Indonesia, Nigeria, Philippines, and Senegal) are "lower middle income," and Kenya is classified as "low income."

The compiled data at the bottom of table 2.1 helps to clarify the data based on the World Bank analytical classification of countries for 2013. In 2013 there is no meaningful pattern that exist between a more specific breakdown of "level of economic development" and the percentage of those polled who stated that GCC is a "major threat" to their country. However, the "major or minor threat" category for 2013 revealed an interesting, although conceptually counterintuitive, *curvilinear pattern* whereby the economic development extremes illustrate a greater level of agreement. A noticeable pattern exists with respect to 2017. In both response categories, "major" and "major or minor threat," there is prima facie evidence that greater "level of economic development" is positively associated with public opinion regarding the threat of GCC. An interesting observation is that the signing of the landmark 2015 Paris Agreement and subsequent entry into force in 2016 materialized between the administration of these two Pew polls. While not wishing to exaggerate the importance of the Paris Agreement to the 2017 poll results, Article 12 of the Agreement called on the parties to implement measures that highlight the problem of GCC and to

> cooperate in taking measures, as appropriate, to enhance climate change education, training, public awareness, public participation and public access to information, recognizing the importance of these steps with respect to enhancing actions under this Agreement. (Paris Agreement, 2015)

OECD AND NON-OECD COUNTRY PERCEPTIONS OF RESPONSIBILITY

Perceptions as to which countries are most responsible for environmental decline in the twenty-first century also suggest a divide between OECD and non-OECD countries. The 2007 and 2008 Pew Global Attitudes Project asked the question, "Which of the following, if any, is hurting the world's environment the most."[9] In 2007, all but two countries in the forty-seven-nation study suggested that the US was the most hurtful. While 20 percent of Israeli respondents thought the US was mostly responsible, 21 percent named China as the most hurtful. Moreover, 25 percent of respondents in India noted the United States. In a somewhat self-deprecating style, however, 29 percent of respondents in India held themselves accountable for hurting the global environment the most. Similarly, a plurality of Americans (33 percent) suggested that the US was most responsible.

Table 2.2 provides the average percentage responses of OECD and non-OECD countries regarding their perceptions as to which country is hurting the global environment the most: the US or China. Interesting divides exist both within and between OECD and non-OECD countries when assessing the 2007–2008 data. In 2007, fifteen of seventeen OECD countries considered the US to be hurting the environment more than China (41 percent to 21.4 percent of respondents). Moreover, OECD countries polled in both years all lessened considerably the extent to which they blamed the US from 2007 to 2008 (nearly a 10 percentage point drop). Conversely, OECD countries as a whole increased considerably (a 14 percentage point increase) the blame that they assigned to China, moving from 21.4 percent to 35.4 percent. The most dramatic shift in orientation was by the Japanese, who decreased their identification of the US by over half (36 percent to 17 percent) while assigning increased blame to China (almost doubling from 34 percent in 2007 to 67 percent in 2008). The same pattern exists for non-OECD country perceptions of the US during this time, as the decrease registered was over 8 percentage points (39.6 percent to 31.5 percent). Moreover, identification of China by non-OECD countries increased, albeit by considerably fewer percentage points (4.1).

An interesting division also exists when comparing OECD and non-OECD country perceptions directly. Unlike OECD countries, not every non-OECD country singled out the US as most hurtful of the global environment in 2007. As aforementioned, respondents in India pointed to themselves as the most hurtful (29 percent) while listing the US second (25 percent). Moreover, while all OECD countries polled in both years lessened their blame of the US in 2008, four non-OECD countries actually increased the extent to which they blamed the US. Respondents in Argentina (49 percent to 54 percent), Jordan (22 percent to 24 percent), Pakistan (41 percent to 51 percent), and Russia (26 percent to 28 percent) increasingly pointed to the US as the most hurtful in 2008. Additionally, while all OECD countries increasingly pointed to China as the most hurtful in 2008, four non-OECD countries did not. While Jordanian and Pakistani perceptions of China remained constant from 2007

Table 2.2. Percentage of Respondents in OECD and Non-OECD Countries Indicating Which Country Is Hurting the World's Environment the Most

	Non-OECD 2007 (n=20)	*Non-OECD 2008 (n=13)*	*OECD 2007 (n=17)*	*OECD 2008 (n=11)*
US	39.6	31.5	41.0	31.6
China	8.7	12.8	21.4	35.4

Sources: Pew Research Center (2008). *Global Attitudes Project: Some positive signs for US image.* https://www.pewresearch.org/wp-content/uploads/sites/2/2008/06/2008-Pew-Global-Attitudes-Report-1-June-12-2pm.pdf; (2007). *Global Attitudes Project: Rising environmental concern in 47-nation survey.* https://www.pewresearch.org/global/2007/06/27/global-unease-with-major-world-powers

to 2008, Lebanese perceptions decreased slightly (19 percent to 18 percent) as Chinese perceptions of itself also declined (11 percent to 9 percent). The latter was not unusual, as India (29 percent to 19 percent), Brazil (16 percent to 14 percent), Japan (7 percent to 3 percent), and the US (33 percent to 22 percent) all saw a lesser percentage of respondents say that their own country was most hurtful of the world's environment in 2008 than in 2007.

This evaluation of subjective perceptions is insightful if not less than encouraging. Public opinion in the US only appears to be greatly concerned with the GSE under two conditions: when the economy is perceived to be performing well and when the environmental issue is perceived to be in close proximity to oneself. The news on the international front, however, is somewhat mixed. The countries reported in table 2.1, in total, illustrate that the majority of their population is quite worried about global warming. However, while concern in the OECD countries increased over the 2013–2017 period, the level of concern in non-OECD countries actually declined. It is plausible that these differences may reflect differences in the time that it takes for developed and developing country economies to emerge from a major recessionary period.

The public opinion data presented provide a very rough gauge of the relative importance of economic, energy, and GSE concerns before, during, and after significant recessionary periods. However, they do little to inform about the objective rate at which the consumption of vital environmental services is taking place. Our focus now turns to documenting the objective state of VES, broken down by the type of VES and relevant country subsets.

NOTES

1. The juxtaposition of "economic priority" and "environmental priority" can be loosely interpreted to represent what EM theory refers to as *economic rationality vs. ecological rationality* at the individual, company, and governmental levels of analysis.

2. Gallup asked, "With which one of these statements do you most agree: protection of the environment should be given priority, even at the risk of curbing economic growth (or) economic growth should be given priority, even if the environment suffers to some extent?"

3. Gallup asked, "With which one of these statements about the environment and energy production do you most agree: protection of the environment should be given priority, even at the risk of limiting the amount of energy supplies—such as oil, gas, and coal—which the US produces (or) development of US energy supplies—such as oil, gas and coal—should be given priority, even if the environment suffers to some extent?"

4. Gallup asked, "Right now do you think the quality of the environment in the country as a whole is getting better or getting worse?"

5. Various environmental concerns were presented as mutually exclusive. Gallup asked, "I'm going to read you a list of environmental problems. As I read each one, please tell me if you personally worry about this problem a great deal, a fair amount, only a little, or not at all. First, how much do you personally worry about ____________________?"

6. The cited examples are from the 2018 Air Quality Index of the top ten US cities that have the worst/best statistics for air pollution.

7. The methodology section of the Gallup Organization World Poll addresses several of these concerns and how their polling process attempts to deal with them.

8. The 2017 Pew report, "Globally, People Point to ISIS and Climate Change as Leading Security Threats," polled thirty-eight countries, thirty-four of which were also polled in the 2013 Pew report and thus provide comparative data. Pew asked, "I'd like your opinion about some possible international concerns for *(survey country)*. Do you think that global climate change is a major threat, a minor threat, or not a threat to *(survey country)*?"

9. Respondents were prompted with India, Germany, China, Brazil, Japan, the US, and Russia as options. The percentage of German (1/1) and Russian (16/16) respondents who named their own country remained constant from 2007 to 2008. The Pew Global Attitudes Project ceased asking this question in 2008. Moreover, other major organizations, such as the Gallup Organization, do not ask a comparable question. Consequently, there exist very limited data on the subject.

Chapter 3

The *Objective* Condition

ARE WE SERIOUSLY CLAIMING TO BE *OBJECTIVE*?

The earlier overview of *subjective perceptions* indicates differences both within and between OECD and non-OECD countries with respect to various environmental issue-areas. These differences of opinion also exist when trying to identify the *objective* state of the global sustainable environment. Measurement differences, time periods emphasized, assumptions about economic growth and development, and other factors are some of the variables that have allowed environmental and development ideologues on all sides of environmental issues, the ability to prejudice data in an effort to establish supporting evidence for their respective arguments. There is no getting around the fact that multiple arguments surrounding most any environmental issue-area are plausible and/or supportable dependent on how the entity conducting the inquiry presents the *objective* state of the GSE. The debate over the impact of anthropogenic activity on global warming is perhaps the most noteworthy of examples. On one side of the issue is the eminent Frank Sherwood Rowland (2001), 1995 Nobel Prize laureate in chemistry,[1] who maintains that

> the Earth's climate is changing, in large part because of the activities of humankind. The simplest measure of this change is the average temperature of the Earth's surface, which has risen approximately 0.7 degrees Celsius over the past century, with most of the increase occurring in the past two decades. In other words, the Earth is undergoing global warming. . . . The concentration of CO_2, the most important greenhouse gas, has increased by more than 16 percent in the past 40 years and by more than 30 percent since the beginning of the industrial revolution 200 years ago. This additional CO_2 comes from the burning of coal, oil, and natural gases, which together account for about 85 percent of the industrial energy used by humans. (pp. 29–30)

Alternatively, while most critics believe that global warming exists, they do not necessarily agree that it is primarily a function of anthropogenic activity. Renowned scientists Siegfried Fred Singer and Dennis Avery (2007) state that

> the Earth is warming but physical evidence from around the world tells us that human-emitted CO_2 (carbon dioxide) has played only a minor role in it. Instead, the mild warming seems to be part of a natural 1,500-year climate cycle (plus or minus 500 years) that goes back at least one million years. . . . By the mid-1980s, however, the First World had already convinced itself of the Greenhouse Theory and believed that puny human industries had grown powerful enough to change the planet's climate. There was little media interest in the frozen findings of obscure, parka-clad Ph.D.s in far-off Greenland. (pp. 1–2)

While one scientific camp suggests that anthropogenic activity has significantly sped up global warming, another presents contrary evidence, based on different measurement instruments, assumptions, and so forth, leading to a different conclusion—that naturogenic forces are responsible—and onward, ad nauseam, it goes. The implications of these arguments, however, are quite severe. If one assumes that decline in the GSE, generally speaking, is mostly the result of "naturally occurring cycles" and not anthropogenic activity, then there isn't much sense in undertaking research that seeks to understand the causal impact that different anthropogenic activities may have and the effectiveness of policy initiatives. For example, it would be useless to evaluate the argument contained in ecological modernization (EM) theory that technological innovation can offset the ill effects that development has on the GSE. Moreover, the environmental policymaking process would simply be a futile exercise, as the notion of *environmental determinism* or *environmental fatalism* would prevail. Unfortunately, there is no skirting the argument that any proposed *objective* state of the GSE will inevitably be dismissed by those not in agreement with the data and purported "evidence" advanced by their perceived "opposition." A litany of perceived problems by opposing camps, revolving around data acquisition, biased data interpretations, methodological concerns, and the like will likely never be sufficiently reconciled. Given this understanding, the tables in this chapter depict an array of VES, provided by the GSE and more specific country subsets, and the ability of humankind to provide/manage the VES over a nearly fifty-year time frame.[2] In effect, the presentation of the data is in the service of understanding the extent to which humankind has demanded (i.e., anthropogenic desires) that the GSE provide VES. Moreover, the identification of patterns related to such provision/management allows valuable insight about trends and the status of the *objective* GSE.

THE CONSTITUTION OF COUNTRY SUBSETS

The chapter tables present a variety of country subset data in an effort to make comparisons between country subsets that occupy different status positions vis-à-vis the GSE. They provide, moreover, a descriptive trend overview of VES (i.e., consumption) by different country subsets—expressed in lustrum periods—during 1966–2016. An evaluation of total global (WORLD) VES will serve as a reference point for the further comparative assessment of country subsets. Given the perceived environment/economic tradeoffs revealed in chapter 2, it is prudent to investigate the extremes with respect to economic development at the country subset level. To facilitate this, there is a comparison of the wealthiest (OECD)[3] and poorest least developed country (LDC) subsets. Before embarking on the investigation of ecological unequal exchange (EUE) theory in chapters 5 and 6, it would appear prudent to outline the level of VES provided by the major country subsets associated with EUE theory, namely, the core (CORE), semiperiphery (SEMI), and periphery (PERI) subsets. Finally, there is an assessment of three country subsets that represent concerns specific to their existence that may arguably affect the level of VES that they provide. For example, the assessment of landlocked countries[4] (LLDCs) and small island developing states (SIDS) represents the potential variable impact of geographical considerations and associated limits that they impose on the provision of VES. While not a geographical consideration, low-income food-dependent countries (LIFDCs) represent an important, twofold exigency the existence of which may play an important role in understanding the variable level of VES provided. While SIDS and LLDCs are mutually exclusive subsets, no fewer than six SIDS and eighteen LLDCs are also LIFDCs, thus introducing a *threefold exigency* for those twenty-four countries that further complicates their development and well-being objectives.

The presentation of the different country subsets is also important because the global system of states no longer falls into a relatively easily interpreted dichotomy such as "East versus West" or "North versus South." Arguably, the latter dichotomy is one that has experienced several "fractures" within both the "developed" and "developing countries" as it pertains to environmental issue-areas such as climate change (Ciplet and Roberts, 2017). For example, while the European Union, Canada, Japan, and Australia committed to binding emissions targets during the 2008–2012 phase of the Kyoto Protocol, the US chose not to ratify the Protocol that then President Clinton had signed. It was a "top-down" environmental protocol, and not all states from the global "North" could accept its legally binding impact on those who would ratify it. This fissure among developed countries would become more severe as Japan and New Zealand chose to forgo additional targeted levels for the 2013–2020 commitment period, and Canada outright withdrew from the Protocol, effective in 2012.

The 2015 Paris Agreement—the successor instrument to the Kyoto Protocol—further indicates the extent to which the global North is not unified in its efforts pertaining to climate change. The "bottom-up" approach to climate change inherent in the Paris Agreement, whereby the concepts of "binding" and "legality" are mostly banished,[5] still hasn't resulted in the global North being unified in its insistence to appropriately tackle global warming. For example, an ongoing conflict pits Turkey against its Annex I status under the 1992 UNFCCC.[6] Perhaps an even more significant fracture within the global North was the outright refusal of the US to remain a party to the Paris Agreement. In lieu of US Senate ratification, then president Obama signed a letter to the UN indicating US acceptance of the Paris Agreement, effectively making the US a party. However, the subsequent 2017 announcement by the US, indicating its intention to withdraw from the Paris Agreement (and its subsequent withdrawal) is inconsistent with the vast majority of the global North who continue to support the agreement.[7]

The recent experience of the global "South" also points to the need to evaluate different country subsets of the developing world. In conjunction with EUE theory, Ciplet and Roberts (2017) argue that at least three tensions can be identified as reasons for dismissing the global South as an appropriate analytical tool. Tensions between countries in the periphery and semiperiphery, within the semiperiphery, and within the periphery all highlight the extent to which the global South is fractured (pp. 381–388). The authors point to the 2009 Copenhagen Summit as evidence of discord between countries in the periphery and semiperiphery as Brazil, South Africa, India, and China (BASIC) largely sided with the US in writing an accord that would not reflect legally binding commitments, one that was in large part condemned by the vast majority of countries from the periphery. Moreover, the authors make the case that periphery countries such as those that are members of the Organization of Petroleum Exporting Countries (OPEC) are in direct competition with others, such as SIDS. These conflicts specifically focus the need for a more specific, intrusive assessment of the outdated North/South division as it pertains to the GSE and VES rendered (Ciplet and Roberts, 2017, pp. 388–391).

THE *OBJECTIVE* STATE OF VITAL ENVIRONMENTAL SERVICES

Cropland Services[8]

Table 3.1 provides lustrum data over the 1966–2016 period,[9] broken down into the aforementioned country subsets, for the *total amount of cropland services provided* and *cropland services provided on a per capita basis*.[10] Cropland services are of obvious importance in terms of, for one thing, the production of adequate foodstuffs for various populations. Cropland services have been under environmental attack by numerous entities, including but not limited to nitrates, fertilizers, and wind erosion.

The data make overly obvious the conclusion that total WORLD cropland services have expanded while population growth has considerably lessened the rate of cropland services per capita. Total cropland services increased 13.7 percent from 1.401 billion hectares (*ha*) to 1.593 billion *ha* over the entire period. Growth was consistent with the exception of 1991–1996, which was largely a result of the global recession of the early 1990s, brought on in part by a doubling of oil prices in the wake of the 1990 Iraqi invasion of Kuwait. Overall, the average five-year percentage growth (AFYPG) was 1.2 percent, with a rather large increase of 4.2 percent in 1986. Conversely, WORLD cropland services per capita were nearly halved (−48.8 percent) decreasing from 0.41 *ha* in 1966 to 0.21 *ha* in 2016. The role of increasing WORLD population is evident, as the impact of technological innovation and cropland services growth did not outpace the impact of the concurrent 119 percent growth (from 3.408 billion *ha* to 7.467 billion *ha*) in WORLD population during the period.

The comparison of OECD and LDC subsets provides a good deal of contrast. In their position as the richest countries of the world, OECD countries only slightly expanded (3.6 percent) total cropland services between 1966 and 1996 (with 1996 being the period high of 470.8 million *ha*) but witnessed a dramatic decline (−12.4 percent) throughout 2016. Overall, OECD countries decreased (−9.3 percent) total cropland services from 454.6 million *ha* in 1966 to 412.3 million *ha* in 2016. The AFYPG for the period was −1 percent, with major downward pressure ranging between three times and five times the average in the post-1996 period. OECD cropland services per capita during the period decreased 38.5 percent, from 0.52 *ha* to 0.32 *ha*. This relatively smaller percentage decline than the WORLD is in part due to technological innovation (Rudel et al., 2009) combined with a smaller rate of population growth (48.5 percent) during the period.

By contrast, total LDC cropland services grew consistently, without interruption, during the 1966–2016 period. Unlike the OECD experience, total

Table 3.1. Total Cropland Services (Million *ha*) and per Capita (*ha*), 1966–2016

	1966	*1971*	*1976*	*1981*	*1986*	*1991*	*1996*	*2001*	*2006*	*2011*	*2016*
WORLD	1,401	1,436	1,444	1,450	1,511	1,532	1,529	1,536	1,544	1,560	1,593
	.41	.38	.35	.32	.30	.28	.26	.25	.23	.22	.21
OECD	454.60	466.6	460.5	464.7	468.0	465.7	470.8	456.0	432.9	415.9	412.3
	.52	.51	.48	.46	.45	.43	.42	.39	.36	.33	.32
LDC	126.60	130.0	132.2	134.0	137.5	142.7	151.0	154.9	169.5	189.8	194.1
	.45	.41	.37	.33	.30	.27	.25	.23	.22	.22	.20
CORE	294.70	304.8	298.7	302.2	302.7	298.6	292.0	287.8	270.4	257.9	258.7
	.50	.50	.47	.46	.45	.43	.41	.39	.36	.33	.32
SEMI	478.30	492.6	500.0	504.0	543.8	559.4	555.1	570.3	581.6	590.4	609.8
	.28	.26	.23	.21	.21	.20	.18	.18	.17	.16	.16
PERI	629.40	639.2	646.3	645.0	665.7	675.0	682.5	679.2	692.5	712.8	725.0
	.34	.30	.28	.25	.24	.22	.20	.19	.18	.18	.17
LLDC	48.10	49.5	51.1	52.2	54.7	59.0	64.9	68.1	73.9	81.2	83.3
	.60	.55	.50	.45	.42	.40	.38	.35	.33	.32	.29
SIDS	6.80	7.9	8.7	9.1	9.5	9.8	10.1	10.5	10.2	10.2	9.9
	.21	.22	.22	.21	.20	.19	.19	.18	.16	.15	.14
LIFDC	360.10	367.7	369.8	366.4	383.3	392.1	413.3	420.9	438.6	454.8	459.1
	.40	.36	.32	.28	.26	.24	.22	.20	.19	.18	.16

Source: United Nations Food and Agriculture Organization, *FAOStat*.

LDC cropland services expanded by 53.3 percent, from 126.6 million *ha* in 1966 to 194.1 million *ha* in 2016. Similar to the OECD, the 1991–2001 period witnessed great change in the orientation of LDCs. Unlike the OECD, however, this period resulted in *greater* LDC expansion of total cropland services. While LDC cropland services during 1966–1996 increased by 19.3 percent, the period saw an even larger increase of 28.5 percent. While AFYPG for the period was 4.5 percent, the 1966–1996 period was considerably less (3.1 percent) while the post-1996 period was over twice as great (6.6 percent). LDC cropland services per capita during the 1966–2016 period decreased 55.6 percent, from 0.45 *ha* to 0.20 *ha.* Unlike the OECD, this decline is *significantly higher* than the WORLD experience and is in large part due to the impact of the concurrent 252.8 percent increase in LDC population (over twice that of the WORLD and five times OECD population percentage increases) during the period. Finally, it is worth noting that the OECD percentage of WORLD cropland services declined (from 32.4 percent to 25.9 percent) over the period while the percentage accounted for by LDCs increased (from 9 percent to 12.2 percent).

The comparison of CORE, SEMI, and PERI also provide notable disparities. As a subset of the OECD, CORE provides a somewhat predictable set of data. Overall, CORE countries decreased total cropland services (−12.2 percent), from 294.7 million *ha* in 1966 to 258.7 million *ha* in 2016. CORE countries slightly expanded total cropland services by 2.7 percent during 1966–1986 (with 1986 being the period high, at 302.7 million *ha*) but then witnessed a dramatic decline (−17 percent) throughout 2016. AFYPG for the period was −1.3 percent, although two noteworthy trends exist. While the 1966–1986 period witnessed a positive AFYPG of 0.7 percent, the post-1986 period reflected a decidedly negative trend, as the AFYPG was −2.6 percent. CORE cropland services per capita during the 1966–2016 period decreased 36 percent, from 0.50 *ha* to 0.32 *ha*, virtually identical to the OECD experience. Similar to the OECD, this relatively smaller decline than the WORLD experience is in part due to the implementation of technological innovation combined with a smaller rate of population growth (36.2 percent) during the period (more than three times less than the WORLD population percentage growth). In part, these combined factors led to the CORE share of WORLD cropland services, decreasing from 21 percent to 16.2 percent over the 1966–2016 period.

Total cropland services provided by PERI grew mostly consistent over the 1966–2016 period, with insignificant setbacks in 1981 and 2001. Unlike CORE—but similar to LDCs—total services grew by 15.2 percent, from 629.4 million *ha* in 1966 to 725 million *ha* in 2016. The increase in PERI cropland services during 1966–1986 was over twice that of CORE (5.8

percent vs. 2.7 percent). Contrary to the subsequent CORE decreases, however, the 1986–2016 period continued to see positive change (8.9 percent). While the latter was slower than the LDC experience (41.2 percent during 1986–2016), PERI data largely mirrored the WORLD experience. The AFYPG for the 1966–2016, 1966–1986, and 1986–2016 periods was flat, at 1.4 percent. PERI cropland services per capita during the 1966–2016 period decreased substantially (−50 percent), from 0.34 *ha* to 0.17 *ha.* Unlike CORE, this decline is essentially the same as the WORLD experience and is in large part due to the 131.9 percent increase in PERI population during 1966–2016 (over 1.1 times that of the WORLD and 3.5 times that of CORE). Lastly, the PERI percentage of WORLD cropland services, unlike the CORE decline but similar to the LDC trend, increased slightly, from 44.9 percent in 1966 to 45.5 percent in 2016.

The experience of SEMI countries shares mostly the characteristics of PERI. Like PERI, SEMI countries expanded total cropland services (at a higher rate than PERI), from 478.3 million *ha* in 1966 to 609.8 million *ha* in 2016, a 27.5 percent increase. Moreover, the AFYPG in SEMI cropland services during 1966–1986 was 3.3 percent, considerably larger than the 2.5 percent AFYPG for the 1966–2016 period. Unlike PERI, however, while remaining positive, the AFYPG in SEMI cropland services decreased to 1.9 percent during the 1986–2016 period. Most important is that growth in services still occurred, albeit at a slower rate. This “decreasing rate of growth” trend began with the aforementioned 1991–1996 WORLD decline. The 42.9 percent decrease in SEMI cropland services per capita during the 1966–2016 period more closely mirrored both the experience of PERI and the WORLD, moving from 0.28 *ha* in 1966 to 0.16 *ha* in 2016. Similar to PERI, this is in large part a function of the SEMI population increase of 120.2 percent during the period (virtually the same as the WORLD but more than 3.3 times that of CORE percentage population growth). Finally, the percentage of WORLD cropland services accounted for by SEMI more closely approximates the PERI experience, increasing from 34.2 percent in 1966 to 38.3 percent in 2016.

LLDCs and SIDs represent country subsets where geographical encumbrances exist and thus represent distinct subsets of developing countries that have concerns that are not of primary importance to the remaining developing countries. Moreover, LIFDCs have a considerable twofold quandary revolving around income levels and food insecurity that may influence the level of environment services that they provide in a manner different from other developing countries. As stated earlier, these “distinctions” allow for potential rifts within the global South, provide additional pressure on country policies pertaining to cropland services and merit an investigation into how they have provided/managed said services over time.

The LLDC[11] total cropland services data largely mirror those of LDCs, as growth was consistently positive, without interruption, throughout the period. Total LLDC cropland services grew by 73.2 percent, from 48.1 million *ha* in 1966 to 83.3 million *ha* in 2016. Moreover, the AFYPG in LLDC cropland services during 1966–1986 was 3.2 percent, while the expansion during 1986–2016 was over twice as great, at 7.2 percent. These two shorter time periods represent a great departure from the 5.7 percent AFYPG for the period. LLDC cropland services per capita closely mirrored the LDC data as the period witnessed a significant decline (51.7 percent) from 0.60 *ha* in 1966 to 0.29 *ha* in 2016. The dramatic 385.4 percent LLDC population increase during 1966–2016 most assuredly provided substantial downward pressure on the "intensity" measure. LLDC population percentage growth was the largest of any of the country subsets and was 1.5 times greater than LDCs and 3.2 times that of the WORLD. Lastly, similar to LDCs, LLDCs increased their percentage of WORLD cropland services, moving from 3.4 percent in 1966 to 5.2 percent in 2016.

The historical record of SIDS is also very similar to LDCs with one major qualification. Total SIDS cropland services expanded by 45.6 percent, from 6.8 million *ha* in 1966 to 9.9 million *ha* in 2016. Overall AFYPG for the period was 4 percent. The 1966–2001 period (2001 being the period high, at 10.5 million *ha*) saw SIDS cropland services consistently increase by an AFYPG of 6.5 percent. The 2001–2016 period, however, broke significantly from the pattern when a consistently negative trend with an AFYPG of −1.9 percent emerged. This negative tailing off is quite similar to both OECD and CORE data. SIDS cropland services per capita also presented a major difference when compared to the data of every other country subset. The SIDS data, generally speaking, approximates the PERI and SEMI data with a 33.3 percent decline over the period (0.21 *ha* to 0.14 *ha*). The 2016 level is awfully close to the "intensity" measure for both PERI (0.17 *ha*) and SEMI (0.16 *ha*). Of particular intrigue is the fact that SIDS cropland services per capita actually increased during 1966–1971 (0.21 *ha* to 0.22 *ha*) and was largely constant during 1966–1981 even though SIDS population increased 10 percent during 1966–1971, 29.9 percent during 1966–1981, and 112.5 percent during 1966–2016. Overall, the SIDS percentage of WORLD cropland services was minimal and remained virtually unchanged, from 0.5 percent in 1966 to 0.6 percent in 2016.

Total LIFDC cropland services grew by 27.5 percent, from 360.1 million *ha* in 1966 to 459.1 million *ha* in 2016. This, along with an AFYPG of 2.5 percent, was identical to SEMI in terms of total cropland services and percentage growth during the 1966–2016 period. However, the similarities with SEMI stop when separately assessing the pre-1986 and post-1986 periods, as LIFDC saw an increasing AFYPG in cropland services from the 1966–1986 period (1.6 percent) to the 1986–2016 period (3.1 percent), whereas SEMI experienced greater growth in the earlier period (3.3 percent) than in the latter period (1.9 percent). In fact, the pattern for LIFDC more closely resembles the respective experiences of PERI (1.4 percent and 1.4 percent), LDC (2.2 percent and 6 percent), and LLDC (3.3 percent and 7.3 percent). LIFDC cropland services per capita also more closely emulated the PERI, LDC, and LLDC experiences. LIFDC per capita cropland services decreased (−60 percent)—more significantly than any other country subset—moving from 0.40 *ha* in 1966 to 0.16 *ha* in 2016. This in large part reflects the impact of LIFDC population growth of 211 percent during the period. Finally, the LIFDC percentage of WORLD cropland services increased from 25.7 percent to 28.8 percent over the period.

Although already mentioned in passing, one cannot minimize the role of population growth and technological innovation and implementation in the provision of cropland services and the agricultural sector in general. *Countries less fortunate than the wealthiest evince a consistent pattern whereby the relative lack of effectively checking population growth and/or the lack of appropriate technological infusion result in cropland services steadily increasing in absolute terms yet declining significantly on a per capita (i.e., intensity) basis*. The magnitude of this trend appears most pronounced for LIFDCs, LDCs, and LLDCs. It is again worth emphasizing that the totality of cropland services provided during the 1966–2016 period significantly increased for the WORLD and all country subsets save OECD and CORE. *This reality, even with the implementation of technological innovation in the agricultural sector, can only serve to overstress the ability of the GSE to provide the cropland services necessary to produce sufficient foodstuffs for a growing population.* Ceteris paribus, current trends indicate that those who would be most hurt, and perhaps would experience such hurt the soonest, are LIFDCs, LDCs, and LLDCs, due to their relatively extreme population increases combined with relative less technological innovation and implementation. It follows that incompatible, unbefitting policy decisions about the GSE may potentially be most injurious to these countries.

Alternatively, one might argue that the data indicate a prima facie case for the proposition that OECD and CORE countries are really in the worst position with respect to the provision of cropland services. Ceteris paribus, while their population increased by relatively low rates over the 1966–2016 period, cropland services actually declined by 9.3 percent and 12.2 percent, respectively. Moreover, both the OECD and CORE percentage of WORLD cropland services declined drastically during 1966–2016, while all other country subsets increased their respective percentages of WORLD cropland services during the period. However, as EUE theory claims, all other things are not equal, as one must evaluate the role that international trade has in the provision, and consumption, of VES. The United Nations Environment Programme (UNEP) has spoken to the important interplay between cropland services, population, and technology, and the inevitable impact on the GSE (UNEP, 2011):

> Global food production has continued to keep pace with and even exceed population growth over the past two decades. Gains in production have come primarily from improved yields and to a lesser extent from new agricultural land. However, despite solid gains made in food security, millions in developing countries still face chronic hunger and malnutrition. More significant gains in agricultural production will be necessary to meet continued global population growth. These will require expanding farm land and using more intensive production techniques. Such practices have known negative impacts on the environment, including loss of biodiversity and pollution from nitrogenous fertilizers and other agricultural chemicals. (p. 61)

More recently, the United Nations Food and Agriculture Organization (UNFAO, 2017) addressed the interplay of these factors and the importance of globalization (i.e., trade):

> Agriculture and food systems have already changed significantly, but will need to adjust further in this evolving global environment. Agricultural production more than tripled between 1960 and 2015, owing in part to productivity-enhancing Green Revolution technologies and a significant expansion in the use of land, water and other natural resources for agricultural purposes. The same period witnessed a remarkable process of industrialization and globalization of food and agriculture. Food supply chains have lengthened dramatically as the physical distance from farm to plate has increased. . . . Expanding food production and economic growth have often come at a heavy cost to the natural environment. Almost one half of the forests that once covered the Earth are now gone. Groundwater sources are being depleted rapidly. Biodiversity has been deeply eroded. Every year, the burning of fossil fuels emits into the atmosphere billions of tonnes of greenhouse gases (GHG), which are responsible for global warming and climate change. All of these negative trends are accelerating in pace and intensity, and agriculture is an important part of the problem. Deforestation, mainly for farming, produces a significant share of global GHG emissions. . . . The lengthening of food chains and changes in dietary patterns have further increased the resource-, energy-, and emission-intensity of the global food system. These trends threaten the sustainability of food systems and undermine the world's capacity to meet its food needs. Although the full implications of climate change on agriculture, forestry and fisheries are difficult to predict, it is expected that the impacts will be of different levels and of a different nature in each region, ecological zone and production system. (pp. 4–5)

Grazing Services[12]

Table 3.2 provides data during 1966–2016, broken down by the aforementioned country subsets, for the *total amount of grazing services provided* and *grazing services provided on a per capita basis*. Grazing land is important to the stability of livestock farming, regardless of whether the latter is in the service of meat, dairy, wool, and/or hide production. A net loss in the provision of grazing services could lead to an increase in grain-fed livestock production. Such a development would call into question the stability of the earlier numbers on cropland services, and concerns related to food security as cropland services become more focused on animal, rather than human, consumption. Moreover, drastic increases in grazing animals over the past twenty years, and their consequent impact on topsoil erosion, makes it likely that fragile grasslands will become increasingly depleted (UNEP, 2011, p. 67; UNFAO, 2017).

The data in table 3.2 indicate that total grazing services increased 5.4 percent, from 3.11 billion *ha* in 1966 to 3.28 billion *ha* in 2016. Within this are two distinct trends. The first is an expansion trend that ran during 1966–2001. The 3.11 billion *ha* devoted to grazing services in 1966 increased 9.8 percent to approximately 3.42 billion *ha* in 2001. The second trend, from 2001 through 2016 reveals a negative shift, as grazing services declined 4.1 percent to 3.28 billion *ha* in 2016. While the AFYPG of the first period was 1.4 percent, the latter period saw an AFYPG of −1.4 percent. The latter trend reinforces the aforementioned concern regarding the potential for diverting cropland production from human to animal needs. WORLD grazing services per capita decreased by 51.6 percent during the period, moving from 0.91 *ha* in 1966 to 0.44 *ha* in 2016. This consistent, uninterrupted decline increased in magnitude as the AFYPG increased from −6.9 percent in the earlier period to −7.2 percent in the 2001–2016 period. Unlike cropland services, the net reduction in grazing services per capita is a consequence of relative WORLD population growth as well as the recent diminution of grazing. The more than doubling of WORLD population during the 1966–2016 period combined with the recent trend toward lessening grazing services speaks loudly to the pressures exerted on the GSE.

The comparison of the OECD and LDCs illustrates some points of consistency and divergence. Overall, the OECD decreased (−14.5 percent) total grazing services, from 900.8 million *ha* in 1966 to 770.6 million *ha* in 2016. While there are insignificant blips in 1976 and 1996, the trend is undeniably negative and stands in opposition to the historical experience of the WORLD. The historical experience of the OECD during 1966–1996 witnessed a negative AFYPG (−0.6 percent). However, the magnitude of this negative AFYPG increased to −2.9 percent during 1996–2016. OECD grazing services per

Table 3.2. Total Grazing Services (Million *ha*) and per Capita (*ha*), 1966–2016

	1966	*1971*	*1976*	*1981*	*1986*	*1991*	*1996*	*2001*	*2006*	*2011*	*2016*
WORLD	3,110.3	3,140.8	3,178.6	3,201.0	3,252.3	3,308.5	3,382.3	3,415.9	3,380.4	3,318.9	3,276.9
	.91	.83	.77	.71	.66	.61	.58	.55	.51	.47	.44
OECD	900.8	888.4	895.2	880.5	869.8	859.6	867.9	847.9	834.2	810.1	770.6
	1.04	.97	.93	.87	.83	.79	.77	.73	.69	.65	.60
LDC	608.9	609.5	609.7	611.1	617.3	625.5	615.4	627.6	634.5	591.4	591.4
	2.18	1.93	1.71	1.51	1.34	1.19	1.02	.92	.82	.68	.60
CORE	319.3	299.4	300.6	291.1	294.1	290.4	284.9	285.1	294.2	296.8	295.9
	.55	.49	.47	.45	.44	.42	.40	.39	.39	.38	.37
SEMI	1,204.1	1,241.5	1,282.4	1,308.3	1,323.1	1,346.0	1,380.4	1,361.8	1,326.5	1,303.8	1,265.8
	.71	.65	.60	.56	.51	.47	.45	.42	.39	.36	.34
PERI	1,586.8	1,600.0	1,595.6	1,601.6	1,635.1	1,672.1	1,717.0	1,769.0	1,759.7	1,718.4	1,715.1
	.85	.76	.68	.63	.58	.54	.51	.50	.46	.42	.39
LLDC	378.5	380.0	367.2	368.6	373.9	377.4	374.8	393.5	382.4	382.2	379.8
	4.70	4.18	3.58	3.19	2.88	2.54	2.21	2.03	1.72	1.51	1.32
SIDS	7.9	7.6	7.9	8.1	8.3	8.4	8.0	7.8	7.9	8.0	8.0
	.24	.21	.20	.19	.18	.17	.15	.13	.13	.12	.12
LIFDC	645.4	644.5	645.0	647.3	654.1	662.6	688.6	700.1	706.7	663.6	663.4
	.72	.64	.56	.50	.44	.40	.36	.33	.30	.26	.24

Source: UNFAO, *FAOStat.*

capita during the 1966–2016 period decreased 42.3 percent, from 1.04 *ha* to 0.60 *ha*, and is a function of population percentage growth—albeit relatively less than that of other country subsets save CORE—and the consistent contraction of total grazing services.

Total LDC grazing services fell (−2.9 percent) from 608.9 million *ha* in 1966 to 591.4 million *ha* in 2016. Unlike the OECD, total LDC grazing services witnessed a consistent expansion, albeit small, during a large part of the 1966–2006 period (AFYPG of 0.5 percent) before experiencing a remarkable 6.8 percent decline in 2011. The identification of these two different trends is terribly similar to the WORLD data while also standing in opposition to the continuous negative trend evinced by the OECD. LDC grazing services per capita followed the same negative pattern as the OECD (−42.3 percent) but was of considerably greater magnitude due to relatively larger LDC population increases. Overall, LDC grazing services per capita during the 1966–2016 period decreased 72.5 percent from 2.18 *ha* to 0.60 *ha.* This decline is also significantly higher than the WORLD percentage (−51.6 percent). Most remarkable is the fact that LDCs provided grazing services at over twice the per capita rate of the OECD in 1966 (2.18 *ha* to 1.04 *ha*) only to fall back to OECD levels in 2016 (0.60 *ha*) in part due to the five times greater percentage rate of population growth. Finally, it is worth noting that both the OECD and LDC percentage of WORLD grazing services provided declined (from 29 percent to 23.5 percent, and 19.6 percent to 18 percent, respectively) over the 1966–2016 period.

A quick perusal of CORE, SEMI, and PERI data provides an overall conclusion that the experience of CORE is considerably different from SEMI and PERI. For example, CORE slightly decreased total grazing services (−7.3 percent) during 1966–2016, whereas both SEMI and PERI slightly increased grazing services (5.1 percent and 8.1 percent, respectively). There do exist, however, important trends within each of these three country subsets. CORE generally trended negative (−10.8 percent), from 319.3 million *ha* in 1966 to 284.9 million *ha* in 1996 (the period low), an AFYPG in grazing services of −1.9 percent, which closely paralleled the OECD. However, during 1996–2016, AFYPG trended positive at 1 percent. Contrary to this, the experiences of both SEMI and PERI are at first positive on average before turning negative in the post-1996 and post-2001 periods, respectively. SEMI saw grazing services expand by 14.6 percent during 1966–1996 (AFYPG of 2.3 percent) but experienced an 8.3 percent decline during 1996–2016 (AFYPG of −2.1 percent). Likewise, PERI experienced grazing services growth of 11.5 percent during 1966–2001 (AFYPG of 1.6 percent)—with the majority of it during 1976–1996 (2.5 percent)—before witnessing −3 percent growth through 2016 (AFYPG of −1 percent). The CORE decrease and SEMI and PERI increases in total provision of grazing services have also produced different directional changes in their respective percentages of WORLD grazing services. CORE saw a moderate decline, from 10.3 percent to 9 percent, while PERI saw a moderate increase from 51 percent to 52.3 percent—the only country subset to record an increase. SEMI, however, remained relatively constant throughout the period, moving from 38.7 percent in 1966 to 38.6 percent in 2016.

The data on grazing services per capita reveal that population growth has negatively affected CORE, SEMI, and PERI. For example, CORE grazing services per capita during the 1966–2016 period decreased substantially, from 0.55 *ha* to 0.37 *ha*, a 32.7 percent decline. This most closely mirrors the experience of the OECD, though the magnitude is greater. SEMI grazing services per capita decreased even more extensively, moving from 0.71 *ha* to 0.34 *ha*, a 52.1 percent decrease. Finally, PERI data reflect the greatest impact, moving from 0.85 *ha* to 0.39 *ha*, a 54.1 percent reduction. While the CORE decline most closely mirrors that of the OECD, the SEMI and PERI leanings more closely approximate the WORLD trend.

Similar to that found when looking at cropland services, total LLDC[13] grazing services largely mirror that of LDCs. Total LLDC grazing services stood mostly stagnant at 0.3 percent, from 378.5 million *ha* in 1966 to 379.8 million *ha* in 2016. There is, however, a dual trend evinced similar to LDCs. The AFYPG in LLDC grazing services during 1966–2001 was positive (0.6 percent), while the AFYPG during the 2001–2016 period turned negative (−1.2 percent). LLDC grazing services per capita also resemble the LDC experience with a significant decline (−71.9 percent), from 4.70 *ha* in 1966 to 1.32 *ha* in 2016. The magnitude of the trend was greater in the 2001–2016 period (AFYPG of −13.4 percent) compared to the 1966–2001 period (AFYPG of −11.3 percent). LLDC percentage of total WORLD grazing services decreased over the period, moving from 12.2 percent in 1966 to 11.6 percent in 2016, again mimicking the LDC experience.

The SIDS data present a case that is remarkably similar to LLDCs when looking at the total provision of grazing services. SIDS grazing services remained very stable, moving from 7.9 million *ha* in 1966 to 8 million *ha* in 2016, a slight, 1.3 percent increase. The AFYPG was also quite low (0.2 percent) during the period. These numbers, however, mask two incredibly significant periods. The 1971–1991 period, for example, greatly outpaced growth during the entire period (AFYPG of 2.5 percent), only to be followed in 1991–2001 by a considerable retrenchment in total grazing services (AFYPG of −3.7 percent). SIDS grazing services per capita most closely approximate the WORLD, as these countries experienced an exact halving, from 0.24 *ha* 1966 to 0.12 *ha* in 2016, reflecting the role of population growth combined with spatial limitations on expanding grazing services. Moreover, the AFYPG during the period was very steep (−6.6 percent). SIDS percentage of total WORLD grazing services was minimal, at 0.3 percent in 1966, and remained virtually unchanged at 0.2 percent in 2016.

Total LIFDC grazing services grew slightly (2.8 percent), from 645.4 million *ha* in 1966 to 663.4 million *ha* in 2016, resembling that of both LLDCs and SIDS. However, the trend within the period is quite variable and isn't analogous to any other country subsets, as there are three distinct periods evident. During 1966–1976, the AFYPG in grazing services was remarkably stable (0 percent). During 1976–2006, however, the AFYPG was 1.6 percent, with 1996 recording an exceptional 4 percent growth in grazing services. The 2006–2016 period then saw a significant negative orientation (AFYPG of −3.1 percent). The idiosyncratic nature of these three intraperiod trends presents an explanatory enigma. One might make the argument that the overall growth rate during 1966–2016 is comparable to those of SIDS and LLDCs, but the reality is that the aforementioned twofold exigency (i.e., income levels and food insecurity) has made the interpretation of LIFDC grazing services more complex. The trend in LIFDC grazing services per capita looks similar to the experience of LDCs and LLDCs. LIFDC grazing services per capita decreased (−66.7 percent) significantly moving from 0.72 *ha* in 1966 to 0.24 *ha* in 2016, reflecting greatly the relative exorbitant LIFDC population growth during this period. Finally, the LIFDC percentage of total WORLD grazing services dipped slightly, from 20.8 percent in 1966 to 20.2 percent in 2016.

The data in table 3.2 illustrate that every country subset experienced a significant net decline in the "intensity" measure, grazing services per capita. Also notable is that only developing countries recorded any growth in total grazing services during the 1966–2016 period. The OECD and CORE, while having the lowest population growth rates, also recorded decreases in their total grazing services as well as in their percentage of total WORLD grazing services. LDCs and LLDCs were the most significantly impacted during the period. While neither of these groups saw a significant increase in grazing services, they both recorded greater than 70 percent declines in grazing services per capita.

Forest Services[14]

Table 3.3 contains limited data for *total forest services* and *total forest services per capita* from 1991 through 2016 for the various country subsets. The importance of sustainable forest services to timber-related products, cropland, and biodiversity is considerable but is perhaps most important with respect to terrestrial carbon sequestration and the "creation" of sink capacity. The overall impact of absolute losses in forest services in this regard should be obvious. Its relationship to global warming, cropland services, and economic development was captured by the UNEP (2011), when it stated,

> Around 13 million hectares of forest were converted to other uses or loss through natural causes each year between 2000 and 2010, compared to 16 million hectares per year during the preceding decade. This results not only in biodiversity loss, but also contributes 12–15% to global warming by releasing CO_2 into the atmosphere and hampering further CO_2 storage. . . . Between 1990 and 2010, 3% of mangrove extent was lost, mostly as a result of coastal development and conversions to agriculture and aquaculture (rice fields, shrimp farms). (p. 37)

Contrary to the earlier findings pertaining to cropland and grazing services, the data in table 3.3 reflect an absolute and continual decline in forest services for the WORLD, as total hectares declined (−3 percent), from 4.121 billion *ha* to 3.996 billion *ha* from 1991 through 2016. The AFYPG for the 1991–2016 period was −0.6 percent, with considerably larger percentage losses during 1991–2001. WORLD forest services per capita have consistently decreased by −28.9 percent (AFYPG of −6.4 percent) over the 1991–2016 period, from 0.76 *ha* in 1991 to 0.54 *ha* in 2016.

The comparison of OECD and LDCs provides a stark differentiation in terms of the trend in total forest services over the twenty-five-year period. The OECD expanded the provision of forest services, in uninterrupted

Table 3.3. Total Forest Services (Million *ha*) and per Capita (*ha*), 1991–2016

	1991	*1996*	*2001*	*2006*	*2011*	*2016*
WORLD	4,121.0	4,084.7	4,051.0	4,029.3	4,012.4	3,995.8
	.76	.70	.65	.61	.57	.54
OECD	1,056.7	1068.9	1,072.1	1,073.6	1,076.1	1,081.7
	.97	.95	.92	.89	.86	.84
LDC	614.3	598.8	583.7	570.4	557.6	545.2
	1.17	1.00	.86	.74	.64	.56
CORE	740.4	742.5	743.8	746.4	750.4	752.5
	1.07	1.04	1.01	.98	.96	.95
SEMI	1,208.8	1,197.2	1,187.9	1,186.4	1,180.3	1,180.3
	.43	.39	.37	.35	.33	.31
PERI	2,171.0	2,145.0	2,119.3	2,096.5	2,081.6	2,063.0
	.70	.64	.59	.55	.51	.47
LLDC	264.3	270.0	261.0	253.3	253.1	245.7
	1.78	1.18	.99	.84	.74	.63
SIDS	80.8	81.1	81.3	81.6	81.8	81.8
	1.61	1.49	1.40	1.31	1.24	1.17
LIFDC	625.3	613.5	598.1	585.2	571.4	558.5
	.38	.32	.28	.25	.22	.20

Source: UNFAO, *FAOStat.*

fashion, from 1.057 billion *ha* in 1991 to 1.082 billion *ha* in 2016, a 2.4 percent increase from start to finish. Conversely, total LDC forest services decreased consistently over the 1991–2016 period and resulted in the largest percentage decline of any country subset. Total LDC forest services declined (−11.2 percent), from 614.3 million *ha* in 1991 to 545.2 million *ha* in 2016. The OECD AFYPG was 0.5 percent, while that of LDCs was consistent, at −2.3 percent. Overall, the OECD percentage of total WORLD forest services increased from 25.6 percent to 27.1 percent, while that of LDCs decreased from 14.9 percent to 13.6 percent. OECD forest services per capita mirrors the WORLD decline, although the percentage decline was half as large. During the 1991–2016 period, OECD forest services per capita declined from 0.97 *ha* in 1991 to 0.84 *ha* in 2016, a 13.4 percent reduction. Similarly, the trend for LDC forest services per capita was also staunchly negative, moving from 1.17 *ha* in 1991 to 0.56 *ha* in 2016. The 52.1 percent decline—nearly four times that of the OECD—reflects the importance of the 86.6 percent LDC population percentage increase during the twenty-five-year period. The AFYPG in OECD forest services per capita (−2.9 percent) and that of LDCs (−13.7 percent) further represent the magnitude of the disparity.

The data in table 3.3 provide great disparity regarding CORE, SEMI, and PERI, as CORE was a microcosm of the OECD while SEMI and PERI closely approximated the WORLD and LDCs. CORE slightly increased total forest services (1.6 percent) from 740.4 million *ha* in 1991 to 752.5 million *ha* in 2016. The AFYPG was very stable throughout the period, at 0.3 percent. Contrary to this, both SEMI and PERI observed net decreases during the 1991–2016 period. Total SEMI forest services declined (−2.4 percent) from 1.21 billion *ha* in 1991 to 1.18 billion *ha* in 2016. PERI experienced a deeper decline (−5 percent), dropping from 2.17 billion *ha* in 1991 to 2.06 billion *ha* in 2016. Although intuitive, it is worth noting that these trends stand in direct contrast to CORE, SEMI, and PERI data, representing total cropland services and total grazing services, although the time frame covered but twenty-five years. The CORE percentage of total WORLD forest services, like that of the OECD, increased from 18 percent to 18.8 percent over the period, while PERI declined from 52.7 percent to 51.6 percent. Conversely, the SEMI percentage of total WORLD forest services increased ever so slightly, from 29.3 percent in 1991 to 29.5 percent in 2016. The AFYPG of CORE, SEMI, and PERI were 0.3 percent, −0.5 percent, and −1.2 percent, respectively, and didn't reveal any masked trends within the 1991–2016 period.

All three country subsets experienced consistent negative trends in forest services per capita during the 1991–2016 period. The severity of these declines, however, were again very similar to the OECD and WORLD data. CORE total forest services per capita moved from 1.07 *ha* in 1991 to 0.95 *ha* in 2016, an 11.2 percent decrease. Proportionately, the CORE data represented a virtual mirror image of OECD data. The SEMI numbers fell from 0.43 *ha* in 1991 to 0.31 *ha* in 2016, a 27.9 percent reduction. Similarly, the PERI numbers fell from 0.70 *ha* in 1991 to 0.47 *ha* in 2016, a 32.9 percent decrease that effectively replicated the WORLD data. Forest services per capita of CORE, SEMI, and PERI were −2.4 percent, −6.3 percent, and −7.7 percent, respectively, and did not reveal any within-period trends.

Total LLDC[15] forest services were the sole country subset that did not exhibit a consistent trend over the 1991–2016 period. Total forest services increased (2.2 percent), from 264.3 million *ha* in 1991 to 270 million *ha* in 1996. However, a consistent negative trend represented the 1996–2016 period, as total hectares declined (−9.4 percent) to 245.7 million *ha* in 2016 with the AFYPG also remaining negative for the latter period (−2.3 percent). LLDCs recorded the deepest percentage fall (−64.6 percent) of any country subset in forest services per capita, moving from 1.78 *ha* in 1991 to 0.63 *ha* in 2016. The AFYPG was −18.4 percent with positive growth only occurring during 1991–1996. Moreover, the LLDC percentage of total WORLD forest services also declined during the period, from 6.4 percent to 6.1 percent.

The SIDS data reflect a very slight (1.2 percent) but consistent growth (AFYPG range of 0 percent to 0.4 percent), from 80.8 million *ha* in 1991 to 81.8 million *ha* in 2016. It is worth noting that SIDS were the only developing country subset that recorded expansion in total forest services. While conceptually an oddity, it's also worth noting that SIDS have expanded in cropland services, grazing services, and forest services. SIDS forest services per capita decreased (−27.3 percent), dipping from 1.61 *ha* in 1991 to 1.17 *ha* in 2016. Although the magnitude isn't as great, the SIDS data mirror PERI, SEMI, and the WORLD. SIDS percentage of total WORLD forest services remained constant, at 2 percent throughout 1991–2001.

Total LIFDC forest services decreased (−10.7 percent), from 625.3 million *ha* in 1991 to 558.5 million *ha* in 2016. The AFYPG changes were quite constant throughout the entire period, ranging from −1.9 percent to −2.5 percent with a mean of −2.3 percent. The consistency in the AFYPG decreases, given the aforementioned twofold exigency present in LIFDCs, may well reflect the need to utilize (i.e., consume) forest services for personal use, as the data in tables 3.1 and 3.2 illustrate that LIFDCs increased both cropland services and grazing services during this time frame. LIFDC forest services per capita also reflected a consistent decline (−47.4 percent), from 0.38 *ha* in 1991 to 0.20 *ha* in 2016, with an AFYPG of −12 percent. The latter represents the lowest level of forest services per capita of any of the country subsets, perhaps speaking to the relative extreme situation in which LIFDCs find themselves. Lastly, only LDCs experienced both a greater percentage decline than LIFDCs in both total forest services and forest services per capita.

Fisheries and Aquaculture Services[16]

The data in table 3.4 indicate that every country subset except CORE expanded its fisheries and aquaculture services greatly during the 1966–2016 period. The net effect of the dramatic increases in total fisheries and aquaculture services comes into focus when one considers the extent to which fish stocks have been exploited. Fully exploited marine fish stocks have remained somewhat stable, at 50 percent since the 1970s. In 2010, however, the UNFAO (2010) sounded the alarm that fisheries and aquaculture services were evincing a negative trend with respect to sustainability when it stated that

> the proportion of stocks estimated to be underexploited or moderately exploited declined from 40 percent in the mid-1970s to 15 percent in 2008. . . . In contrast, the proportion of overexploited, depleted or recovering stocks increased from 10 percent in 1974 to 32 percent in 2008. . . . In 2008, 15 percent of the stock groups monitored by FAO were estimated to be underexploited (3 percent) or moderately exploited (12 percent) and, therefore, able to produce more than their current catches. This is the lowest percentage recorded since the mid-1970s. Slightly more than half of the stocks (53 percent) were estimated to be fully exploited and, therefore, their current catches are at or close to their maximum sustainable productions, with no room for further expansion. (p. 35)

The UNFAO would continue to sound the earlier alarm by stating that the "percentage of stocks fished at biologically unsustainable levels increased from 10 percent in 1974 to 33.1 percent in 2015, with the largest increases in the late 1970s and 1980s" (UNFAO, 2018b, p. 40). While not a particularly large increase, the 1.1 percentage point increase from 32 percent in 2008 still represents movement toward *eventual unsustainability*. The UNFAO (2018b) would continue to sound the alarm with a more calamitous tone:

> In 2015, maximally sustainably fished stocks accounted for 59.9 percent and underfished stocks for 7.0 percent of the total assessed stocks. The underfished stocks decreased continuously from 1974 to 2015, whereas the maximally sustainably fished stocks decreased from 1974 to 1989, and then increased to 59.9 percent in 2015. (p. 40)
>
> It seems very unlikely that the world's fisheries can rebuild the 33.1 percent of stocks that are overfished in the very near future, because rebuilding requires time, usually two to three times the species' life span. (p. 46)

Table 3.4 provides data on total WORLD fisheries and aquaculture services from both marine and inland waters. Since 1950, inland waters have typically accounted for 5–10 percent of total fisheries and aquaculture services (UNFAO, 2010). In 2016, inland waters constituted 12.8 percent of total

Table 3.4. Fisheries and Aquaculture Services (1,000 *t*) and per Capita (*kg*), 1966–2016

	1966	*1971*	*1976*	*1981*	*1986*	*1991*	*1996*	*2001*	*2006*	*2011*	*2016*
WORLD	54,464	66,220	69,556	75,298	93,455	98,293	121,952	127,184	139,992	155,616	172,363
	16.0	17.5	16.7	16.6	18.8	18.1	20.9	20.4	21.1	22.1	23.1
OECD	24,662	28,681	31,781	36,779	41,846	39,788	39,704	35,601	33,980	31,611	29,282
	28.4	31.3	32.9	36.5	39.9	36.5	35.2	30.5	28.1	25.2	22.7
LDC	2,277	2,840	2,791	2,936	3,502	3,980	4,511	6,547	9,000	10,874	13,124
	8.2	9.0	7.8	7.3	7.6	7.6	7.5	9.6	11.6	12.5	13.4
CORE	14,599	17,455	17,984	19,872	22,261	19,871	17,242	16,132	15,717	13,980	13,842
	25.0	28.6	28.3	30.4	33.1	28.7	24.1	21.9	20.7	17.9	17.4
SEMI	15,113	17,787	21,847	23,030	28,745	35,808	57,625	64,150	73,062	86,530	104,467
	8.9	9.2	10.2	9.8	11.1	12.6	18.9	19.8	21.4	24.1	27.8
PERI	24,759	30,985	29,732	32,403	42,457	42,616	47,086	46,903	51,215	55,107	54,020
	13.2	14.7	12.7	12.7	15.1	13.7	14.1	13.1	13.4	13.5	12.4
LLDC	418	512	538	518	588	691	780	938	1,219	1,545	1,836
	5.2	5.6	5.2	4.5	4.5	4.6	3.4	3.6	4.0	4.5	4.7
SIDS	209	345	510	546	764	747	766	1,014	1,605	1,566	1,672
	6.4	9.5	12.9	12.8	16.5	14.8	14.1	17.4	25.8	23.7	23.9
LIFDC	2,352	3,313	3,562	3,883	4,703	6,065	7,701	9,165	10,988	13,250	17,352
	2.6	3.3	3.1	3.0	3.2	3.7	4.1	4.3	4.7	5.2	6.2

Source: UNFAO, Global Capture and Production 1950–2019..

fisheries capture (UNFAO, 2018b, p. 2). The WORLD data indicate extensive growth in total fisheries and aquaculture services, growing from 54.5 million tons (*t*) in 1966 to 172.4 million *t* in 2016. Somewhat surprising is the extent to which this 216.5 percent increase in total fisheries and aquaculture services far outpaced the 119 percent increase in WORLD population over the same period, indicating the extent to which this aspect of the GSE has become increasingly crucial to meeting the food consumption needs of developing countries, especially SIDS and LIFDCs. While the AFYPG (12.5 percent) for the period was impressive, a more intrusive look at the data reveals that the largesse of growth during the period occurred in 1971 (21.6 percent), 1986 (24.1 percent), and 1996 (24.1 percent). Finally, WORLD fisheries and aquaculture services per capita were quite variable during the period but ultimately increased (44.4 percent), from 16 kilograms (*kg*) in 1966 to 23.1 *kg* in 2016. Moreover, the AFYPG in fisheries and aquaculture services per capita was 4 percent, while once again the three aforementioned years accounted for a goodly amount in the gains made in population growth (9.4 percent, 13.3 percent, and 15.5 percent, respectively).

The comparison of OECD and LDCs revealed some differences in the patterned behavior. Overall, OECD fisheries and aquaculture services increased by 18.7 percent, from 24.7 million *t* in 1966 to 29.3 million *t* in 2016. This general observation, however, is masking a good deal of variability in the provision of these services, as two distinct trends are present. OECD fisheries and aquaculture services first expanded greatly (69.7 percent) from 1966 through 1986 but then precipitously declined (−42.9 percent) through 2016. The AFYPG of 2.1 percent also significantly masked these two trends, with the early trend evincing a 14.1 percent AFYPG, while the latter trend was −5.9 percent. OECD fisheries and aquaculture services per capita data revealed a decline (−20.1 percent), from 28.4 *kg* in 1966 to 22.7 *kg* in 2016. Initially, the trend was extremely positive, increasing 40.5 percent from 28.4 *kg* in 1966 to 39.9 *kg* in 1986. However, from 1986 through 2016, the level consistently decreased (−43.1 percent) reaching 22.7 *kg* in 2016 with an AFYPG of −8.9 percent. Not surprising, the OECD percentage of total WORLD fisheries and aquaculture services declined significantly, from 45.3 percent in 1966 to 17 percent in 2016.

The LDC data provide a stark contrast to the OECD experience. Outside of one minor inconsistency in 1976, LDC data present a uniform, consistent increase (476.4 percent) in the provision of fisheries and aquaculture services, from 2.3 million *t* in 1966 to 13.1 million *t* in 2016. This increase dwarfed LDC population percentage growth for the period (252.8 percent) and again illustrates the importance of this aspect of the GSE for developing countries. The AFYPG of 19.9 percent somewhat masks the extraordinary growth from 2001 through 2016. Having said this, though, it is important to note that LDC fisheries and aquaculture services per capita actually declined (−8.5 percent), from 8.2 *kg* in 1966 to 7.5 *kg* in 1996. The latter figure would, however, nearly double by 2016 (13.4 *kg*, 78.7 percent), as the LDC total provision of these services nearly tripled, far outpacing population percentage growth during 2001–2016. Accordingly, LDC percentage of total WORLD provision of fisheries and aquaculture services increased from 4.2 percent in 1966 to 7.6 percent in 2016.

CORE data on fisheries and aquaculture services reveal the only country subset to have experienced a decline over the 1966–2016 period. Total CORE services fell (−5.2 percent) from 14.6 million *t* in 1966 to 13.8 million *t* in 2016, with an AFYPG of 0.01 percent. Perhaps more important than the directional difference is the fact that the larger CORE trend, like the OECD, masked a more important reality: that the CORE provision of fisheries and aquaculture services mimicked the aforementioned dual OECD trends. A marked increase (52.5 percent) through the 1986 period was evident prior to a precipitous decline (−37.8 percent) through 2016. CORE fisheries and aquaculture services per capita also followed the earlier noted OECD per capita data, increasing (32.4 percent) from 25 *kg* in 1966 to 33.1 *kg* in 1986 before trending extraordinarily negative (−46.3 percent), falling to 17.4 *kg* in 2016. It follows that the CORE percentage of total WORLD fisheries and aquaculture services would fall spectacularly—from 26.8 percent in 1966 to a mere 8 percent in 2016.

SEMI data reveal a glaring disparity with CORE. While CORE reveals great growth in the provision of total fisheries and aquaculture services, followed by a considerable decline, SEMI data illustrate consistent, extremely expansive growth throughout the entire period. Amazingly, total SEMI fisheries and aquaculture services significantly increased (591.2 percent), from 15.1 million *t* in 1966 to 104.5 million *t* in 2016. The AFYPG from 1991 through 1996 registered 60.9 percent alone. It is important to realize the importance of the Chinese contribution to the explosion beginning in 1991. While Chinese fisheries capture increased from 1991 through 1996 and then leveled off through 2016, Chinese aquaculture absolutely exploded during the 1991–2016 period (UNFAO, 2018b, p. 19). This in part explains the dramatic increases in SEMI fisheries and aquaculture services per capita services in the 1991–1996 period (AFYPG of 50 percent). Moreover, the SEMI per capita data rose from 8.9 *kg* in 1966 to 27.4 *kg* in 2016, an increase of 212.4 percent—far outpacing the elevated 131.9 percent increase in SEMI population during the period. Accordingly, while the CORE percentage of total WORLD fisheries and aquaculture services decreased, the SEMI percentage increased outrageously, from 27.7 percent in 1966 to 60.6 percent in 2016.

PERI data closely emulate SEMI with respect to total fisheries and aquaculture services growth but resemble CORE when looking at the per capita provision of these services. Total PERI provision of fisheries and aquaculture increased (118.2 percent), from 24.8 million *t* in 1966 to 54 million *t* in 2016. While insignificant slight pattern interruptions appeared in 1976, 2001, and 2016, the overarching pattern of significant growth is unmistakable, with an AFYPG of 8.6 percent. The evaluation of PERI fisheries and aquaculture services per capita data, however, indicates a good deal of turbulence throughout the fifty-year period even though overall growth was negative (−6.1 percent), dipping from 13.2 percent in 1966 to 12.4 percent in 2016. The AFYPG of −0.2 percent masks at least two years, 1971 and 1986, where great gains emerged in the intensity measure, 11.4 percent and 18.9 percent, respectively. Although the magnitude of the decrease was considerably less, the PERI percentage of total WORLD fisheries and aquaculture services mimicked CORE, dropping from 45.5 percent in 1966 to 31.3 percent in 2016. A worthwhile observation is that PERI produced more fisheries and aquaculture services than the OECD beginning in 1986 and produced more than SEMI from 1966 through 1991 until the extraordinary hyperproduction in services by China.

LLDCs are obviously at a great disadvantage with respect to fisheries and aquaculture services due to the marine element being largely nonexistent. Regardless, LLDCs[17] experienced a major increase (339.2 percent), largely uninterrupted, in the total provision of fisheries and aquaculture services, steadily moving from 418 thousand *t* in 1966 to 1.8 million *t* in 2016. One should be cognizant of the fact, however, that the latter figure represents a virtually nonexistent 1.1 percent of total WORLD fisheries and aquaculture services—albeit an increase from its 0.8 percent share in 1966. LLDC fisheries and aquaculture services per capita saw an overall decline (−9.6 percent), similar to PERI, from 5.2 *kg* in 1966 to 4.7 *kg* in 2016. This speaks to the obvious important role of international trade in fisheries and aquaculture, in particular in inland capture. The UNFAO (2018b) further highlights the importance of fisheries and aquaculture to LLDCs and SIDS:

> The highest per capita fish consumption, over 50 kg, is found in several SIDS, particularly in Oceania, which underlines the diminishing but still important role of geography in the disparities in fish consumption among regions. The lowest levels, just above 2 kg, are in Central Asia and some landlocked countries such as Afghanistan, Ethiopia and Lesotho. International trade has helped to reduce the impact of geographical location and limited domestic production, broadening the markets for many species and offering wider choices to consumers. (pp. 72–73)

Similar to LLDCs, SIDS have greatly increased total fisheries and aquaculture services. More than any other country subset, total services increased by a monstrous 700 percent over the 1966–2016 period, moving from 209 thousand *t* to 1.7 million *t* in 2016. With the exception of two insignificant disruptions, in 1991 and 2011, this positive trend has not wavered. Most notable are the 32.4 percent and 58.2 percent increases from 1996 through 2006, as increased attention was given to marine capture (125 percent increase) from 1996 through 2006 while decreasing focus on inland waters—decreasing precipitously (−36.4 percent) from 1986 through 2016. While the AFYPG was 25.5 percent, three remarkable periods of growth—1966–1976 (AFYPG of 56.5 percent), 1981–1986 (AFYPG of 39.9 percent), and 1996–2006 (AFYPG of 45.4 percent)—account for the vast majority of the overall 1966–2016 growth. SIDS fisheries and aquaculture services per capita data fluctuate greatly during the period. However, there is a marked upsurge (273.4 percent) from 6.4 *kg* in 1966 to 23.9 *kg* in 2016. This dramatic increase, unsurprisingly, is also the largest among the country subsets. The AFYPG is telling of the extreme volatility in production during the period, ranging from −10.3 percent to 48.4 percent. However, one should take note that the SIDS percentage of total WORLD fisheries and aquaculture services actually decreased, from 0.4 percent in 1966 to 0.01 percent in 2016.

LIFDCs were responsible for over 40 percent of world inland capture in 2016. Coupled with the knowledge that developing countries consume roughly 90 percent of the nearly 95 percent of the total world inland fisheries capture, it is easy to see the importance of fisheries and aquaculture services to LIFDCs (UNFAO, 2018b, p. 46). The data for LIFDC reveal a consistent expansion that rivals SIDS. The total LIFDC provision of fisheries and aquaculture services swelled (637.8 percent), unwavering, from 2.4 million *t* in 1996 to 17.4 million *t* in 2016—second only to SIDS. The AFYPG was 22.5 percent and outside of the 1966–1981 period was remarkably stable. Although two minor discrepancies are present in 1971 and 1976, the overall trend with respect to LIFDC fisheries and aquaculture services per capita is also consistently positive during the period (138.5 percent), moving from 2.6 *kg* in 1966 to 6.2 *kg* in 2016. Most notably different from LLDCs and SIDS is the fact that the LIFDC percentage of total WORLD fisheries and aquaculture services increased substantially from 1966 through 2016, from 4.3 percent to 10.1 percent.

CO_2 Emissions

Table 3.5 provides data on *total CO_2 emissions from fossil fuels and cement production* and *CO_2 emissions per capita* that each country subset accounted for during 1966–2016. The obvious concern over CO_2 emissions is with respect to ozone depletion, global warming, and global climate change. Total

CO_2 emissions reflect the absolute magnitude (i.e., scale) of importance to global warming, as was briefly discussed in chapter 1. From an environmental perspective, it is the totality of WORLD CO_2 emissions that ultimately matters in terms of the GSE, as *accumulation* is of primary importance (Jorgenson and Clark, 2012, p. 10; Rosa et al., 2004). Politically speaking, however, it is CO_2 emissions per capita—or the *intensity* with which emissions occur from specific countries or country subsets—that are the most important (Jorgenson and Clark, 2012, p. 12; Jorgenson et al., 2007; Shandra et al., 2004).

Perhaps the most notable international agreement with respect to effectively addressing ozone-depleting substances (ODS) and their effects on global warming and GCC has been the 1987 Montreal Protocol. It paid great dividends in terms of controlling ODS, most specifically chlorofluorocarbons (CFCs)[18] and halons but has been relatively ineffective to date in stopping the increases in either methane or CO_2 emissions. As stated by the UNEP (2011), "Global efforts since 1992 to slow the growth of, and ultimately reduce the total level of CO_2 emissions, have not yet fully succeeded. Those efforts must be strengthened; otherwise, it is very unlikely that the target of limiting temperature increase to 2° C by 2100 to reduce global warming as agreed by global leaders in Cancun in 2010, will be met" (p. 22). Moreover, while the Montreal Protocol was generally effective with respect to CFCs, it did not necessarily foresee that the replacement protocol, first the production of hydro-chlorofluorocarbons (HCFCs) and then hydrofluorocarbons (HFCs), would perhaps increase the presence of CFC-113a. While HFCs are not ODS, they are GHG that, due to their lengthy atmospheric lifetime and relatively large global warming potential (GWP), have a more negative impact than even CO_2 on global warming. While the intent of the 2015 Paris Agreement was to further control GHG, including the most critical one, CO_2, it relied on a nonbinding mechanism that included nationally determined contributions (NDCs). The 2016 Kigali Amendment to the Montreal Protocol, which entered into force in January 2019, not only addresses the aforementioned HFC problem in a binding fashion but, in so doing, also addresses a substance that effectively exacerbates the impact of CO_2 on global warming.

Table 3.5 reveals that total WORLD and CO_2 emissions per capita have increased substantially (196.2 percent and 35.4 percent, respectively) from 1966 through 2016. Total WORLD CO_2 emissions consistently increased from 12,046 million metric tons (*mt*) in 1966 to 35,675 million *mt* in 2016, with an AFYPG of 11.8 percent. Most alarming are the major percentage increases from 1966 through 1976 (AFYPG of 21.7 percent) and from 2001 through 2011 (AFYPG of 16.5 percent). CO_2 emissions per capita increased from 3.53 *mt* per capita in 1966 to 4.78 *mt* in 2016, with an AFYPG of 3.3 percent. The two aforementioned time frames are critical as CO_2 emissions

Table 3.5. Total CO_2 Emissions from Fossil Fuels and Cement Production (Million *mt* of Carbon), and per Capita (*mt*), 1966–2016

	1966	*1971*	*1976*	*1981*	*1986*	*1991*	*1996*	*2001*	*2006*	*2011*	*2016*
WORLD	12,046	15,410	17,801	18,787	20,396	22,429	23,523	25,138	30,287	34,357	35,675
	3.53	4.08	4.28	4.14	4.11	4.19	4.03	4.04	4.57	4.88	4.78
OECD	7,759	9,813	10,737	10,813	10,780	12,036	12,949	13,446	13,867	13,098	12,597
	9.06	10.86	11.27	10.86	10.41	11.18	11.55	11.57	11.52	10.50	9.81
LDC	31	45	46	55	64	72	95	119	172	238	319
	.11	.14	.13	.14	.14	.14	.16	.17	.22	.27	.33
CORE	6,650	8,319	8,862	8,684	8,480	9,537	10,171	10,470	10,594	9,782	9,282
	11.37	13.62	13.97	13.29	12.61	13.75	14.22	14.21	13.97	12.55	11.66
SEMI	1,594	2,391	3,189	3,831	4,831	5,992	7,634	8,326	12,018	16,044	16,903
	.94	1.24	1.49	1.63	1.87	2.11	2.51	2.57	3.52	4.47	4.50
PERI	3,802	4,700	5,750	6,272	7,085	6,900	5,718	6,342	7,675	8,531	9,490
	2.03	2.23	2.46	2.45	2.51	2.22	1.71	1.78	2.01	2.10	2.18
LLDC	12	18	22	26	30	38	40	44	57	91	123
	.15	.20	.21	.23	.23	.26	.18	.17	.19	.27	.31
SIDS	34	74	113	115	123	140	160	171	181	219	244
	1.03	2.04	2.86	2.69	2.65	2.78	2.94	2.94	2.91	3.31	3.49
LIFDC	380	538	665	804	1,019	1,188	1,375	1,627	1,970	2,539	3,176
	.42	.53	.58	.62	.69	.72	.72	.77	.84	.99	1.13

Sources: United Nations Food and Agriculture Organization, *FAOStat;* Global Carbon Project, 2017.

per capita AFYPG was exceptional at 10.3 percent and 9.9 percent, respectively. Admittedly, the 1966–2016 period has seen uneven growth in intensity, but the general trend is difficult to ignore. Perhaps most troublesome is that the international community, unlike its sustained success in limiting ODS via the Montreal Protocol framework, hasn't been able to sustain such binding international success/commitment to GHG emissions, especially CO_2.

The evaluation of OECD and LDCs reveals notable differences in the patterned behavior of the richest and poorest countries of the world. Total OECD CO_2 emissions increased considerably (62.4 percent) from 7,759 million *mt* of carbon in 1966 to 12,597 million *mt* in 2016. However, a more intrusive look identifies two distinct trends present in the data. Save for a very minor regression in 1986, OECD increases were consistent through 2006, when they reached their pinnacle of 13,867 million *mt*, a 78.7 percent increase, before declining (–9.2 percent) to the lower 2016 level.[19] Likewise, the AFYPG of 5.3 percent revealed two rather exceptional periods of growth, from 1966 through 1976 (AFYPG of 18 percent) and 1986 through 1996 (AFYPG of 9.7 percent). Total OECD CO_2 emissions per capita increased (8.3 percent) over the same period, from 9.06 *mt* to 9.81 *mt*. Again, the AFYPG masks a substantial amount of variation (AFYPG ranging from −8.9 percent to 19.9 percent). Total OECD CO_2 emissions as a percentage of total WORLD CO_2 emissions decreased considerably, from 64.4 percent in 1966 to 35.3 percent in 2016.

Total LDC CO_2 emissions grew remarkably (929 percent) from 31 million *mt* in 1966 to 319 million *mt* in 2016. Moreover, the LDC data reveal a pattern that not only shows consistent increases throughout the period but significantly larger increases during the 1966–1971 (AFYPG of 45.2 percent) and the 1991–2016 periods (i.e., 31.9 percent, 25.3 percent, 44.5 percent, 38.4 percent, and 34 percent, respectively). Also noteworthy is that the rate of growth in LDC CO_2 emissions from 2006 through 2016 has slowed. Even with a minor deviation in 1971, the pattern for LDC CO_2 emissions per capita also grew (200 percent) consistently moving from 0.11 *mt* in 1966 to 0.33 *mt* in 2016, with an AFYPG of 12.4 percent. Total LDC CO_2 emissions moved from 0.3 percent of total WORLD CO_2 emissions to 0.9 percent over the 1966–2016 period. While the consistent percentage increases in LDC CO_2 emissions are spectacular and undeniable, one must remain cognizant of the point of reference—total OECD emissions were *250 times greater* than LDC emissions in 1966 while only *39.3 times greater* in 2016.

The comparison of CORE, SEMI, and PERI also provides a more insightful look at the pattern of CO_2 emissions and intensity. CORE parallels, with respect to both total CO_2 emissions and CO_2 per capita, the earlier overview of OECD data. Total CORE emissions increased (39.6 percent) over the 1966–2016 period, moving from 6,650 million *mt* to 9,282 million *mt*, with an AFYPG of 3.8 percent. The latter, however, masks a rather large increase in CO_2 emissions from 1966 through 1976 (AFYPG of 15.8 percent) as well as a significant period of decline from 2006 through 2016 (AFYPG of −6.4 percent). Moreover, the same falloff seen for the OECD in 2011 and 2016 was again evident for CORE. Contrary to the OECD, however, all ten CORE countries exhibited this decrease in CO_2 emissions since 2006. CORE intensity, similar to the OECD, was quite variable, even though the 1966–2016 increase (2.6 percent) was minimal, moving from 11.37 million *mt* to 11.66 million *mt*. The variability is evident, however, in looking at the 25.1 percent change from 1966 through 1996 before declining precipitously through 2016 (AFYPG of −18 percent). Finally, CORE also resembled the OECD in terms of its percentage of total WORLD CO_2 emissions, decreasing from 55.2 percent to 26 percent during the period.

The SEMI experience is quite different from CORE in that there is an exceptional increase (960.4 percent) in CO_2 emissions, from 1,594 million *mt* in 1966 to 16,903 million *mt* in 2016. Moreover, total SEMI CO_2 emissions overtook OECD levels in 2006.[20] The AFYPG in SEMI CO_2 emissions (27.3 percent) more closely paralleled that revealed for LDCs (27 percent) than it did CORE (3.8 percent). SEMI CO_2 emissions growth was most notable during the 1966–1976 (AFYPG of 41.7 percent) and 2001–2011 periods (AFYPG of 38.9 percent). Remarkably, SEMI CO_2 emissions grew from 24 percent of CORE in 1966 to 182 percent in 2016. Finally, the SEMI percentage of total WORLD CO_2 emissions increased radically, from 13.2 percent to 47.4 percent during the period. SEMI CO_2 emissions per capita also witnessed a dramatic increase (378.7 percent), from 0.94 million *mt* in 1966 to 4.5 million *mt* in 2016—tripling SEMI population percentage growth during the 1966–2016 period. As noted earlier, the 1966–1976 and 2001–2011 periods disproportionately influenced the whole of the period, as AFYPG was 26.1 percent and 32 percent, respectively. This growth was also largely the result of the dramatic upsurge in Chinese CO_2 emissions, by 37 percent and 27 percent in 2006 and 2011, respectively.

PERI CO_2 emissions data reveal an enigma. Overall, the 1966–2016 period evinced an increase (149.6 percent), from 3,802 million *mt* in 1966 to 9,490 million *mt* in 2016. From 1966 through 1986, total emissions expanded, consistently increasing (86.3 percent) to 7,085 million *mt*. From 1986 through 1996, however, a decrease (−19.3) occurred, as emissions fell to 5,718 million *mt*. The subsequent 1996–2016 period saw a resurgent increase (66 percent) in CO_2 emissions. The 1966–2016 AFYPG of 10.3 percent was on a par with WORLD. The negative PERI AFYPG during the 1986–1996 period, however, is an oddity distinct not only from CORE and SEMI but also from every country subset. The PERI percentage of total WORLD CO_2 emissions decreased from 31.6 percent in 1966 to 26.6 percent in 2016. Similar to

CORE, SEMI CO_2 emissions per capita changed relatively little (7.4 percent), moving from 2.03 million *mt* in 1966 to 2.18 million *mt* in 2016. It is important to note that while SEMI recorded an increase, CORE CO_2 emissions in 1966 were 560 percent of SEMI and in 2016 were still 535 percent of SEMI. The PERI CO_2 emissions per capita AFYPG was 1.3 percent but still evinced the same anomaly during the 1986–1996 period (AFYPG of −17.3 percent).

Total LLDC CO_2 emissions and CO_2 intensity are both a near mirror image of the LDC subset. Without interruption, total LLDC[21] emissions increased from 12 million *mt* in 1966 to 123 million *mt* in 2016, an incredible 925 percent expansion. To place this extraordinary increase in perspective one need only realize that the bookend values only represented 0.1 percent and 0.3 percent of total WORLD CO_2 emissions, less than 1 percent of SEMI CO_2 emissions and less than 40 percent of LDC CO_2 emissions. The period AFYPG (27.2 percent) saw exceptional growth, during 1966–1971 (AFYPG of 50 percent) and during 2001–2016 (AFYPG of 41.4 percent). LLDC CO_2 emissions per capita also increased during the period (106.7 percent) doubling from 0.15 million *mt* in 1966 to 0.31 million *mt* in 2016. While the AFYPG of the period was 9.3 percent, it masked a significant negative trend during 1991–2001 (AFYPG of −18.2 percent).

SIDS CO_2 emissions data is somewhat similar to LLDCs. Although not nearly as dramatic, the 617.6 percent rise in emissions from 34 million *mt* in 1966 to 244 million *mt* in 2016 is nonetheless quite astonishing. Like both LDCs and LLDCs, the trend is, without interruption, consistent throughout the period, with an AFYPG of 25.2 percent. Exceptional AFYPG increases are evident during 1966–1976 (AFYPG of 85.2 percent). The SIDS percentage of total WORLD CO_2 emissions is also quite similar to LDCs at 0.3 percent in 1966 and 0.7 percent in 2016. SIDS CO_2 emissions per capita increased (238.8 percent)—similar to the experience of SEMI—moving from 1.03 million *mt* in 1966 to 3.49 million *mt* in 2016. The AFYPG was also like SEMI, although the 1976–1986 period exhibited significant negative growth (–3.7 percent) suggesting that population increases outpaced CO_2 emissions growth.

LIFDC data was remarkably similar to that of LDCs, LLDCs, and SIDS. One notable exception is that LIFDCs experienced absolutely no interruptions in either total CO_2 emissions or CO_2 emissions per capita. Total LIFDC CO_2 emissions increased robustly (735.8 percent) from 380 million *mt* in 1966 to 3,176 million *mt* in 2016 with an AFYPG of 23.9 percent. After an initial 41.6 percent increase in AFYPG, the remainder of the 1966–2016 period was surprisingly quite stable, relatively speaking. Similarly, LIFDC CO_2 emissions per capita increased (169 percent) from 0.42 million *mt* in 1966 to 1.13 million *mt* in 2016 with an AFYPG of 10.6 percent. Both the 1966–1971 (AFYPG of 26.2 percent) and 2006–2016 periods (AFYPG of

16 percent) were aberrational periods of relatively greater CO_2 emissions per capita growth. Finally, the LIFDC percentage of total WORLD CO_2 emissions did increase, similar to the aforementioned country subsets, from 3.2 percent to 8.9 percent in 2016.

The foregoing five areas by no means constitute an exhaustive inquiry into the *objective* state of the GSE. Nor are they meant to. However, they do provide a descriptive glimpse into five VES that are typically examined in determining the health of the GSE. Each is an increasingly important aspect in the quest to promote a GSE while concurrently providing for the economic growth, development, and well-being of all. The presentation of a multitude of trends and patterns regarding the totality of VES and related intensity measures, while cumbersome, is important. Many of the intensity measure trends point to an increasingly problematic situation with respect to the intersection of population, technology, and the GSE. While EM theory posits the importance of technological innovation and implementation to curtail environmental decline, the population increases associated with certain country subsets demand that the potential positive role of technology is realized sooner than later. Moreover, EUE theory maintains that the structure of international trade greatly disadvantages developing countries vis-à-vis their developed counterparts. While that relationship is evaluated in chapter 7, the data presented here can be interpreted to constitute prima facie evidence for the position. For example, it is somewhat curious that CORE cropland services have radically declined over the 1966–2016 period while PERI countries have measurably increased cropland services over the same period. The same outcome applies to grazing services and fisheries and aquaculture services as well. These trends certainly suggest a more intrusive investigation into the merit of both EM and EUE theory in these respective areas.

We have thus far considered the importance of subjective perceptions and objective realities, pointing out some of the linkages that they hold to both EM and EUE theory. While these theories are later evaluated for their utility in providing explanation to the economic growth, development, and GSE nexus, we next turn our attention to exploring a fuller understanding of what is meant by "development." Considerable attention is paid to the underlying foundational basis for the traditional view of growth and development, born out of the post-WWII politicization of development theories. While the traditional view of growth and development, with its sole emphasis on economic considerations, is still dominant in the literature, a broader view of what constitutes "development" is necessary to better understand the earlier stated relationship. Consequently, we now turn our attention to reconceptualizing development.

NOTES

1. Rowland shared the honor with fellow scientists, Mario Molina and Paul Crutzen, "for their work in atmospheric chemistry, particularly concerning the formation and decomposition of ozone."

2. This overview of VES closely mirrors the component parts of the *ecological footprint*. The latter is addressed more fully in chapter 6.

3. The makeup of the country subsets utilized in formulating the following tables are in appendix A. Every attempt has been made not to bias the *objective* numbers of different country subsets by arbitrarily adding countries to the subset at that point during the 1966–2016 period when they became a formal member of the subset. For example, the OECD subset includes data for the current thirty-eight member states with the exception of Colombia (admitted in 2020) and Costa Rica (admitted 2021)—for every five-year interval—even though only twenty-one of these states were OECD members during the entire fifty-year period. Consequently, data for Lithuania, although not a member until 2018, is included in the OECD subset for every five-year recording of data regardless of its formal membership in the organization. This ensures that the data, and associated percentage growth figures, are not biased upward.

4. Data pertaining to the LLDC subset is perhaps the most worrisome concern with respect to not biasing the *objective* data presented over the time period covered. The LLDC classification originated in 1957. However, several countries did not achieve their independence and were subsequently not included in the LLDC subset until much later. For example, South Sudan would only have data since 2011 and Eswatini since 1968. More problematic to record are the ex-Soviet countries and North Macedonia, all of which achieved statehood in 1991. The decision was made not to include the countries that became independent in 1991 because (1) disaggregated data was not available for these countries prior to 1991 and (2) their inclusion would have significantly biased upward the more objective condition of LLDC environmental services from 1966 through 2016. Finally, it is important to note that Kosovo is not included due to it being a "partially recognized state." Several landlocked countries, such as Belarus, the Czech Republic, Hungary, Liechtenstein, Luxembourg, Slovakia, and Switzerland, are not "developing" and are also excluded from the LLDC subset.

5. Generally speaking, the "substance" is nonbinding while "reporting" is binding. For example, the intended nationally determined contributions that countries submitted are not legally binding, as the treaty indicates that they *should* aim to achieve them, not that they *shall* achieve them. Moreover, the countries *shall* report their emissions. The latter reporting requirement, however, is simply a restatement from the 1992 UN Framework Convention on Climate Change (UNFCCC) that requires the same. It is worth noting that the US Senate ratified that agreement—and continues to be legally obligated to it—when then president George H. W. Bush presented it to the Senate for action.

6. Turkey was originally both an Annex I and Annex II country under the Kyoto Protocol since it was a founding member of the OECD. In 2001, it was delisted from Annex II after lengthy discussions wherein Turkey argued that it was a "developing" rather than "developed" country.

7. The 2015 Paris Agreement entered into force on November 4, 2016. Sections 1 and 2 of Article 28 make clear the process by which a country may formally withdraw. Given the protocol for withdrawal, the earliest that the US could have formally withdrawn from the Accord was November 4, 2020—and it did exactly that.

8. The UN Food and Agriculture Organization (UNFAO, 2018a) defines *cropland* as "land used for cultivation of crops. The total of areas under 'Arable land' and 'Permanent crops.'" *Arable land* is "the total of areas under temporary crops, temporary meadows and pastures, and land with temporary fallow. Arable land does not include land that is potentially cultivable but is not normally cultivated." *Permanent crops* is "land cultivated with long-term crops which do not have to be replanted for several years (such as cocoa and coffee), land under trees and shrubs producing flowers (such as roses and jasmine), and nurseries (except those for forest trees, which should be classified under 'Forestry'). *Permanent meadows and pastures* are excluded from land under permanent crops."

9. Future references to "the period" refer specifically to the 1966–2016 period unless otherwise noted.

10. The presentation of *per capita services* is one way by which to gauge the importance of population growth to the provision of VES (i.e., *intensity*). However, other considerations such as the role of technology implementation and government policy with respect to "increasing" VES are also important to understanding the trends evinced in the tables that follow. One might consult the Digital Adoption Index from the World Bank for information regarding how people, businesses, and governments have adopted digital technology to this end.

11. The reported 73.2 percent increase noted forthwith would have been nearly three times higher, at 203.7 percent, if the ex-Soviet countries and North Macedonia were included as of 1996. The data on LLDC cropland services per capita, coincidentally, would not have been severely biased, as it would have been 0.30 *ha* in 2016 rather than the 0.29 *ha* reported straightaway.

12. The UNFAO (2018a) defines *grazing services* with land under permanent meadows and pastures. The latter is defined as "land used permanently (five years or more) to grow herbaceous forage crops through cultivation or naturally (wild prairie or grazing land). Permanent meadows and pastures on which trees and shrubs are grown should be recorded under this heading only if the growing of forage crops is the most important use of the area. Measures may be taken to keep or increase productivity of the land (i.e., use of fertilizers, mowing or systematic grazing by domestic animals.) This class includes:

- Grazing in wooded areas (agroforestry areas, for example)
- Grazing in shrubby zones (heath, maquis, garigue)
- Grassland in the plain or low mountain areas used for grazing: land crossed during transhumance where the animals spend a part of the year (approximately 100 days) without returning to the holding in the evening: mountain and subalpine meadows and similar; and steppes and dry meadows used for pasture."

13. The reported 0.3 percent increase noted forthwith would have reported as 80.9 percent if the ex-Soviet countries and North Macedonia were included as of 1996. The data on LLDC grazing services per capita, coincidentally, would not have been severely biased, as it would have been 1.39 *ha* in 2016 rather than the 1.32 *ha* reported straightaway.

14. The UNFAO (2018a) defines *forest land* as "land spanning more than 0.5 hectares with trees higher than 5 metres and a canopy cover of more than 10 per cent, or trees able to reach these thresholds in situ. Excludes land that is predominantly under agricultural or urban land use, and land that is predominantly used for maintenance and restoration of environmental function."

15. The reported −7 percent decrease noted forthwith would have actually turned positive (5.7 percent) had the ex-Soviet countries and North Macedonia been included as of 1996. The data on LLDC forest services per capita, coincidentally, would not have been as severely biased, as it would have been 0.57 *ha* in 2016 rather than the 0.63 *ha* actually reported.

16. *Fisheries and aquaculture services* include both inland and marine capture as well as inland and marine aquaculture.

17. The reported 339.2 percent growth noted forthwith would have been biased a bit higher (382.8 percent) if the ex-Soviet countries and North Macedonia were included as of 1996. The data on LLDC fisheries and aquaculture services per capita, coincidentally, would not have been severely biased, as it would have been 4.1 *mt* in 2016 rather than the 4.7 *mt* reported.

18. The discovery of CFC-113a in the 1960s is an obvious exception to this very general statement. CFC-113a levels have increased over the 2012–2017 period and are suspected to be related to one of four sources including the production of HFCs (specifically HFC-134a and HFC-125). Research indicates a potential linkage between the existence of CFC-113a and HFC-producing entities in eastern China and the Korean peninsula (Adcock et al., 2018, pp. 4747–4750).

19. While the decrease was evident for the OECD subset, several OECD countries actually continued the pattern of increasing CO_2 emissions through the 2011–2016 period. Among these are Chile, Iceland, South Korea, Norway, and Turkey.

20. This development was mostly due to the increase in Chinese CO_2 emissions, from 3.5 billion *mt* in 2001 to 6.5 billion *mt* in 2006, exceeding 50 percent of total SEMI CO_2 emissions.

21. The reported 925 percent increase, while extraordinary, would have ballooned to 5,408.3 percent if the ex-Soviet countries and North Macedonia were included as of 1996. The data on LLDC CO_2 emissions per capita would also have been biased higher, at 1.34 million *mt* in 2016 instead of the more accurate 0.31 million *mt* reported.

PART II

Sustainability, Development, and Theory

Chapter 4

On Development, *Eudaimonia*, and Sustainable Well-Being

CHARACTERIZATIONS OF DEVELOPMENT

Development is undoubtedly one of the most contentious, convoluted, and clumsily understood concepts in international relations history (Pye, 1965; Seers, 1969; Sen, 1988, p. 12). This history is chockful of disagreements over its origins, what constitutes it, whether it is a desirable goal, and whether the existence of development is synonymous with being *modern*. Our understanding of "development" is quite variable, taking on numerous characteristics dependent on a goodly number of factors. The concept is discernibly germane to any level of analysis as we consider the personal development of individuals, the development of organizational groups, the development of local, state, and national governments, and the development of the international system of states. Comprehension becomes further difficult given the realization that different characteristics are often the primary focus of research that involves different levels of analysis. For example, attention is often focused on the moral development of the individual, the sociocultural development of organizational groups, the political development of government institutions, and the economic development of the international system of states.

The characteristics of development are also arguably dependent upon the academic training and ideological orientation of those "clarifying" its meaning as well as the defining policy goals and initiatives of political leadership. As will be seen shortly, this "politicization" of what constitutes development has been counterproductive. The numerous manifestations of "development" paraded by a substantially large number of disciplinary-based orientations reflect this unfortunate reality. For example, *development economics* has had a long history of defining development in terms of economic growth, while *political development* has placed disproportionate emphasis on explaining the emergence, maintenance and transition, and decline of governing institutions within and between societies. Moreover, *development sociology* examines development in terms of the processes underlying societal transition and the desire for change, while the related discipline of *development geography* has long viewed development in terms of the materially different spatial patterns that emerge between societal groups. *In effect, "development" is the bastard child of multiple disciplinary parents, each of whom has a storied history of deeming their academic predisposition as the dominant influence in both the conception and life of the child.*

Development in the context of the current enterprise revolves primarily around the nation-state and international levels of analysis, and it incorporates many aforementioned disciplinary emphases. Still, effectively distinguishing the meaning of "development" is a seemingly difficult enterprise that cannot possibly render a satisfactory explanation given the plethora of informed opinions that exist. Nobel laureate Gunnar Myrdal (1974), however, rebuked this all-too-often stated conclusion by stating that concept-definitional clarity prior to conducting the analysis is an absolute requirement (p. 729). To that end, numerous scholars and/or practitioners have offered copious categorization schemes differentiating the peculiarities of development.

Cowen and Shenton (1996) distinguished between *intentional* and *immanent development*, with the former being policy directed while the latter reflects progress that accrues from activity that has not been intentionally directed (pp. 443–448). Arndt (1981) also offered a distinction based on whether development *happens*, via government initiative, as opposed to something that *happened* either with or without government direction (p. 462). In a similar vein as these, Hart (2001) distinguished between *Big D Development* and *little d development*. While the former reflects the "post–second world war project of intervention in the 'third world' that emerged in the context of the cold war" the latter pertains to "the development of capitalism as a geographically unequal, profoundly contradictory set of historical processes" (p. 650). While these analyses put forth several examples of development, reflecting their larger orientations to development, the primary focus is not on the constituent elemental makeup of development per se. Moreover, Lewis (2019) has questioned the utility of the Hart distinction based on its lack of conceptual clarity, a result of it having "travelled" or "stretched"[1] too greatly to accommodate numerous development-oriented constituencies (p. 14).

Still others have effectively tried to understand development by putting forth "clean-cut" categories for which almost everyone agrees are not mutually exclusive. For example, in an attempt to illustrate how the concept is "qualified," Bellu (2011) gives four nonexhaustive categories of development including economic, human, sustainable, and territorial, with economic being considered the "first form of development" (p. 3). These categories are by no means mutually exclusive, yet the "disaggregation" of development in this manner is an effort to provide enhanced definitional clarity and more easily derived policy initiatives targeting each particular focus. The same is true in our conceptualization and subsequent categorization of *developing countries* based on different elements said to either reflect their "level of development" or a particular "situational characteristic" (e.g., landlocked countries) that sets them apart from other countries. Fialho and van Bergeijk (2017) have tracked the "proliferation" of developing country classification schemes as they apply to development policy and found that "internal proliferation is associated with lacking a clear rationale, no definition of country characteristics, and possibly the direct involvement of developing countries in designing the category." Moreover, they suggest a "need to consider development from a multidimensional perspective rather than the predominantly used per capita income indicators" (p. 99). It is to that end, a reconceptualization of the traditional view of development, one that is multidimensional and better reflects a holistic conception of human well-being, that this chapter is focused.

ARISTOTLE, DEVELOPMENT, AND EUDAIMONIA

The vast majority of literature regarding development and *development studies* stands as an affront to the aforementioned Fialho and van Bergeijk (2017) recommendation in that it is exceptionally reductionist with an emphasis on the importance of per capita income (i.e., growth) indicators in the post-WWII period (e.g., Baran, 1957; Hirschman, 1958; Lewis, 1955). Given the aforementioned diversity of disciplinary foci, the incorporation of this limited understanding stands as an affront to a historical, holistically informed conceptualization of development. Importantly, the absence of a more holistic understanding of development will necessarily translate into suboptimal development policies. Currie-Alder (2016) recognized the inherent problems associated with only identifying development with the post-WWII period and thus admirably offered a categorization of development studies that spanned over two centuries and included two identifiable "waves" of emphasis. While the eighteenth-century wave focused on development in the service of a "better society at home," the post-WWII wave turned its attention to development in the service of "reconstruction, decolonization and newly independent but poor countries" (p. 6). Currie-Alder (2016) provides an especially useful categorization of the historical importance of the economic emphasis in development studies and suggest that this history predates the eighteenth century by briefly referencing Aristotle's idea of "flourishing lives" and the Tunisian-born historiographer/philosopher Ibn-Khaldun's ideas pertaining to the rise and fall of nations (p. 6).

Indeed, the origins of a more holistic focus on development and development studies dates to Aristotle and his focus on the attainment of the ultimate "good" of eudaimonia (i.e., well-being). Early, and arguably faulty, translations strictly equated eudaimonia with "happiness." The concept of happiness conveys a subjective reality, whereas Aristotle conceived of the nature of eudaimonia as objective. Cooper (1975) suggests that a more appropriate translation is "flourishing" from which the often-used interpretation of "flourishing life" is derived (pp. 89–90). Marangos and Astroulakis (2010) maintain that "well-being" is preferable to "happiness" because it is less committal in that it doesn't immediately reflect a sense of pleasure (pp. 552–553). Aristotle, himself, indicated that eudaimonia is constituted by a flourishing life—to live well and do well. The problem lies in how one defines "living well and doing well" (Aristotle, 1908, bk. 1, ch. 4). Unlike the Stoics, Aristotle believed that both virtue *and* externalities such as good friends and wealth were required to facilitate being *eudaimon*. The *desirability* of such externalities, such as wealth, must be great, given this observation:

> Yet evidently, as we said, it needs the external goods as well; for it is impossible, or not easy, to do noble acts without the proper equipment. In many actions we use friends and riches and political power as instruments; and there are some things the lack of which takes the lustre from happiness, as good birth, goodly children, beauty; for the man who is very ugly in appearance or ill-born or solitary and childless is not very likely to be happy, and perhaps a man would be still less likely if he had thoroughly bad children or friends or had lost good children or friends by death. As we said, then, happiness seems to need this sort of prosperity in addition; for which reason some identify happiness with good fortune, though others identify it with virtue. (Aristotle, 1908, bk. 1, ch. 8)

The argument can be made that eudaimonia is constituted by a sense of "well-being" that pertains to a modern sense of development at all of the previously identified levels of analysis. Aristotle, however, repeatedly emphasizes that while positive, the eudaimonia of the individual is second to that of society, suggesting that the state, through its own virtuous actions, can acquire well-being.

> And politics appears to be of this nature; for it is this that ordains which of the sciences should be studied in a state, and which each class of citizens should learn and up to what point they should learn them; and we see even the most highly esteemed of capacities to fall under this, e.g., strategy, economics, rhetoric; now, since politics uses the rest of the sciences, and since, again, it legislates

> as to what we are to do and what we are to abstain from, the end of this science must include those of the others, so that this end must be the good for man. For even if the end is the same for a single man and for a state, that of the state seems at all events something greater and more complete whether to attain or to preserve; though it is worth while to attain the end merely for one man, it is finer and more godlike to attain it for a nation or for city-states. (Aristotle, 1908, bk. 1, ch. 2)

The major Aristotelian premise of any intellectual inquiry into a subject matter, such as development, is that it requires a number of investigative, knowledge-based tools and proceeds from that already known. Arguably, the understanding of most any societal issue involves the investigation of multiple relevant factors and a commitment to stay clear of more parsimonious but yet overly reductionistic explanatory paths.

Dubbed by Dante as the "master of those who know," Aristotle inaugurated a tripartite classification of scientific disciplines (i.e., knowledge-based tools) by which matters of significance are "calculated and contemplated." Inter alia, Aristotle identified in *The Nicomachean Ethics* the *theoretical, practical, and productive* "intellectual virtues"[2] (see Aristotle, 1908, bk. 6). The theoretical sciences (i.e., *epistêmê*) reflected the acquisition of knowledge for the sake of knowledge/universals and included a broad range of disciplines dealing with the natural universe such as mathematics, biology, theology, astronomy, physics, and botany. This knowledge is invariable (e.g., the square root of 16 is 4).[3] Alternatively, the practical sciences (i.e., *phronesis*) reveal the importance of wise human *action* and include such pragmatic disciplines as ethics and politics. Finally, the productive sciences (i.e., arts and crafts—*technê*) transcend both the theoretical and practical in that they illustrate the importance of *making* as opposed to *acting*. Unlike the theoretical sciences, the nature of knowledge in both the practical and productive sciences is variable (i.e., subjective). In effect, Aristotle identified three broad categories of knowledge-based tools utilized in fully comprehending the *multidimensionality* of a subject. In effect, there cannot exist one "science" that represents/explains the idea of the "ultimate good" for either the individual or society.

> Further, since "good" has as many senses as "being" (for it is predicated both in the category of substance, as of God and of reason, and in quality, i.e. of the virtues, and in quantity, i.e. of that which is moderate, and in relation, i.e. of the useful, and in time, i.e. of the right opportunity, and in place, i.e. of the right locality and the like), clearly it cannot be something universally present in all cases and single; for then it could not have been predicated in all the categories but in one only. Further, since of the things answering to one Idea there is one science, there would have been one science of all the goods; but as it is there are many sciences even of the things that fall under one category, e.g., of

> opportunity, for opportunity in war is studied by strategics and in disease by medicine. (Aristotle, 1908, bk. 1, ch. 6)

It is easy to see how the idea of "well-being," expressed in sync with more modern conceptions of *multidimensional development*, is representative of eudaimonia. Take the role of health care in development. Known universals exist from which the acquisition of other knowledge stems. For example, it is a truth that the human body requires adequate nutrition to prevent such conditions as kwashiorkor, emaciation, and starvation. Consequently, individuals, as well as governments, incorporate the practical sciences when debating the best means by which to address nutritional requirements for their population. Moreover, the importance of the productive sciences lies in the subsequent development and incorporation of high-yielding technologies into agricultural practices. The goal of adopting a policy to meet the nutritional needs of the population as well as the creation/incorporation of new agricultural technologies represents the first of two types of Aristotelian goals, those that are a means to an end. Conversely, the goal of overall "well-being," whether of the individual or society as a whole, is illustrative of the second type of goal, that which is an end in and of itself. Moreover, it would be difficult to see how the overall development of the society could constitute anything other than an end unto itself.

While perhaps a relatively novel interpretation of eudaimonia, Marangos and Astroulaskis (2010) in furthering the field of development ethics have recommended that the Aristotelian conception of eudaimonia, interpreted loosely as "well-being," be advanced to "the macro level of international development" in order to achieve the "good society" (pp. 551–552). Moreover, the relevance of Aristotle to a multidimensional perspective on development (i.e., well-being) is reflected by Nobel laureate Amartya Sen (1988) while reflecting on various aspects of "functionings":

> The well-being of a person can be seen as an evaluation of the functionings achieved by that person. This approach has been implicitly used by Adam Smith (1776) and Karl Marx (1844) in particular, and more recently in the literature on "the quality of life." . . . It can be more explicitly developed, conceptually defended, and empirically applied. . . . The functioning achievements are, of course, causally related to commodity possession and use, and thus the constituent elements of the GNP do enter the *determination* of functioning achievements. Indeed, these elements are the means of which the functionings are the ends—a point of view clearly presented by Aristotle in *Nicomachean Ethics* and *Politics*. (pp. 15–16)

THE CLASSICISTS: DEVELOPMENT AS ECONOMIC GROWTH

Economic growth is unquestionably a key component of development (Sen, 1983, p. 748; 1988, p. 12). The early historical assessment of the constituent elements of development, however, largely reduced it to economic concerns, in particular *economic growth*, while discounting other relevant factors. Moreover, "economic growth" and "development" were in large part considered synonymous terms. The acceptable measurement for economic growth transitioned from the mercantilist era with the introduction of *An Inquiry into the Nature and Causes of the Wealth of Nations*, by Adam Smith (2007). Prior to this seminal publication, economic growth was perceived as best evaluated based on aggregate economic production (Robbins, 1968, pp. 5–9). Moreover, while investigating the relationship between prosperity (i.e., development and indirect measures of wealth) and population growth, Lord Robbins (1968) stated that "more often than not it is *aggregate* rather than *average* wealth which seems to be the criterion." (p. 24)[4]

Smith's (2007) review of the principle of division of labor in book I of *The Wealth of Nations* provides the basis for evaluating how "per person production" can increase dramatically given increased task specialization. The classic pin-making example provides a useful transition from an emphasis on aggregate production to average production (and potential consumption) per person. This is reflected in the beginning paragraphs of the *Introduction and Plan of the Work.*

> The annual labour of every nation is the fund which originally supplies it with all the necessaries and conveniences of life which it annually consumes, and which consist always either in the immediate produce of that labour, or in what is purchased with that produce from other nations. . . . According therefore, as this produce, or what is produced with it, bears a greater or smaller proportion to the number of those who are to consume it, the nation will be better or worse supplied with all the necessaries and conveniences for which it has occasion. (p. 10)

One should note that the blurriness between economic growth and development was inconsequential to whether development was to be valued in and of itself. Mercantilist philosophy, while concerned with power and plenty, did facilitate development in the aforementioned aggregate sense albeit basing the wealth of the nation solely upon the wealth of the aristocracy. However, while the origination of the nation-state system created a perception that development was a *desirable* policy objective of the state, the overly centralized mercantilist system only desired development to the extent that it benefited the ruling classes and merchants (Robbins, 1968, pp. 158–160). In contrast, philosophers, such as David Hume, and classical development theorists, in particular Adam Smith, David Ricardo, and John Stuart Mill, entertained the desirability of development as a policy directive incorporating the whole of society.[5] It should be noted that these theorists did not, however, suggest that development should be pursued at any cost. This is reflected in Lord Robbins's (1968) comment regarding Smith's (2007) desire for development:

> It is to be remembered that *The Wealth of Nations* itself was part of a course in which he taught, to use the words of one of his pupils, not only "the principles of expediency" but also those "of morality and justice." One has only to remember his insistence, already cited, on the necessity of counteracting by education the unfortunate effects on character of industrial specialisation, to realise that his was not a support of economic development no matter what it cost in other connections; and we know that his attitude in this respect was shared by his followers in the nineteenth-century classical tradition. It is clear that the members of this school would not have favoured growth at the expense of intelligence or health. . . . To me at least it is equally clear that they would not have favoured growth at the expense of freedom. (p. 168)

DEVELOPMENT STUDIES: THE EMERGENCE OF CONCEPT CLARIFICATION?

The distinguishing characteristics providing conceptual clarity between economic growth and development remained somewhat blurred by the classical development theorists. Although still largely based in economic terms, the pivotal distinctions would eventually become clearer during the advent and growth of *development studies* in the mid-twentieth century. Moreover, the associated measurement of concepts would also become more refined as a result. However, the immediate post-WWII period remained "fuzzy" with respect to whether distinctions were adequately informed, and accepted, by the majority of scholars, practitioners, and policymakers alike.

The emergence of concept clarification built on the work of classical development theorists but also on the tenets advanced in the work of Joseph Schumpeter. *Schumpeterian development* emerges from a transformation of socioeconomic institutions and structures, while economic growth accrues due to factor changes within the existent economic structure. Temporal concerns are inherent in the nature of the concepts, as economic growth accrues relatively quickly and is easily quantified and measured, while development gains are not as easily measured and require a substantially longer period to realize (Feldman et al., 2016, pp. 6–8).

Many post-WWII commentaries were influenced by the Schumpeterian distinction between continuous (i.e., "static," the theory of continuous flow) and discontinuous (i.e., "dynamic," the theory of development) processes.[6] In essence, Joseph Schumpeter (1949) drew a difference between continuous incremental growth, as reflected in the actions of managerial talent, and discontinuous economic development, as represented by the entrepreneurial class:

> By "development," therefore, we shall understand only such changes in economic life as are not forced upon it from without but arise by its own initiative, from within. Should it turn out that there are no such changes arising in the economic sphere itself, and that the phenomenon that we call economic development is in practice simply founded upon the fact that the data change and that the economy continuously adapts itself to them, then we should say that there is no economic development. By this we should mean that economic development is not a phenomenon to be explained economically, but that the economy, in itself without development, is dragged along by the changes in the surrounding world, that the causes and hence the explanation of the development must be sought outside the group of facts which are described by economic theory. Nor will the mere growth of the economy, as shown by the growth of population and wealth, be designated here as a process of development. For it calls forth no qualitatively new phenomena, but only processes of adaptation of the same kind as the changes in the natural data. Since we wish to direct our attention to other phenomena, we shall regard such increases as changes in data. . . . We do this because these changes are small per annum and therefore do not stand in the way of the applicability of the "static" method. Nevertheless, their appearance is frequently a condition of development in our sense. But even though they often make the latter possible, yet they do not create it out of themselves. (p. 63)

> Our question is: does this whole development which we have been describing proceed in unbroken continuity, is it similar to the gradual organic growth of a tree? Experience answers in the negative. It is a fact that the economic system does not move along continually and smoothly. Counter movements, setbacks, incidents of the most various kinds, occur which obstruct the path of development, there are breakdowns in the economic value system which interrupt it. . . . The counter movements do not merely obstruct development, they put an end to it. A great many values are annihilated; the fundamental conditions and presuppositions of the plans of the leading men in the economic system are changed. . . . And the development which then starts again is a new one, not simply the continuation of the old. It is true, experience teaches that it will move more or less in a similar direction to the earlier, but the continuity of the "plan" is interrupted. The new development proceeds from different conditions and in part from the action of different people; many old hopes and values are buried forever, wholly new ones arise. (pp. 216–218)

The extent to which Schumpeter's work laid a basis for a variety of post-WWII conceptualizations of economic growth and development is reflected in a relatively comprehensive evaluation of the period. Flammang (1979) highlighted the extent to which relevant communities could not agree on the defining characteristics of both economic growth and development as he attempted to understand better whether the two concepts were facilitating one another or effectively competing. Based on multiple post-WWII writings, nine general orientations toward economic growth and development were identified, including one that opted not to offer discernible definitions of each concept but would arrogantly speak to the theories of development nonetheless. This reflects the importance of the aforementioned Myrdal (1974) insistence that concept clarification/definition must come prior to undertaking the analysis. A second orientation equated the two concepts by measuring both based on their "total or per capita income or output" (p. 48). The third identifiable orientation reflects a perceived distinction that developed countries "grow" while developing countries "develop." A fourth approach addresses the "origins of the process" and finds no agreement as to whether economic growth, or development, derives from endogenous factors, exogenous factors, or some combination of the two.

A fifth orientation addresses the question as to whether economic growth and development are "alternating processes," while the sixth approach furthers this question by positing the existence of "threshold" levels for both economic growth and development that must be met before the other "process" ensues. The seventh orientation focuses on the extent to which "structural change" occurs, with most studies postulating that development requires structural change that includes not just economic but also social and political concerns. Stemming from this is the eighth orientation that focuses on income distribution, suggesting that development reflects a more equitable distribution. Finally, there is an orientation that focuses on the "range of economic choice" accorded to individuals whereby development is presumed to increase the range of options (pp. 48–49).[7]

While the earlier noted orientations reflect a preoccupation with economics and concept equivalence, the latter identified orientations are those that begin to depart from the idea that economic growth and development are virtually indistinguishable. The most notable orientations related to Schumpeter are those positing "alternating processes" and "structural change." Moreover, it would be correct to suggest that Schumpeter also spoke to the "origins of the process," income distribution, and the "range of economic choice" afforded to individuals, all of which speak to conceptual distinctions.

Still others attempted to be more concise in their attempts to distinguish between economic growth and development. Seers (1972), for example, suggested that development is seen by most as a normative concept that is largely synonymous with the idea of *improvement* (pp. 21–22); it is reflected more concretely in the following passage:

> The questions to ask about a country's development are therefore: What has been happening to poverty? What has been happening to unemployment? What has been happening to inequality? If all three of these have declined from high levels, then beyond doubt this has been a period of development for the country concerned. If one or two of these central problems have been growing worse, especially if all three have, it would be strange to call the result "development," even if per capita income doubled. This applies of course to the future too. A "plan" which conveys no targets for reducing poverty, unemployment and inequality can hardly be considered a "development plan." . . . Of course, the fulfilment of human potential requires much that cannot be specified in purely economic terms. I cannot spell out all the other requirements, but it would be very unbalanced if I did not mention them at all. They include adequate educational levels, freedom of speech, citizenship of a nation that is truly independent, both economically and politically, in the sense that the views of other governments do not largely predetermine his own government's decisions. (Seers, 1969, p. 5)

Nobel laureate Simon Kuznets (1973) also distinguished between economic growth and development, although by predominantly focusing on the economic-related aspects, stating that economic growth is constituted by "a long-term rise in capacity to supply increasingly diverse economic goods to its population, this growing capacity based on advancing technology and the institutional and ideological adjustments that it demands. The sustained rise in the supply of goods is the result of economic growth, by which it is identified" (p. 247). Kuznets would further state that economic growth can potentially give rise to negatives that economic development policy solutions will target with effective technologies (i.e., material and social technology) (pp. 247–248). This characterization embodies the Schumpeterian difference between "static" and "dynamic" processes, but both Kuznets and Seers remained overly focused on conceptual distinctions as they applied only to the economic field (e.g., economic growth versus poverty, inequality, and unemployment). Bradlow (2004) identifies this limited orientation as the "traditional view" with respect to the conceptualization of economic growth and development.

> There was a time when there was a general consensus that development was about economic growth, which, at least analytically, could be treated as a separate problem from other social, cultural, and political issues in society. Today, however, that consensus has broken down. The competing views of development now cluster around two distinct approaches. We can refer to these two

views as "the traditional view" and the "modern view." The differences between these views of development revolve around a few key issues. The most relevant are: (1) the appropriate role and responsibilities of the state and the other actors in development decision-making; (2) whether development is primarily an economic process or is a holistic process of transformation; and (3) the relationship between international and national regulation in the development process. (p. 199)

EUDAIMONIA REVISITED

The Modern View of Development

The "modern view" of development, while not dismissing the role of economics, broadens the focus in an attempt to be more holistic in evaluating the "objective" state of development. In essence, economic aspects are integrally related to the "social, political, environmental, and cultural aspects.. . . . From this perspective, development projects and policies should be treated not so much as discrete economic events but as episodes of social, economic, and environmental transformation that are part of an ongoing process of change" (Bradlow, 2004, p. 207).

In addressing the relatedness of entitlements, capabilities, and control, Sen (1983) had also identified a fundamental problem with the traditional view:

> Perhaps the most important thematic deficiency of traditional development economics is its concentration on national product, aggregate income and total supply of particular goods rather than on "entitlements" of people and the "capabilities" these entitlements generate. Ultimately, the process of economic development has to be concerned with what people can or cannot do, e.g., whether they can live long, escape avoidable morbidity, be well nourished, be able to read and write and communicate, take part in literary and scientific pursuits, and so forth. It has to do, in Marx's words, with "replacing the domination of circumstances and chance over individuals by the domination of individuals over chance and circumstances." (p. 754)

The modern view of development recognizes the necessity of a multidisciplinary approach to understand the dimensions of development more accurately and how best to achieve it. It also places emphasis on the long-term transformation of socioeconomic, political, cultural, and environmental structures. This emphasis on structural transformation is consistent with the idea that Myrdal (1974) advanced nearly decades earlier, regarding the meaning of "development":

> By *development* I mean the *movement upward of the entire social system*, and I believe this is the only logically tenable definition. This social system encloses, besides the so-called economic factors, all noneconomic factors, including all sorts of consumption by various groups of people; consumption provided collectively; educational and health facilities and levels; the distribution of power in society; and more generally economic, social, and political stratification; broadly speaking, institutions and attitudes—to which we must add as an exogenous set of factors induced policy measures applied in order to change one or several of these endogenous factors. (pp. 729–730)

Still others have identified specific elemental components of an expanded view of development. The selection of these elemental components is undoubtedly highly subjective and, once again, somewhat reflect disciplinary emphases. Goulet (1971) speaks of an *authentic development* whereby three axiomatic needs must be satisfied: the ability to provide basic needs, the ability to be a person, and the ability to make your own choices (p. 448). In his construction of the *Physical Quality of Life Index* (PQLI), Morris (1978) drew a distinction between economic growth and development, positing that the confluence of three indicators—literacy, infant mortality, and life expectancy—effectively reveal development levels (p. 225). Of particular note is the fact that the PQLI eliminated all economic factors from its construction. The United Nations Development Programme (UNDP, 2019) improved the PQLI construction by rectifying the dismissal of economic factors as important to development. In 1990, under the leadership of Pakistani economist Mahbub ul Haq, the Human Development Index[8] (HDI) was originated that incorporated life expectancy, literacy, and per capita income measures.[9]

Development as Sustainable Well-Being

Development is eudaimonia constituted by a subjective multidimensional assessment of *sustainable well-being*. As was mentioned earlier, Aristotle placed considerable focus on the role of eudaimonia in the lives of individuals and society. He proposed that those who are eudaimon have achieved an *objectively* derived standard of existence. As aforementioned, however, considerable debate continues as to the precise meaning of the concept. Does eudaimonia mean happiness, flourishing, well-being? Aristotle believed it meant to live well and to do well. In effect, "to live well" suggests that the individual, the group, the society, and the nation have acquired a certain objective standard of living.

Although detractors exist who bemoan its use (Kraut, 1979), eudaimonia is in this analysis equated with the concept of well-being, but with qualification. Maintaining the existence of an objective standard appears somewhat idealistic given the great disparities in current "development" levels as well as contrarian opinions as to the relative importance of the constituent elements—whether conceptualized in general or specific terms—comprising said development. Perhaps a more prudent approach evaluates the state of development in situationally relevant terms and the ability to *sustain the gains* under the new structure. For example, a government who has instituted a fundamental change in its system of governance from a military junta to a constitutional democracy will have experienced development. However, it would be foolish to think that the fledgling democracy would be on a par with a constitutional democracy that has existed for two centuries. What is critical, however, is the ability to *sustain the gains* made by institutionalizing the words and behaviors of a constitutional democracy (i.e., the *process* of democratic consolidation).

Central to this discussion is the idea that development (i.e., well-being) should result in the net improvement of people's lives. Currie-Alder (2016) defines development as being "fundamentally about improving the human condition" (p. 6). Moreover, "what constitutes success in development now spans per capita income, equity, sustainability, realization of human rights, empowerment, and happiness" (p. 16). Willis (2013) suggests that "at the heart of the concept of 'development' are notions of improvement or betterment." Bellu (2011) says that development is usually construed as improvement in either the system holistically or with respect to its elemental makeup (p. 2).

However, there are also those who believe that equating development with a modern conception of well-being, taken alone, is insufficient. For example, Barder (2012) maintains that well-being is not an absolute quality but one that continuously evinces both positive and negative occurrences and that the generic incorporation of "well-being" only reflects positive development while ignoring retrenchment.

> But to define development as an improvement in people's well-being does not do justice to what the term means to most of us. Development also carries a connotation of lasting change. Providing a person with a bednet or a water pump can often be an excellent, cost-effective way to improve her well-being, but if the improvement goes away when we stop providing the bednet or pump, we would not normally describe that as development. This suggests that development consists of more than improvements in the well-being of citizens, even broadly defined: it also conveys something about the capacity of economic, political and social systems to provide the circumstances for that well-being on a sustainable, long-term basis. (Barder, 2012)

On this point there really is no controversy. Development (i.e., sustainable well-being) can result in both positives and negatives. Witness health-care systems. Restructuring a free-market health-care system to a socialized medicine system will impact positively the well-being of individuals who could not previously afford to purchase health care in the private marketplace while negatively impacting the well-being of the wealthiest members of society (assuming redistribution based on increased taxation of the wealthiest). Likewise, restructuring the health-care system from a socialized medicine system to one that is fundamentally based on the free market will inevitably result in negatively impacting the well-being of those who cannot afford the higher economic cost while positively impacting the wealthiest via decreased taxation/redistribution. In effect, development (i.e., well-being) isn't an exclusively positive, linear path of progression devoid of potential negative effects. What is crucial is sustaining the positive aspects of well-being while minimizing the negative developments that will inevitably make themselves known. Barder (2012) recognizes this same characteristic quality of development (i.e., well-being):

> Development is more than improvements in people's well-being: it also describes the capacity of the system to provide the circumstances for that continued well-being. Development is a characteristic of the system; sustained improvements in individual well-being are a yardstick by which it is judged. This has important implications for development policy, both for developing countries themselves wishing to put their economy and society onto a path of faster development, and for outsiders who want to help that process. We are at an early stage of exploring those implications. (Barder, 2012)

THE POST–WORLD WAR II POLITICIZATION OF DEVELOPMENT THEORY

Historical Precursors

The founding and maintenance of *mercantilism* was premised on the acquisition of wealth defined in terms of aggregate production/usurpation. The centralization of the system facilitated a "development policy" whose emphasis centered on maximizing national power via wealth acquisition. This *philosophy of economic absolutism* dictated that the nature of political interaction between nations would be vastly competitive and that government regulation of both the economic and political spheres would be necessary to win such competitions. Consequently, protectionist economic policies and imperialist wars based on the assumption of a zero-sum game were normal and acceptable interactions to aid in achieving the aforementioned increases in wealth for the ruling classes and merchants.

Inter alia, the *classical school* of economic philosophy would significantly debunk the mercantilist assumption of a zero-sum game and the associated belief that the nation should always seek a positive balance of trade via protectionist policies and the like. In the *Political Discourses*, David Hume would convincingly illustrate how the mercantilist preoccupation with increasing bullion reserves would not translate into increased wealth or with the creation of new wealth (i.e., development of society in general). Moreover, in *Discourse V, Of the Balance of Trade*, Hume (1906, pp. 51–66) succinctly stated in conceptual terms the process by which the idea of maintaining a positive balance of trade was faulty. Specifically:

> Suppose four-fifths of all the money in *Britain* to be annihilated in one night, and the nation reduced to the same condition, with regard to specie, as in the reigns of the Harrys and Edwards; what would be the consequence? Must not the price of all labour and commodities sink in proportion, and everything be sold as cheap as they were in those ages? What nation could then dispute with us in any foreign market, or pretend to navigate or to sell manufactures at the same price, which to us would afford sufficient profit? In how little time, therefore, must this bring back the money which we had lost, and raise us to the level of all the neighbouring nations? where, after we have arrived, we immediately lose the advantage of the cheapness of labour and commodities; and the further flowing in of money is stopped by our fulness and repletion . . . Again, suppose that all the money in *Britain* were multiplied fivefold in a night, must not the contrary effect follow? Must not labour and commodities rise to such an exorbitant height that no neighbouring nations could afford to buy from us, while their commodities, on the other hand, became so cheap in comparison that, in spite of all the laws which could be formed, they would be run in upon us, and our money flow out till we come to a level with foreigners, and lose that great superiority of riches which had laid us under such disadvantages? (p. 53)

Adam Smith (2007) and David Ricardo (2015) would build on the Hume indictment and further illustrate the aforementioned benefit of the division of labor as well as introduce how absolute and comparative advantages would facilitate the accumulation of greater wealth. Moreover, the *desirability* of development was now based on the benefits accruing to the whole of society and on international free market competition that presupposed the existence of a positive-sum game.

The Post-WWII Transition and Beyond

In addition to identifying two historical "waves" of global development, Currie-Alder (2016) provides a useful categorization of three traditions of *development studies* in the United States that reflect the target of such development. For example, *national development* is inward looking as it focuses on nation building and other domestic concerns. Conversely, *international development* is outward looking with a primary focus on the relatively poor countries of the world. Finally, Currie-Alder maintains that *global development*, which thrived in the 1990s, focuses on the interdependencies of both developed and developing countries due to common problems (i.e., environmental decline, etc.) (2016, pp. 7–8).

While not intended for this purpose, the Currie-Alder categorization is perhaps a useful classification for looking at the politicization of development approaches since WWII. One can identify in *modernization theory*, for example, a stated need to both repel the communist threat and enhance markets—thus providing a good to the US—as well as the suggestion that the US is genuinely interested in the "development" of developing countries. Hence, it *might* be argued that the modernization period is representative of an emphasis on global development. Alternatively, one *might* argue that neo-Marxist theories of development lean toward a preoccupation with national development by implementing import-substitution policies, protectionism, and so forth. One *might* also argue the same with respect to the era of neoliberalism, as the developed countries and the moneyed classes benefited greatly from capital redistribution. Moreover, it is arguable that the postdevelopment era of development is representative of international development, as the apparent emphasis seemingly focused on common development problems throughout global society. Although not detailed further, this categorization scheme is useful when addressing the positions of various actors and the politicization of development.

The foundation for the post-WWII introduction of *development studies* in the US was in large part triggered by the 1949 inaugural speech of President Harry Truman. The "Four Points" discourse highlighted the role of both economic and political development in the "worldwide effort for the achievement of peace, plenty, and freedom." Developing and increasing both the strength and effectiveness of international institutions by demonstrating unwavering support for the UN and a North Atlantic collective security agreement underscored the importance of political development. Similarly, a strategic focus on world trade and economic recovery, coupled with the dissemination of both "scientific advances and industrial progress," underscored the importance of economic development (Truman, 1949). The reinforcing role of both political and economic advances is evident in the following summary passages from the inaugural speech:

> The American people desire, and are determined to work for, a world in which all nations and all peoples are free to govern themselves as they see fit, and to achieve a decent and satisfying life. . . . We are moving on with other nations to build an even stronger structure of international order and justice. We shall have as our partners countries which, no longer solely concerned with the problem of national survival, are now working to improve the standards of living of all their people. . . . Greater production is the key to prosperity and peace. And the key to greater production is a wider and more vigorous application of modern scientific and technical knowledge. Only by helping the least fortunate of its members to help themselves can the human family achieve the decent, satisfying life that is the right of all people. Democracy alone can supply the vitalizing force to stir the peoples of the world into triumphant action, not only against their human oppressors, but also against their ancient enemies—hunger, misery, and despair. (Truman, 1949)

Admittedly, this understanding of development was a component part of the larger policy goal of thwarting the growth of communism by promoting the interests of the US and Western Europe. George Kennan, the deputy chief of mission of the US to the USSR from 1944 to 1946, would become a major player in the formation of this postwar policy of *containment* and its relevance to development policy. Kennan penned *The Long Telegram*[10] of February 1946 as a response to the US government desire to understand Soviet nonsupport of the new economic pillars of the Bretton Woods system, the International Bank for Reconstruction and Development (IBRD; i.e., World Bank), and the International Monetary Fund (IMF). This analysis would frame the policy recommendations in the Clifford-Elsey report submitted to President Truman in September 1946,[11] which specifically mentioned "restricting" the Soviet Union. Kennan's *The Sources of Soviet Conduct* (i.e., the *X* article) in 1947 outlined how *containment* of the Soviet Union and communism in general could occur[12] and, coupled with the proclamation of the Truman Doctrine in March 1947, solidified US foreign policy, and support for it, for decades to come.

The *desirability* of development was now predicated on the ability to contain Soviet expansionism and the spread of communism in the newly independent, developing countries. Although Truman highlighted the importance of development, defined in both economic and political dimensions, the economic reductionist field of development economics overshadowed this viewpoint. The focus on the economic dimension (i.e., the traditional view of development) was perhaps understandable though, as scholars, practitioners, and future policymakers would largely equate development with economic development and the latter with economic growth. Moreover, the economic emphasis was a consequence of having measurable indicators that politicians and others could incorporate into model building and public policy (Seers, 1969, p. 1). Inter alia, this speech inferred, if not dictated, that the US was the model for economic growth and development and that it was the moral responsibility of US policy to facilitate similar results for a variety of less fortunate nations. Moreover, the free market, orthodox approach was lauded as universally valued for its ability to encourage liberal democracy and peace.

The immediate post-WWII period emphasis on the containment of communism included an emphasis on the *Economic Growth Paradigm* (EGP). In brief, the paradigm fostered a belief that "economic growth is good, imperative, essentially limitless, and the principal remedy for a litany of social problems" (Dale, 2019). This was coupled with the idea that rapid economic growth would be associated with increased legitimacy of the social system, prevent the expansion of communism, and enhance international peace. It was thought that economic behavior (i.e., economic growth and development) would closely follow natural law as posited by the classical economists. In effect, economic growth in the *developing world* would facilitate the policy of containment by discrediting the economic philosophy of the Soviet Union relative to that of the United States.

This primary focus on economics, as opposed to noneconomic aspects of economic growth and development, is evident in the implementation of the Marshall Plan from 1948 through 1951.[13] The vast majority of the $13 billion provided targeted economic growth efforts. The results of the program have always met with mixed interpretations, with some suggesting that the direct (i.e., measurable) economic results of the program had a minimal impact on economic growth (Crafts, 2011; Magid, 2012). However, Tarnoff (2018) maintains that the economic growth success of the program is dependent upon whether comparisons are made to the pre-WWII era or to the beginning of the program: 1947. The latter four-year period reveals an average 33 percent growth in GDP, approximately 37 percent increase in aggregate agricultural production, and 55 percent growth in industrial production (p. 16). However, no one could debate the proposition that it inhibited the threat of Soviet expansionism in the region.

The Orthodox Paradigm and Modernization Theory

The perceived direct success of the Marshall Plan greatly influenced subsequent political discussions regarding how best to facilitate the economic growth and development objectives of developing countries. Nobel laureate Arthur Lewis (1955) would set the tone for how the evaluation of development would be managed during the late 1950s and 1960s when he stated,

"First it should be noted that our subject matter is growth, and not distribution. It is possible that output may be growing, and yet that the mass of the people may be becoming poorer. We shall have to consider the relationship between the growth and the distribution of output, but our primary interest is in analysing not distribution but growth" (p. 9). This sentiment reinforced the EGP and encouraged a pathway toward development facilitated purely by the perceived importance of economic growth. It would ultimately influence political leaders to adopt, in a qualified sense, different theories and policies espoused under the rubric of the orthodox paradigm. The orthodox paradigm, and the variety of modernization theories espoused within it, has its roots in the positivist tradition and liberal thought. Moreover, the orthodox paradigm emphasizes that development occurs via a process of unilinear, evolutionary, materialistic growth (Chilcote, 1981, pp. 55–80).

Modernization, as an orthodox theory of development, had numerous proponents but none greater than the version espoused by Walt Rostow. Born largely out of the success of the Marshall Plan and the perceived failure of an increased emphasis on military aid throughout the 1950s, Rostow's construction would curry favor with a Kennedy administration that sought enhanced goodwill between the US and Latin America.[14] This is evident in the following excerpts from the "Alliance for Progress" speech before Congress and the diplomatic corps of Latin American republics in March 1961. Inter alia, Kennedy (1961) stated:

> Throughout Latin America, a continent rich in resources and in the spiritual and cultural achievements of its people, millions of men and women suffer the daily degradations of poverty and hunger. They lack decent shelter or protection from disease. Their children are deprived of the education or the jobs which are the gateway to a better life. And each day the problems grow more urgent. Population growth is outpacing economic growth—low living standards are further endangered and discontent—the discontent of a people who know that abundance and the tools of progress are at last within their reach—that discontent is growing. (Kennedy, 1961)

> If we are to meet a problem so staggering in its dimensions, our approach must itself be equally bold—an approach consistent with the majestic concept of Operation Pan America. Therefore I have called on all people of the hemisphere to join in a new Alliance for Progress—Alianza para Progreso—a vast cooperative effort, unparalleled in magnitude and nobility of purpose, to satisfy the basic needs of the American people for homes, work and land, health and schools—techo, trabajo y tierra, salud y escuela. (Kennedy, 1961)

> The living standards of every American family will be on the rise, basic education will be available to all, hunger will be a forgotten experience, the need for

> massive outside help will have passed, most nations will have entered a period of self-sustaining growth. (Kennedy, 1961)

> Let me stress that only the most determined efforts of the American nations themselves can bring success to this effort. They, and they alone, can mobilize their resources, enlist the energies of their people, and modify their social patterns so that all, and not just a privileged few, share in the fruits of growth. (Kennedy, 1961)

> Thus if the countries of Latin America are ready to do their part, and I am sure they are, then I believe the United States, for its part, should help provide resources of a scope and magnitude sufficient to make this bold development plan a success—just as we helped to provide, against equal odds nearly, the resources adequate to help rebuild the economies of Western Europe. (Kennedy, 1961)

In 1957, Max Millikan and Rostow penned *A Proposal: Key to an Effective Foreign Policy.* Within it they identified two major objectives of US foreign policy: "To meet effectively the threat to our security posed by the danger of overt military aggression, a threat now inherent in the present capabilities and possible future intentions of the Communist bloc countries," and "to promote the evolution of a world in which threats to our security and, more broadly, to our way of life are less likely to arise" (1957, p. 3). While not ignoring the importance of the former, Millikan and Rostow (1957) focused their attention on the latter, maintaining that past US efforts have "put relatively too much emphasis in recent years on pacts, treaties, negotiations, and international diplomacy and too little on measures to promote the evolution of stable, effective, and democratic societies abroad which can be relied upon not to generate conflict because their own national interests parallel ours and because they are politically healthy and mature" (p. 4). Underlying this belief was the proposition that the US only desires military preparation and aggression and power politics, and was no longer concerned with the "social and economic improvement" and the creation of a social system that can facilitate such outcomes (1957, p. 6). *A Proposal* argued that the US should take leadership in an expanded, long-term assistance program targeting economic development in developing countries that would best facilitate the aforementioned objectives. The establishment of a threefold classification of developing countries—preconditions for economic progress, economic takeoff, and self-sustained growth—facilitated the identification of how countries could best utilize the assistance while also conveying that the assistance isn't about securing military or political favors (1957, p. 127).

While both liberal and conservative[15] "modernization treatises" were being offered at the time (see Apter, 1965; Heilbroner, 1963; Lerner, 1958; La

Palombara and Weiner, (1966); Levy, 1966; McClelland, 1961; Millikan and Rostow, 1957; Rostow, 1960, 1971), the incoming Kennedy administration "adopted" the conception offered by Millikan and Rostow. Rostow would subsequently serve the administration in several capacities, including deputy special assistant to the president for national security affairs, chairman of the policy planning council at the State Department, and an "ambassadorial" post on the Inter-American Committee on the Alliance for Progress. In 1966, he would be appointed national security advisor by President Johnson.

The Millikan and Rostow orientation struck a chord for several reasons, including the apparent want of the Kennedy administration to foster a policy similar to Roosevelt's *Good Neighbor Policy* toward the countries of Central and South America. The supposition that chaos and conflict would not accompany the demise of traditional institutions also appealed to an administration that did not desire increased foreign military intervention. Moreover, the idea that democratization would be facilitated by a more equitable distribution between the elites and commoners (e.g., greater educational opportunities) appealed to the Kennedy administration. In sum, Millikan and Rostow offered a treatise that paralleled greatly the more liberal orientation of the Kennedy administration. As Ish-Shalom (2006) states,

> Rostow's theory is a clear liberal variant of the development theory. Liberalism was especially attractive to Kennedy, a democrat president who entered the White House in full swing on a liberal ticket hoping to enhance deteriorating American relations with the developing world, especially with Latin America. Under these circumstances, it is no wonder that Kennedy sought guidance on development from the halls of academic scholarship. With his liberal agenda and beliefs, no wonder either that he preferred a more liberal version of development and inclined toward its most prominent writer, Rostow and his theory of modernization. (p. 297)

The wording utilized in many speeches given by President Kennedy reflect the extent to which Millikan and Rostow informed the administration's orientation toward economic growth and development. Kennedy would often refer to the belief that poverty and maldistribution in developing countries were undermining the viability of the social and political structures necessary to ward off totalitarianism and ensure US national security. Moreover, Kennedy would reiterate the importance of a US policy that assisted in facilitating the efforts of Latin American republics to modernize and obtain the stage of "self-sustained growth" (Ish-Shalom, 2006, p. 298).

Just as Lewis (1955) had maintained, *economic growth* was the primary emphasis of those promoting modernization, and *economic growth* would be its associated measure of success. The *desirability* of economic growth remained extremely high. Moreover, Millikan and Rostow's (1957) conception focused greatly on the need to obtain certain rates of economic growth in order to progress through the stages. For example, a country evincing an average per capita growth rate of between 1 percent and 2 percent over a five-year period was said to be transitioning from stage 1 to stage 2 (p. 49). Indeed, the goal of the proposal was to ensure that all countries would grow real per capita incomes by 1.5 percent to 2 percent (p. 126). There is no lack of direction on how to generate said economic growth, but there existed a paucity of operational details on how economic growth would then facilitate development. Refashioning a well-known adage, the assumption inherent in modernization theory appeared to be "build economic growth, and development will come."

The Radical Paradigm and the Neo-Marxist Response

President Kennedy called for the UN to embrace Rostow's conception of modernization. On December 19, 1961, the UN General Assembly would designate the 1960s as the *UN Development Decade*, stating that development efforts during the 1950s had resulted in increasing the development gap—*as measured by per capita income growth*—between developed and developing countries.[16] The influence of the Kennedy administration is palpable, as several passages reflected direct inclusion of Rostow's modernization approach:

> Member States and their peoples will intensify their efforts to mobilize and to sustain support for the measures required on the part of both developed and developing countries to accelerate progress towards self-sustaining growth of the economy of the individual nations and their social advancement so as to attain in each under-developed country a substantial increase in the rate of growth, with each country setting its own target, taking as the objective a minimum annual rate of growth of aggregate national income of 5 per cent at the end of the Decade. (General Assembly resolution 1710/16)

The emphasis on economic growth, "self-sustaining growth," as well as the idea that developing countries have primary responsibility for their own development illustrates the influence of the Kennedy administration. However, a notable difference is the fact that the UN General Assembly envisioned a much more ambitious, 5 percent economic growth by the end of the decade, while the Kennedy administration, as mentioned earlier, foresaw 1.5 percent to 2 percent.

Many in the developing world were frustrated by the results of the first development decade, claiming that the economic growth that occurred was insufficient (Jolly et al., 2009, p. 259) and did not reach the poorest half of the developing world (Nafziger, 2007, p. 52). While the focus was on economic growth (Seers, 1969, p. 1), the level of development was considered unacceptable, as noted in the 1970 establishment of the *second development decade*:

> However, the level of living of countless millions of people in the developing part of the world is still pitifully low. These people are often still undernourished, uneducated, unemployed and wanting in many other basic amenities of life. While a part of the world lives in great comfort and even affluence, much of the larger part suffers from abject poverty, and in fact the disparity is continuing to widen. This lamentable situation has contributed to the aggravation of world tension. (General Assembly resolution 2626/25)

The inability of the first development decade to facilitate adequate economic growth in developing countries that would enhance the *well-being* (i.e., development) of the whole society caused great consternation over Rostow's modernization theory of development. To be fair, however, the initial resolution was largely an "exhortatory statement" (Fomerand, 2004, p. 175) that provided relatively little in terms of specific processes, goals, and the like. Moreover, an institutional framework for the acquisition of goals was virtually nonexistent in the 1961 resolution.

Exhortatory or not, the lack of effective progress led to developing countries making demands that stood opposed to several key aspects of modernization theory. In 1974, the UN General Assembly would pass the *Declaration for the Establishment of a New International Economic Order* (General Assembly resolution 3201/S-6) and the *Programme of Action on the Establishment of a New International Economic Order* (General Assembly resolution 3202/S-6) that provided for, inter alia, the nationalization or expropriation of foreign business interests as well as the establishment of commodity cartels. In effect, the system of free trade and the related assumption of a positive sum game espoused by the classical development economists was rebuffed by many in the developing world. The cooperative system in pursuit of development, envisioned by the Kennedy administration, was returning to a system characterized by state/state conflict.

The dominance of the EGP under modernization theory came into question, as further dissatisfaction with the progress of development occurred. Emerging was a combative view of development born out of the radical paradigm, which contrary to the orthodox paradigm, emphasized multilinear, revolutionary, materialistic growth (Chilcote, 1981, pp. 55–80). The orthodox belief in a cooperative system of states was now in Kuhnian crisis, as the radical, neo-Marxist belief of states in conflict was growing stronger (Billet, 1993, pp. 3–5).

It is important to note that the neo-Marxist affront to modernization theory was not due to the emphasis of the latter on economic growth. Inter alia, the goals of the second development decade, for which developing countries had increasing influence over, still revolved primarily around "economic growth," as it stipulated a 6 percent minimum average annual rate of GDP and 3.5 percent growth in GDP per capita income. Alternatively, the increasing ideological belief that the application of modernization theory was "predatory capitalism" in disguise—seeking expanding markets, increasing control over natural resources, enlarging the privileged position of developed countries as evinced by a widening "development gap"—was the foundational argument for the paradigmatic challenge. Facilitating this challenge was the UN Economic Commission for Latin America (UNECLA) and a plethora of Latin American development theorists who argued that the global structure of production and trade resulted in the exploitation of developing countries.[17] The Alliance for Progress was heralded a failure (Gill, 1971, p. 244; Levinson and De Onis, 1970, pp. 7–16), and governments began to implement structuralist policies such as agrarian reform and protectionism in order to accentuate their accurate perception of relatively low levels of power.

The Basic Needs and Capabilities Approaches

The second development decade and the radical paradigm represented a political refutation of the orthodox paradigm, Rostow's modernization theory, and its implementation by both Kennedy and Johnson. The *third development decade* would build on this challenge via its concern about the ongoing use of a flawed measure of development (Overseas Development Institute, 1978, p. 1). The orthodox emphasis on economic growth as the defining factor of development was first challenged by proponents of the *Basic Needs Approach* (BNA) and then by various conceptualizations of the *Capabilities Approach* (CA).[18] While the focus of this section is not on the politicization of a particular development theory per se, the brief focus on the *measurement of development* problem is one that derives from the politicization of earlier development approaches, hence its inclusion at this juncture. Perhaps the jargon of Streeten (1981) is best: "In this section an attempt will be made to define the differentiating features of a basic-needs approach. It then becomes not the development strategy but an adjunct to, and a modification of, existing development strategies" (p. 335).

It is important to recognize that the 1980 resolution providing for the third development decade sought to institutionalize the demands of the New International Economic Order (NIEO). Beyond this, the document continued to voice its frustration with the results accruing during the second development decade. Moreover, the document reflected a continued emphasis on economic growth as the key measure of successful development but went on to speak of the importance of specific aspects of "development" that proponents of the BNA and CA argued should be measured and subsequently evaluated. As stated by the UN General Assembly,

> The goals and objectives of the International Development Strategy for the Second Development Decade remain largely unfulfilled. In addition, the present negative trends in the world economy have adversely affected the situation of developing countries and, as a result, have impaired their growth prospects. . . . The stark reality confronting mankind today is that close to 850 million people in the developing world are living at the margin of existence enduring hunger, sickness, homelessness and absence of meaningful employment. . . . In order to achieve the goals and objectives of the International Development Strategy, the average annual rate of growth of gross domestic product for the developing countries as a whole during the [Third Development] Decade should be 7 per cent. . . . If the average annual rate of growth of population in the developing countries were to remain at about 2.5 per cent, an average annual increase of 7 per cent in gross domestic product would lead to an annual increase of about 4.5 per cent in per capita gross domestic product. This would double income per capita in developing countries around the middle of the 1990s. Such a growth in income is necessary if real progress is to be made towards raising substantially the share of the developing countries in world production of goods and services and towards eliminating the growing gap between the standards of living of developing and developed countries. Such growth is equally essential if the people of developing countries are to benefit from development through expanding employment opportunities, rising levels of income and consumption, better housing and expanding facilities for health and education. Accelerated growth in the developing countries is also needed in order to support national policies aimed at achieving a more equitable distribution of income and benefits from development. Further, such growth will contribute significantly to a more balanced growth of the world economy. (General Assembly resolution 35/56)

The resolution made mention of numerous items associated with development, but unlike the emphasis on economic growth, there were no specific "development targets" to be achieved. With the notable exception of infant mortality, very few specific outcomes related to development, or how to achieve it, were presented. The "policy measures to be implemented" section of the resolution similarly reflected the importance that modernization theory placed on gross investment, gross domestic savings, capital formation in general, export expansion via manufacturing growth, and the restructuring of domestic economic structures, all very important tenets of Rostow's modernization theory of development, and its emphasis on economic growth.

Although discussed later in this chapter, perhaps the musing of Nobel laureate Robert Lucas (1988) in his assessment of the neoclassical growth model—giving a theoretical foundation for neoliberalism—is instructive in understanding why economic growth, rather than development, continued to be overemphasized in theory, policy, and application. A neoclassical economist, his words indicated the need to better understand the dimensions of development:

> It seems to be universally agreed that the model I have just reviewed is not a theory of economic development. Indeed, I suppose this is why we think of "growth" and "development" as distinct fields, with growth theory defined as those aspects of economic growth we have some understanding of, and development defined as those we don't. I do not disagree with this judgment, but a more specific idea of exactly where the model falls short will be useful in thinking about alternatives. (p. 13)

The BNA sought to illuminate the *dimensions of development* while providing a usable measure for the same. In making the argument that the emergence of BNA in the early 1970s was not just the latest "fashion" but rather an emphasis on development that would survive, Morawetz (1977) maintained that the emphasis on basic needs was not new but present in the immediate post-WWII period. He also maintained that the initial programs in both Colombia and India, in 1950 and 1952, respectively, illustrated this early emphasis on basic needs (pp. 7–8). Moreover, one could argue further that Aristotle spoke of basic human needs when discussing eudaimonia and the need for individuals to acquire both physical and mental "well-being" prior to becoming eudaimon. This and the Morawetz argument notwithstanding, BNA only became *firmly entrenched in the politicization of development* during 1969–1976, having "arrived" in 1976 when the World Employment Conference "enthroned" basic needs (Jolly, 1976, pp. 31–44).

Perhaps the most informative exposition on the BNA is the work of Streeten and Burki (1978), Streeten (1981), Streeten et al. (1981), and Stewart (1985) whereby, inter alia, specific measurement issues such as income versus basic needs and the problematic delineation of a "basic needs bundle" were elaborated. At its heart is the recognition that the BNA is a *consumption-oriented process*, as it specifically targets the alleviation of basic needs among the poorest, who have not been "reached" by the economic growth generated during the first two development decades. In brief, the BNA involves the measurement of "well-being" based on the minimal level of goods necessary to alleviate such impoverishment. The transition to the BNA emphasis on how to measure development further politicized development, as it constituted a direct challenge to the established orthodox paradigm with respect to what constitutes development and how it is best measured.[19]

Somewhat similar to the BNA, the CA of both Sen and Nussbaum also served to challenge the existing definitional and measurement regime of earlier development theories within the orthodox paradigm. While it would be fair to state that the CA has incorporated a good deal of the BNA in producing a "single coherent philosophical framework" (Clark, 2005, p. 3), one should take care not to conflate the BNA with either the Sen or Nussbaum version of CA. While the BNA was "consumption-oriented" in both its definitional and measurement of development, Sen's CA was more about the "provision of capabilities" (i.e., *genuine* opportunities) and "functionings" (i.e., *beings*—states of existence, and *doings*—the behavioral actions taken). Sen was ultimately more concerned with development (i.e., well-being) as *freedom* in terms of providing real opportunities from which individuals could choose to facilitate their functionings.

It is important at this juncture to note that various conceptions of CA do not constitute explanatory theories with respect to "why development." Rather, they provide a normative basis that assists in the description and conceptualization of development and a plethora of related concepts (i.e., inequality, poverty, quality of life, etc.). Moreover, CA challenged the prominent belief that economic growth would automatically "translate" into development, alternatively suggesting that the most important basis for *genuine development* is the ability (i.e., freedom) of the individual to utilize various resources in achieving a greater sense of well-being.

Both Sen and Nussbaum considered capabilities more important than functionings due to the belief that one bias of modernization theory was that it facilitated enhanced opportunities for developed countries while lessening the *genuine* opportunities for the developing world.[20] In contrast to Sen's focus on enhancing *freedom*, Nussbaum's conception of CA was based on the establishment and measurement of the minimal requirements to meet a basic level of respect for *human dignity*, which is closely identified with the Aristotelian idea of well-being. Nussbaum went on to identify ten capabilities that must exist for the realization of human dignity. In general, these ten revolve around: (1) life, (2) bodily health, (3) bodily integrity, (4) senses, imagination, and thought, (5) emotions, (6) practical reason, (7) affiliation, (8) other species, (9) play, and (10) control over one's environment. Nussbaum maintained that each of these areas of well-being have minimal threshold requirements that must be present and able to be accessed (i.e., capabilities) by individuals for development to have occurred (Nussbaum, 2011, pp. 33–34). Whether a person chooses to exercise the provision of any of these ten capabilities, in essence transitioning an opportunity into a reality, is then their individual choice (i.e., freedom). Sen (1987, pp. 36–37) introduced the idea of *refined functioning* to identify those who are afforded the enhanced freedom (i.e., capability) to take an action that can benefit their personal well-being but choose to forgo it nonetheless.

While Sen and Nussbaum disagreed on the primary aspect of development to focus on, *enhancing freedom* versus *respect for human dignity*, both represented a significant challenge to the status quo, which continued to maintain that development is purely about economic growth. Granted, Sen and Nussbaum agreed about the relevance of economic growth, but they also knew that economic growth alone did not necessarily development make.

Although expressions associated with the NIEO, BNA, and CA provided increased expectations for development during the third development decade, those expectations, by and large, did not materialize. The *lost decade of the 1980s* was due to a plethora of exogenous *and* endogenous factors, especially for sub-Saharan and Latin American countries (Singer, 1989, pp. 46–47). Fundamentals associated with the 1973–1974 oil crisis resulted in stagflation in numerous developing—and developed—countries that were dependent on imported oil. This would be repeated in the wake of the 1979–1980 oil crisis. Those countries who implemented the reforms in conjunction with the dictates of the radical paradigm would soon find that greater state intrusion into the development process did not mean greater success in dealing with the economic crisis (Radice, 2008, pp. 1164–1168). The economic downturn was substantial for those countries dependent on export sectors that suffered relative price declines and, as a consequence, balance of payments hardships. Moreover, countries that suffered greatly from "weakness" with respect to domestic institutions would also feel the pain caused by external shocks (i.e., oil crisis, global recession, etc.) more greatly than would have otherwise been the case (Krasner, 1985).

The process that many oil-dependent, developing countries took to finance their chronic balance of payments deficits—derived from increasingly expensive oil imports—would also hamper their economic growth and development during both the 1970s and 1980s. Due to stagflation, the US abandoned the gold standard in 1971, leading to the creation of the "petrodollar" system whereby any country wishing to purchase oil from a member of OPEC would have to do so in US dollars and be subject to fluctuations in the worth of the US currency. Given the spike in oil revenues, the need for OPEC members to "recycle" surpluses of petrodollars was large and resulted in increased liquidity in US and European financial markets via OPEC investment of petrodollars through commercial banks. Beyond this, many OPEC countries would directly lend part of the petrodollar surplus to developing countries to finance deficits. The net effect of financial institutions making capital available to oil-dependent countries for their balance-of-payments crises led to the establishment of long-term loans (i.e., external debt) that would further tax the economic growth and development potential of developing countries long after the initial crisis subsided. Compounding the problem was a dollar that was precipitously losing its value in 1979, which only exacerbated an already expensive oil dependency by most in the developing world.

Although the growth goals during the third development decade were not remotely close to being achieved for all developing countries, there were positives, from a political viewpoint, that derived from the emergence of the BNA and the CA. For example, the continued focus on economic growth as the solitary determinant of development was largely debunked. Also present was a greater understanding of the constituent elements of development and improvement in the measurement of "development." For example, the construction of the Physical Quality of Life Index and HDI flew in the face of many adherents of the orthodox paradigm in general and modernization theory specifically. In 1990, the more precise usage of terminology in the *fourth development decade* resolution would reflect the "real" importance of economic growth—recognizing the more limited role that it plays in procuring "development" goals—while also focusing more intently on specific aspects of well-being. Moreover, none of the earlier development decade resolutions spoke of doing whatever it would take to assure the "necessary means of survival," a reflection of the growing prominence of the BNA and CA challenge.

> The principal aim of the Strategy is to ensure that the 1990s are a decade of accelerated development in the developing countries and strengthened international co-operation. The decade should witness a significant improvement in the human condition in the developing countries and a reduction in the gap between rich and poor countries. It should be one in which ways are found for the world community to meet its needs without degrading the environment. The Strategy also has important social and political objectives. Development over the decade should enhance the participation of all men and women in economic and political life, protect cultural identities and assure to all the necessary means of survival. Each country is responsible for its own economic policies for development, in accordance with its specific situation and conditions, and for the life and wellbeing of all its citizens. The Strategy should help provide an environment that supports the evolution everywhere of political systems based on consent and respect for human rights, as well as social and economic rights, and of systems of justice that protect all citizens. . . . The Strategy has singled out a number of areas of special priority: the eradication of poverty and hunger, human resources and institutional development, population, the environment and food and agriculture. The pursuit of goals in these areas calls for resolute and vigorous action and for styles of development that establish a mutually reinforcing relationship between rapid economic growth and social objectives. (General Assembly resolution 45/199)

Neoliberalism and the Washington Consensus

The 1970s had brought a host of problematic economic, financial, and trade crises to bear on the prospects for a successful 1980s development decade. Due to the perception that Keynesian economic philosophy was unable to effectively deal with stagflation, increasing unemployment, and declining profit making, among other issues, there also existed a transition to a resurgent economic philosophy couched more in the tradition of classical economics and its neoclassical descendants.[21] The reality is that Keynesianism, and an increased role for the state in development efforts, had been under political attack for a considerable time. State adherents to import substitution industrialization (ISI), protectionism, and other structuralist dictates—derived from the radical paradigm—whether of a quasi-capitalist or command economy, were viewed as anathema to efficiency and effectiveness. The "failures" of these neo-Marxist constructions to realize substantial economic growth and development in the 1970s opened the door to a barrage of criticism from neoclassical economists and other likeminded forces (Harvey, 2007, pp. 29–32). The policy response born out of this criticism, however, had to be careful not to "throw the baby out with the bathwater." According to Connell and Dados (2014),

> what neoliberal policymakers had to attack worldwide, often using Cold-War tools, was other development strategies. The main rivals, adopted by many post-colonial elites in the 1950s and 1960s, were capitalist import-replacement industrialization . . . and Soviet-inspired state-centered command economies. . . . Over time, neoliberal economists, journalists, and politicians by sheer repetition created a widespread impression that these alternatives had "failed" or were "exhausted." There is considerable evidence that IRI, at least, did not fail economically. But there is no doubt that both IRI and command economies involved unequal distributions of income, technocratic views of the state, and small local markets, making them prone to local crises (Kay 1998; Vellinga 2002). It was the social settlements around these strategies, such as labor rights and informal redistributive networks that were at stake in the struggle over development, and were to be disrupted by the triumph of neoliberalism. (p. 123)

In reality, the influence of neoliberalism on development existed long before its emergence in the late 1970s. Twentieth-century neoliberalism was substantively born in the immediate aftermath of WWII at the 1947 founding of the Mont-Pèlerin Society by later Nobel laureate Friedrich von Hayek.[22] According to Hartmann-Mahmud (2009), the principles of neoliberalism revolved around three "policy pillars": (1) laissez-faire economics, (2) free trade, and (3) privatization (p. 745). Laissez-faire economics generally regards the free market as the most effective and efficient mechanism by which to allocate resources. Even within neoliberalism, however, there exist at least three different opinions as to *how free* the market should be. *Public choice* closely approximates the extremes of freedom associated with modern-day libertarians (i.e., government is bad and cannot be trusted in most any matter of concern). At the other end of the continuum is the *market-friendly* approach that presupposes the imperfection of markets, especially in developing countries. International financial institutions (IFIs), such as the IBRD, assume that the state may have to intervene, *minimally*, to correct the imperfections. Between these extremes are the adherents to the *free market* approach, a more moderate orientation relative to both extremes.

Beyond the general emphasis on the free market are a wealth of policies that further characterize the positions of the aforementioned varieties of neoliberalism. For example, measures that decrease the influence of trade unions, collective bargaining (i.e., wage constraints), and government regulation are encouraged. Tax cuts, especially for the rich, are encouraged. Related to minimizing taxes is the dismantling of public services, government-provided social security, and privatization. The foundational basis of all of these measures is the perception of an inherent contradiction between the state and the market, and between the political and economic aspects associated with them (Herrera, 2006).

Although not yet institutionalized in the US, a neoliberal plan was implemented in Chile after the 1973 coup d'etat against the democratically elected "leftist" administration of President Salvador Allende (Petras, 1997, pp. 80–81). The subsequent Pinochet dictatorship would institute a goodly number of neoliberal tenets espoused by the "Chicago Boys" who were trained by 1976 Nobel laureate Milton Friedman—who was a presence at the founding of the Mont-Pèlerin Society. According to Harvey (2007):

> It violently repressed all left-of-center social movements and political organizations and dismantled all forms of popular organization, such as community health centers in poorer neighborhoods. The labor market was "freed" from regulatory or institutional restraints, trade union power, for example . . . the policies of import substitution that had formerly dominated in Latin American attempts at economic regeneration, and that had succeeded to some degree in Brazil after the military coup of 1964, had fallen into disrepute. With the world economy in the midst of a serious recession, something new was plainly called for. A group of U.S. economists known as "the Chicago boys," because of their attachment to the neoliberal theories of Milton Friedman, then teaching at the University of Chicago, were summoned to help reconstruct the Chilean economy. They did so along free-market lines, privatizing public assets, opening up natural resources to private exploitation, and facilitating foreign direct investment and free trade. The right of foreign companies to repatriate profits from their Chilean operations was guaranteed. Export-led growth was favored over import substitution.

> The subsequent revival of the Chilean economy in terms of growth, capital accumulation, and high rates of return on foreign investments provided evidence upon which the subsequent turn to more open neoliberal policies in both Britain (under Thatcher) and the United States (under Reagan) could be modeled. Not for the first time, a brutal experiment in creative destruction carried out in the periphery became a model for the formulation of policies in the center. (p. 26)

Politically, the US would institutionalize neoliberalism under the Reagan administration. The Thatcher administration in Britain had also institutionalized the belief in neoliberalism in part by maintaining a slogan professing that "there is no alternative—TINA" (Frangie, 2011, pp. 1183–1184; Thomas, 2001, p. 167). Although differences certainly existed, conceptually and in practice, the ascendance of neoliberalism under Reagan harkened back to the aforementioned dominance of modernization theory in the 1960s (Brohman, 1995, pp. 133–134). In a 1981 speech at the International Meeting on Cooperation and Development in Cancun then president Reagan spoke of his immense support for the principles of the neoliberal revolution:

> Let us meet the challenge of charting a strategic course for global economic growth and development for all nations. . . . The actions we are taking will renew confidence in the dollar, strengthen our demand for imports, hold down inflation, reduce interest rates and the cost of borrowing, and increase resources for foreign investment. . . . History demonstrates that time and again, in place after place, economic growth and human progress make their greatest strides in countries that encourage economic freedom. . . . Government has an important role in helping to develop a country's economic foundation. But the critical test is whether government is genuinely working to liberate individuals by creating incentives to work, save, invest, and succeed. . . . Despite the mid-seventies recession, we were able to liberalize the international trading system under the leadership of the GATT. . . . The IMF remains the centerpiece of the international financial system. . . . The World Bank and other multilateral development banks have dramatically increased their resources and their overall support for development. . . . But we are just as convinced that the way to do this is not to weaken the very system that has served us so well, but to continue working together to make it better. . . . We have yet to unleash the full potential for growth in a world of open markets. . . . In this spirit, we bring a positive program of action for development, concentrated around these principles:
>
> -stimulating international trade by opening up markets, both within countries and among countries;
>
> -tailoring particular development strategies to the specific needs and potential of individual countries and regions;

> -guiding our assistance toward the development of self-sustaining productive activities, particularly in food and energy;
>
> -improving the climate for private capital flows, particularly private investment;
>
> -creating a political atmosphere in which practical solutions can move forward, rather than flounder on a reef of misguided policies that restrain and interfere with the international marketplace or foster inflation.
>
> The program deals not in flashy new gimmicks, but in substantive fundamentals with a track record of success. It rests on a coherent view of what's essential to development—namely political freedom and economic opportunity. (Reagan, 1981)

Although neoliberalism became the dominant development approach, it still lacked in terms of the distinction between economic growth and development. This comes as no surprise, given that the neoclassical school, from which it derived, was also void of such a distinction (Brinkman, 1995, p. 1171). Just like modernization theory decades before, neoliberalism as a Western-based orientation posited a universal path that all countries should follow and largely assumed the existence of development given successful economic growth. Thomas (2001) stated this in no ambiguous terms, maintaining that "neoliberalism supports global economic integration and presents it as the best, the most natural and the universal path towards economic growth, and therefore towards development, for all humanity" (p. 167).

The neoliberalism reversion back to the primacy of economic growth stood in stark contrast to the BNA and the CA and would be accompanied by *structural adjustment programs* (SAPs) to deal with the inordinate amount of developing country debt that had accrued during the earlier development decades. State and/or International Financial Institutions (IFI) intervention was successful—and necessary according to the aforementioned *market-friendly* adherents of neoliberalism—to the extent that the new foundational structures constructed facilitated the implementation of neoliberal policies (Brohman, 1995, pp. 134–135). The willingness to impose SAPs indicates that the *desirability* of economic growth remained extremely high, especially for the developed countries whose position vis-à-vis the developing countries was enhanced greatly, given the redistribution (i.e., redirection) of global capital flows to their benefit.

The policies of neoliberalism, born out of neoclassical economic theory, are often considered synonymous with the *Washington Consensus*, a term that triggered great debate as to its meaning and relatedness to neoliberal development policy. British economist John Williamson (1990) established the moniker in identifying and evaluating the relevance of ten free-market policy instruments to Latin America. The point of the Williamson inquiry was to determine those economic reforms (i.e., policy instruments) that "Washington"[23] considered important in establishing a baseline to measure Latin American compliance with IFI directives (i.e., SAPs). Williamson was generally interested in the relevance of the ten instruments: (1) fiscal deficits, (2) public expenditure priorities, (3) tax reform, (4) interest rates, (5) exchange rates, (6) trade policy, (7) foreign direct investment, (8) privatization, (9) deregulation, and (10) property rights. The liberalization bias with respect to each of these concerns was certainly a response to the prevalence of the high degree of state ownership of enterprise and high regulation of business interests in developing countries (Williamson, 2005, p. 197).

Troubling for Williamson was the manner by which different communities interpreted the Washington Consensus.[24] That there were so many interpretations of what types of liberalization policies would work most effectively appeared to substantiate Williamson's concern that there didn't appear to be a "consensus." Naim (2000) substantiated Williamson's fear of a lack of consensus when overviewing a litany of "disagreements among some of the most respected and influential individuals in the field and ones that share favorable ideological pre-dispositions towards markets, private capital and free trade and investment, while harboring a deep distrust of socialist ideas, central planning and government intervention" (p. 508). Williamson contended that at least two alternative conceptions wrongly mistook his words and furthered the perception that the Washington Consensus was nothing more than a restatement of neoliberalism.[25] Williamson (2005) first objected to those who equated it with the policies of the IFIs and, perhaps, the US government in the post-1989 period, as three concrete differences had emerged:

> First, the Bretton Woods institutions increasingly came to espouse the so-called bipolar doctrine toward exchange rates . . . according to which countries should either float their exchange rate "cleanly," or else fix it firmly by adopting some institutional device such as a currency board. This is directly counter to my version of the Washington Consensus, which called for a competitive exchange rate. . . . Second, the Bretton Woods institutions, or at least the International Monetary Fund (IMF), came in the mid-1990s to urge countries to liberalize their capital accounts, whereas . . . my version had deliberately limited the call for liberalization of capital flows to FDI. But, third, there was also one highly positive difference (or set of differences), as the World Bank and the IMF came to take up the institutional issues that I had not included in 1989. (p. 200)

The second misrepresentation as to its meaning, suggesting that these were policy instruments for which there was consensus, appeared even more troubling for Williamson:

> Whatever else the term "Washington Consensus" may mean, it should surely refer to a set of policies that command a consensus in some significant part of Washington, either the U.S. government or the IFIs or both, or perhaps both plus some other group. Even in the early years of the Reagan administration, or during the administration of George W. Bush, it would be difficult to contend that most of the distinctively neoliberal policies, such as supply-side economics, monetarism, or minimal government, commanded much of a consensus, certainly not in the IFIs. Yet most of the political diatribes against the Washington Consensus have been directed against this third concept, with those using the term this way apparently unconcerned with the need to establish that there actually was a consensus in favor of the policies they love to hate. (p. 201)

The Washington Consensus was not a blueprint, an agenda for policy action, according to Williamson (2005, p. 195). Nonetheless, the Camdessus "silent revolution" of SAPs and the Washington Consensus share some common elements regardless of whether they are synonymous in meaning. For example, both reflect the need to downsize the role of state ownership of enterprises and a large regulatory environment for business as well as increasing capital availability whether or not it is limited only to foreign direct investment (Boughton, 2001). One key difference, in terms of "development" studies, is the enhanced emphasis that the Washington Consensus appeared to have with respect to economic growth and development. While neoliberalism appeared to "assume" that development will just naturally flow from the pursuit of economic growth, Williamson's (2005) conception of the Washington Consensus made very apparent that economic policy should go beyond its narrow focus on economic growth. Moreover, Williamson recommended that the traditional mechanism for advancing income distribution (i.e., redistribution based on increasing taxation on the rich) be enhanced by incorporating approaches that would facilitate the growth of human capital among the poor and realizing "the potential of microcredit, land reform, and asset titling" (p. 204).

Significant neoliberalists, such as Nobel laureate Robert Lucas (1988), maintained that the approach needed to go further than the promotion of economic growth but yet appeared not to get far in their "reaching" for a policy of development. The following sentiments by Lucas (1988) indicate the focus on economic growth, the importance of a theory of economic development, and the seeming inability to derive the latter.

> By the problem of economic development I mean simply the problem of accounting for the observed pattern, across countries and across time, in levels and rates of growth of per capita income. This may seem too narrow a definition, and perhaps it is, but thinking about income patterns will necessarily involve us in thinking about many other aspects of societies too. (p. 3).

> A successful theory of economic development clearly needs, in the first place, mechanics that are consistent with sustained growth and with sustained diversity in income levels. . . . But there is no one pattern of growth to which all economies conform, so a useful theory needs also to capture some forces for change in these patterns, and a mechanics that permits these forces to operate. (p. 41).

The increasing politicization of development during the period of neoliberalism is also evident in the varied reactions as to the success of policies emanating from IFIs and the United States. As aforementioned, the *lost decade of the 1980s* produced extraordinarily little objective evidence for policy success, especially in sub-Saharan and Latin American countries. The 1990s decade, while a slight improvement in economic growth rates, generally speaking, did not significantly alter the balance with respect to "development." Rather, some have argued that it restored privileged class interests in both developed and developing countries (Fine, 2009; Frangie, 2011). Connell and Dados (2014) maintain that "one need not accept Amin's preferred alternative (an autonomous command economy) to agree that neoliberal development strategy produces a distinctive pattern of growth with important social consequences" (p. 124). Moreover, neoliberalism cared not about addressing exogenous factors such as "basic inequalities in international economic and geopolitical structures" (Brohman, 1995, p. 135). Neoliberalism has not only deepened inequalities both between developed and developing countries as well as within the latter group, "but more dangerously it is legitimizing global inequalities of life-chance, legitimizing a situation where inequalities are greater than at any period in history (Thomas, 2001, pp. 167–168). Finally, Herrera (2006) goes further in stating most assuredly the disastrous impact of neoliberalism while also positing that the approach doesn't constitute a development policy but serves the larger interests of the developed countries: "These polices have been harmful to most of humanity. The global South especially has suffered from odious debt repayments, capital flight, and the repatriation of profits on foreign investments. Neoliberalism is not a development model; it is the strategy put into practice by high finance to plunder the South while achieving slow capital accumulation in the North" (p. 8).

In the Specter of the Washington Consensus: Postdevelopment Approaches

It was an era of *breakups*, of *collapses*, of *ends*: the Soviet Union, Yugoslavia, Eastern Europe, the US savings and loan industry, the Berlin Wall, apartheid, the Cold War, socialism, communism, and on and on. Indeed, one author prematurely celebrated the "End of History" or, alternatively, the apparent victory and consolidation of power by a liberal hegemonic power (Fukuyama,

1992). Given the lack of significant progress in "development" throughout the 1980s and 1990s, it should not have come as a great surprise to hear the era declared "the end of the age of development." Sachs (1992) presented the demise unambiguously:

> The last 40 years can be called the age of development. This epoch is coming to an end. The time is ripe to write its obituary. . . . The idea of development stands like a ruin in the intellectual landscape. Delusion and disappointment, failures and crimes have been the steady companions of development and they tell a common story: it did not work. Moreover, the historical conditions which catapulted the idea into prominence have vanished: development has become outdated. But above all, the hopes and desires which made the idea fly, are now exhausted: development has grown obsolete. Nevertheless, the ruin stands there and still dominates the scenery like a landmark. Though doubts are mounting and uneasiness is widely felt, development talk still pervades not only official declarations but even the language of grassroots movements. It is time to dismantle this mental structure. (p. 1)

Esteva (1992) put the eventual demise of development, and that which follows in its wake, in more earthly terms: "Everyone gets confused. By using uncritically such a loaded word, and one doomed to extinction, they are transforming its agony into a chronic condition. From the unburied corpse of development, every kind of pest has started to spread" (p. 6).

Still others have come to consider development as a "zombie-like" category due to it "being declared deceased and then at the same being resuscitated" (Gudynas, 2011, p. 442). Similarly, Fine (2009) characterizes this period as "zombieconomics," as development is alive in the sense that it corrupts other disciplines while at the same time being intellectually dead with nothing "new to offer other than parasitic extension of its principles to new applications" (p. 888).

The *death of development* declaration is in part due to the perception that "development" policies had been largely *redistributive*—as in the aforementioned reestablishment of class—instead of *generative*—producing economic growth at rates sufficient to generate capital for development projects. The abysmal rates of aggregate economic growth, 1.4 percent and 1.1 percent during the 1980s and 1990s, respectively, contributed greatly to the demise (Harvey, 2007, pp. 34–35). Moreover, its most recent caretaker, neoliberalism, was criticized for its preoccupation with measurable indices, in particular economic growth (i.e., aggregate GDP growth) and inflation, while not paying enough attention to relatively more difficult-to-measure development indicators such as access to education and the rights of laborers. As mentioned earlier, others maintained that neoliberalism understated the numerous negative outcomes—such as increasing income inequality and environmental degradation, spending reductions in education, health, and general welfare (i.e., well-being), and a general decline in liberal democracy—to developing countries. Inter alia, these ideas would serve as the foundational basis for the political challenge to neoliberalism—its inability to facilitate the development needs of developing countries.

The 1980s had already brought to bear many anti-neoliberal positions (e.g., the BNA and CA) that sought to show the perversity associated with pursuing economic growth and market fundamentalist policies via, for example, the introduction of SAPs. For example, Sen (1988) spoke to the need to go beyond the traditional EGP evinced by neoliberalism and focus on development needs:

> On the other hand, the success of all this has to be judged ultimately in terms of what it does to the lives of human beings. The enhancement of living conditions must clearly be an essential- if not *the* essential-object of the entire economic exercise and that enhancement is an integral part of the concept of development. . . . Even though an expansion of GNP, *given other things,* should enhance the living conditions of people, and will typically expand the life expectancy figures of that country, there are many other variables that also influence the living conditions, and the concept of development cannot ignore the role of these other variables. . . . Ultimately, the assessment of development achieved cannot be a matter only of quantification of the *means* of that achievement. The concept of development has to take note of the actual achievements themselves. The assessment of development has to go well beyond GNP information, *even when* the other difficulties referred to earlier (such as distributional variation, presence of externalities and non-marketabilities, imperfect price mechanisms, etc.) were somehow overcome. (pp. 11–15)

Moreover, General Assembly assessments of the utility of neoliberalism and development were also becoming more critical of the economic growth emphasis while also identifying the need to focus on the "preconditions" necessary for development:[26] "In 1999, a review of the Decade revealed that development progress had been mixed, with many challenges remaining. Economic growth, by itself, was no longer a sufficient factor of development. The focus had shifted to a number of institutional preconditions for development, including good governance, transparency and accountability, decentralization and participation, and social security" (Jackson, 2007). The inadequate ability of neoliberalism to facilitate the development needs of developing countries only served to increase its detractors. However, the detractors were quite fragmented in terms of their identification of the ills of neoliberalism and what the appropriate response should be. For example, Pieterse (2000) notes the existence of a *postdevelopment* orientation that was said to encompass several different threads of thought, including *antidevelopment*—which focuses exclusively on an angry rejection of the "business as usual" approach of neoliberalism—and the *beyond development* contingent that takes antidevelopment a step further by focusing on what is to be done now (p. 176).

It would also be appropriate to include adherents of the *postgrowth school*[27] to the group of detractors under the postdevelopment umbrella. Neoliberalism, like its modernization theory predecessor, failed to draw an adequate distinction between economic growth and development, alternatively preferring to focus almost exclusively on the virtues of economic growth. Hence, it appears quite suitable to place various proponents of the *postgrowth* school under the postdevelopment moniker. Adherents to the postgrowth school posit that there are limits to both economic and population growth, which consequently necessitates a fundamental shift away from the economic growth paradigm. Moreover, postgrowth adherents maintain that neoliberal economic growth is unsustainable (Rifkin, 2014). Ultimately, adherents to the postgrowth school are characterized by "growth skepticism" due to either the perception that measures of development are flawed (Holmes and Yarrow, 2016, p. 2) or because of "the adverse effect of growth on natural resources coupled with the disconnect between economic growth and "well-being" (Dale, 2019).

Even in the wake of formidable challenges, it is nevertheless the case that development policy, whether "zombielike" or not, has remained in the shadow of neoliberalism. Indeed, some argue that industrialization and economic growth are still the guiding principles of development (Andreasson, 2017, pp. 2636–2637). The establishment of the Millennium Development Goals (MDGs) certainly reflected the incorporation of neoliberalism. Koehler (2015, p. 743) maintains that the four development decades were "productivist-oriented," focusing on increasing employment and economic growth while focusing on decreasing poverty via redistributive policies. Conversely, the MDGs reflected a "market-oriented" approach that was devoid of any policy (Gore, 2010, p. 71), thereby allowing the tenets of neoliberalism to take hold.

The MDGs were largely considered ineffective due to the inability to increase employment and production although successful at facilitating a greater degree of globalist integration (Gore, 2010). The fact that the MDGs were unable to decrease income and wealth inequities led some to regard them as "neoliberalism in guise" (Koehler, 2015, pp. 743–744). The unequal distribution of the costs of globalization and the sharing of benefits derived from it, recognized in the 2000 UN Millennium Declaration (General Assembly resolution 55/2), would largely continue to be a reality for developing countries.

Three noteworthy events do suggest a turn away from development efforts couched in neoliberalism. First, the Great Recession of 2007–2009 did prompt a not-so-subtle retrenchment toward Keynesianism, albeit for a brief time. Second, the construction of the Sustainable Development Goals (SDGs) appears to reflect a departure from the lack of coherent policy, as was evident with the MDGs. Moreover, there is some question whether the 2030 SDGs can survive in the aforementioned shadow of neoliberalism (Kumi et al., 2014) due to the fact that they harken back to the "productivist-orientation" of development. Finally, three members of the IMF research department recently questioned whether two particular components of neoliberalism had been "oversold" as beneficial to country development. According to Ostry et al. (2016),

> There are aspects of the neoliberal agenda that have not delivered as expected. Our assessment of the agenda is confined to the effects of two policies: removing restrictions on the movement of capital across a country's borders (so-called capital account liberalization); and fiscal consolidation, sometimes called "austerity," which is shorthand for policies to reduce fiscal deficits and debt levels. An assessment of these *specific* policies (rather than the broad neoliberal agenda) reaches three disquieting conclusions:
>
> - The benefits in terms of increased growth seem fairly difficult to establish when looking at a broad group of countries.
> - The costs in terms of increased inequality are prominent. Such costs epitomize the trade-off between the growth and equity effects of some aspects of the neoliberal agenda.
> - Increased inequality in turn hurts the level and sustainability of growth. Even if growth is the sole or main purpose of the neoliberal agenda, advocates of that agenda still need to pay attention to the distributional effects. (pp. 38–39)

Ostry et al. (2016) went further by suggesting that greater attention be paid to, ironically, aspects of development as conceptualized by many proponents of the BNA and CA approaches:

> The evidence of the economic damage from inequality suggests that policymakers should be more open to redistribution than they are. Of course, apart from redistribution, policies could be designed to mitigate some of the impacts in advance—for instance, through increased spending on education and training, which expands equality of opportunity (so-called predistribution policies). (p. 41)

The politicization of development approaches will likely continue into the foreseeable future as different orientations vie for preeminence both in terms of economic theory and policy implementation. At present, the tenets of neoliberalism, however "zombie-like," remain a shadowy force facilitating greater globalist integration. The postdevelopment approaches continue to pose a credible challenge but have yet to produce a Kuhnian scientific revolution and thus displace the affinity for neoliberalism that many policymakers ardently retain.

The 2030 Agenda for Sustainable Development is laudable for its stated objectives regarding a "modern view of development." However, as was shown in chapter 3, the emphasis on sustainable growth has yet to overcome the subjective perceptions that many hold of its importance when juxtaposed with the desire for a vibrant economy. Notwithstanding trends regarding the consumption of VES, it appears that formidable obstacles continue to beset a genuine appreciation for the global sustainable environment. Moreover, any increasing prominence of the tenets of neoliberalism in the achievement of the SDGs will likely mean a proportionate decline in the *objective* GSE as it has been presented here. We now turn our attention directly to the historical development of EM and EUE theory, theories that are a direct outgrowth of the conceptualization, measurement, and politicization of the traditional view of development.

NOTES

1. Sartori (1970) argues that we have stretched or strained the definition of concepts to the point that they now represent nothing more than "vague, amorphous conceptualizations" (pp. 1033–1036).

2. While Aristotle stipulated the existence of moral and intellectual virtues, only the latter are emphasized here.

3. This is an obvious oversimplification but one that suffices for present purposes.

4. Lord Robbins (1968) subsequently incorporated per capita production as a measure of development. However, he continued to maintain that there existed troubles in defining and measuring the concept (p. 151).

5. It should be noted, however, that while Smith (2007), Ricardo (2015), and Mill (2004) reflected on the notion of "stationary" (i.e., steady) state development, Mill (2004) entertained this eventuality as desirable given that it would still provide "improvement" (i.e., development) of society but in other ways. For example, stationary state development would require people to learn how to live within their economic and environmental means (pp. 592–596).

6. Schumpeter would later comment that the use of the concept "static," in particular, could be easily confused with a previously constructed idea of a "stationary economy." In reality, Schumpeter's "static" process reflected a norm of economic growth that just continued doing what it always has done. It is in this sense, "continuous growth," that it was a reflection of a "static" process. Moreover, a "dynamic"

process of economic development existed in the sense that the discontinuous changes to the established equilibrium represented a dynamic change from the norm (Schumpeter, 1949, pp. 82–83, note 1).

7. Flammang (1979) ultimately concluded that economic growth and development policies were "complementary" in the long term but "competitive" in the short term (p. 61).

8. Although the measures were revised in 2010 and 2014, the HDI measure still reflects the original three dimensions: "A long and healthy life, knowledge, and a decent standard of living" (UNDP, 2015).

9. Similar indexes would also suppose a difference between economic growth and genuine development, such as the Gender Development Index and Gender Empowerment Index in 1995 (replaced in 2010 by the Gender Inequality Index). The latter looks at reproductive health, empowerment, and the labor market to see what the opportunity cost to the development of a nation is due to gender inequality. The Environmental Sustainability Index also originated in 1995 (replaced in 2002 by the Environmental Performance Index) as an attempt to enhance understanding of how the GSE is crucial to overall well-being.

10. Read the Long Telegram at https://nsarchive2.gwu.edu/coldwar/documents/episode-1/kennan.htm

11. Read the Clifford-Elsey report at https://ysmithcpallen.com//sites/default/files/sites/all/documents/Clark%20Clifford%20Report.pdf

12. Read the *X* article at http://slantchev.ucsd.edu/courses/pdf/Kennan%20-%20The%20Sources%20of%20Soviet%20Conduct.pdf

13. It would be erroneous to suggest that this was the only aid program that emphasized the importance of capital and economic growth in order to thwart the communist menace. In fact, the US government designated the vast majority of $14.6 billion in grants and credits available between July 1945 and the end of 1947 to European recovery (US Bureau of the Census, 1949, p. 846). Moreover, annual funding of the 1951 Mutual Security Act resulted in approximately $60 billion distributed from 1952–1961 (US Bureau of the Census, 1962, p. 862).

14. Some will undoubtedly balk at this statement, given the 1961 Bay of Pigs fiasco. Cuba, however, was a very specific consideration with multiple externalities in play. Overall, the Kennedy administration sought to develop more positively its relationships with Latin American republics.

15. Liberal (i.e., "soft") modernization encourages social justice and democratization, whereas conservative (i.e., "hard") modernization seeks to bolster conservative elites, military regimes, and other such entities that are not interested in democratization but may help the US secure its perceived national security interests. Arguable, Millikan and Rostow (1957), Rostow (1960, 1971), and La Palombara and Weiner (1966) represent the former, while Apter (1965) and Heilbroner (1963) embody the latter.

16. The 1950s, what Koehler (2015, p. 736) refers to as "decade zero," did see a state-oriented, capital formation (i.e., Keynesian) set of policies pursued in order to facilitate the development of developing countries. Little time is currently spent on

"decade zero," as the introduction of modernization theory proper provided the underlying foundation for EM theory. For more, see chapter 5.

17. The foregoing comments suffice in understanding the continuing politicization of development. A fuller elaboration on the measures advocated and implemented (e.g., import substitution, protectionism, etc.) and their underlying foundation for EUE theory can be found in in chapter 5.

18. The BNA and CA represent "approaches" and not "theories" of *well-being*. This stands in contrast to modernization and neo-Marxist theories. Sen (1992, p. 48) spoke to this by stating that the CA is best viewed as a multipurpose framework rather than a theory about well-being. These approaches, particularly the BNA, led to the development of the human development paradigm.

19. This is also true for proponents of the radical paradigm who continued to emphasize economic growth as the primary determinant of development even though they wished to break from the perceived structural oppression associated with the modernization approach.

20. The perceived bias is potentially problematic, as even Sen (1992) observed that it is typically easier to measure functionings than capabilities (pp. 52–53).

21. The assault on Keynesian economics is but one narrative regarding the origins of neoliberalism and the one presented here. European and US economists of various rightist orientations viewed state intervention in the economy as counterproductive and an impediment to economic growth and development. Conversely, only the free market could "effectively" dictate the desired positive outcomes with respect to both economic growth *and* development. For an expanded view of this position as well as a look at an alternative explanation for the origins of neoliberalism—the systems model of capitalism—see Connell and Dados, 2014.

22. One should note that there were attempts prior to the monumental meeting at Mont-Pèlerin, Switzerland. Hayek was a participant in the 1938 gathering, brought together by Ludwig von Mises, of liberal principals in Paris who held a vision similar to that espoused by the Mont-Pèlerin Society nearly ten years later.

23. According to Williamson (1990), "the Washington of this paper is both the political Washington of Congress and senior members of the administration and the technocratic Washington of the IFIs, the economic agencies of the US government, the Federal Reserve Board, and the think tanks."

24. It is important to understand that Williamson's conception of the "Washington Consensus" was very fluid over time. Marangos (2009) provides a very clear picture of the evolution of the Washington Consensus, as Williamson responded to various criticisms of the initial designation of the ten policy instruments.

25. Williamson came to understand that a concept recommended to him, *universal convergence*, would have better reflected the intended meaning of why he introduced his initial ten policy instruments.

26. This was rather ironic, as it harkened back to the second stage of Rostow's modernization theory. See chapter 5 for the parallels.

27. As used here, the postgrowth school is synonymous with the post-GDP school.

Chapter 5

The Intellectual Roots of Ecological Modernization and Ecological Unequal Exchange

THE COMPLEMENTARY UTILITY OF ENVIRONMENTAL THEORY

Although numerous environmental theories seek to shed light on the economic/environment discourse, the focus at present is on EM theory and EUE theory. In further understanding their *historical and intellectual roots*, *major tenets*, and *methods of inquiry*, the stark divisions that exist will become more than obvious. The overview that follows doesn't deny these divisions but makes a case for evaluating these theories in relation to one another. Researchers in various disciplinary fields have repeatedly stated the value in such an approach, as will be seen later. At this juncture, however, the focus is on illuminating the aforementioned aspects of each theory.

Ecological Modernization Theory

Historical and Intellectual Roots

EM theory has its origins in the principles of *industrial production*, *science and technological innovation*, *market-generated ecological restructuring* (i.e., movement from *economic rationality* to *ecological rationality*), *decoupling/delinking*, *evolutionary development*, and *decentralized governance systems*. More specifically, EM derives from the endeavors of a variety of late-twentieth-century, European-based social scientists (Huber, 1982, 1985; Jänicke, 1985; Simonis, 1989) wishing to understand further the perceived positive societal and nation-state *transformation* toward the global sustainable environment.

EM theory is a direct offshoot of the modernization theories of the 1950–1970s. It stems from a belief in the same underlying economic principles (i.e., classical liberalism) from which modernization theories, such as that by Walt Rostow, emerged. For example, EM theory accepts the premises underlying positive economic growth and development (i.e., industrialization) policies but qualifies the excessively economic-based models by incorporating compatible environmental objectives with industrialization.[1] The *1987 Brundland Report*, with its focus on reconciling the traditional perception that industrialization could not assimilate both economic and environmental goals, provided a conceptual impetus for an emergent EM theory. The *Report* focused greatly on the notion that economic growth would not be harmed by the inclusion of environmental concerns due to the role that the dissemination of *science and technological innovation* would play in the process.

> If industrial development is to be sustainable over the long term, it will have to change radically in terms of the quality of that development, particularly in industrialized countries. But this is not to suggest that industrialization has reached a quantitative limit, particularly in developing countries. . . . Technology will continue to change the social, cultural, and economic fabric of nations and the world community. With careful management, new and emerging technologies offer enormous opportunities for raising productivity and living standards, for improving health, and for conserving the natural resource base. (World Commission on Environment and Development, 1987)

The aforementioned sounds eerily similar to the overarching importance that Rostow (1960) attached to *science and technological innovation* as one of the fundamental ingredients of economic growth policies adopted by then president Kennedy. It was purported that countries, historically speaking, sequentially evolve (i.e., in linear fashion) through five stages of economic growth dependent upon a variety of economic, political, and social considerations: (1) the traditional society, (2) the preconditions for take-off, (3) the take-off, (4) the drive to maturity, and (5) the age of high mass-consumption. While Rostow (1960) was primarily concerned with the economic considerations underlying and sustaining economic growth, he envisioned the political and social realms[2] as important contributors *and* consequences of growth (p. 2).

The *traditional society* is a precursor to the EM belief that anthropogenic forces can induce the natural world to effect systematic change and positive outcomes with respect to economic growth. Countries in this stage present with a variety of economic, political, and social "symptoms,"[3] including limited production functions, a ceiling on output per person, and a disproportionate allocation of resources to the agricultural sector. Technology was either present in a minimalist fashion but not readily incorporated in society, existed but was not accessible, or simply did not exist, thus resulting in the aforementioned ceiling on output per person. A sociocultural attitude of fatalism pervaded society and limited meaningful long-term change while still providing for short-term improvements in the life of individuals. This must be seen within the context of the distribution of power whereby centralized political power was the norm, with rich landowners constituting regional power brokers (Rostow, 1960, pp. 4–5).

The transitional *preconditions for take-off* stage is an integral part of the linear growth process, for it is during this stage that the capacity of countries to benefit from modern science and technology, and geometric growth,[4] is acquired. Of considerable importance is the fact that the agricultural and industry sectors will benefit from new production structures, the latter a consequence of the implementation of technology. However, this technology does not pervade the whole of the economy, as low technology production structures largely remain the norm, resulting in limited advancements. The massing of social overhead capital, or that which will be utilized in the building of long-term investments in infrastructure,[5] housing, and so forth is not only a crucial component of this stage but also one that speaks to the importance of political and social concerns. Because private sector profits aren't sufficient to produce the necessary level of social overhead capital, government must play an important role in the process. Concurrent with this is the recognition that both the regionally based political institutions—and distribution of power—and value system associated with traditional society must recede in favor of strong centralization of political power and a belief that progress on both individual and national fronts is possible (Rostow, 1960, pp. 17–28).

The *take-off* stage is the frontier of *modern society*, as innovative technology results not only in the commercialization of the agricultural sector via new production structures but in advancements in industry as well. Moreover, this is largely facilitated by access and implementation of technology *coupled* with social overhead capital, and a political class that is amenable to the requirements of modernization. According to Rostow (1960):

> In Britain and the well-endowed parts of the world populated substantially from Britain (the United States, Canada, etc.) the proximate stimulus for take-off was mainly (but not wholly) technological. In the more general case, the take-off awaited not only the build-up of social overhead capital and a surge of technological development in industry and agriculture, but also the emergence to political power of a group prepared to regard the modernization of the economy as serious, high-order political business. (p. 8)

Generally, the take-off is facilitated by the ability of societies to break the old, established social, political, and cultural orientations originally present in traditional societies and still percolating in the preconditions stage. However, Rostow (1960) also maintained that take-off in a second grouping of societies was delayed less by the aforementioned orientations than by the "high (and even expanding) levels of welfare that could be achieved by exploiting land and natural resources" (p. 36).

Modern technology that permeates all economic activity is the foremost characteristic of the *drive to maturity*. Technology played a pivotal role during the take-off but was limited in the scope of its application. This is overcome in the drive to maturity, however, as the application of technology moves into "more refined and technologically often more complex processes" (Rostow, 1960, p. 9). It is at this juncture where Rostow indicates that the innovation of "modern" technology is continuous through time and that the presence of this technology, along with political forces, will largely determine the "leading sectors" of the economy. The considerable importance attached to technology is evident in his later referring to this stage as "the drive to *technological* maturity" (Rostow, 1971). Consider the following by Rostow (1960):

> This is the stage in which an economy demonstrates that it has the technological and entrepreneurial skills to produce not everything, but anything that it chooses to produce. (p. 10)

> There are a variety of ways a stage of economic maturity might be defined: but for these purposes we define it as the period when a society has effectively applied the range of (then) modern technology to the bulk of its resources. . . . In terms of sectoral development the drive to maturity sees the industrial process differentiated, with new leading sectors gathering momentum to supplant the older leading sectors of the take-off, where deceleration has increasingly slowed the pace of expansion. . . . The leading sectors in the drive to maturity will be determined, then, not merely by the pool of technology but by the nature of resource endowments; by the character of the take-off, and the forces it sets in motion; and it may be shaped to a degree, as well, by the policies of governments. (p. 59)

The *age of high mass-consumption* stage is demarcated as the point whereby greater attention is paid to demand (i.e., consumption) as opposed to supply (i.e., production) considerations in the development of the society. Consequently, the focus on science and technological innovation to further develop production structures and the like was now of relatively lesser importance but is by no means extinguished. On the demand side of the equation, history suggests that the state will act in one of three manners with respect to the surplus of resources generated: (1) an *internal focus*—the welfare state—whereby redistribution of income via progressive taxation policies, (2) an *external focus*—power and influence—whereby resources are allocated to the military and foreign policy endeavors, or (3) an *enhanced consumption focus*—on quality and materialism—whereby consumption of new and/or improved foodstuffs, shelter, and clothing and/or durable goods not previously possessed occurs (Rostow, 1960, pp. 73–74).

While Rostow didn't specifically outline how modern science and technology would "interact" with environmental concerns in either the drive to maturity or age of high mass-consumption stages, it would be erroneous to suggest that he did not see the importance of technological innovation in addressing the environmental problems that modernization had produced throughout the process. In his updated 1971 treatise, *Politics and the Stages of Growth*, Rostow not only spoke specifically to the evolutionary role of science and technology in production processes and the like but also to the expectation that *technological advances* would deliver countries from environmental decline. According to Rostow (1971),

> What distinguishes the world since the industrial revolution from the world before is the systematic, regular, and progressive application of science and technology to the production of goods and services. The resulting flow of innovation has been an additional factor of production which has the special characteristic that it is, so far as we know, indefinitely expansible. And the organized creativity of the human mind appears thus far to be of a productivity capable of compensating for limitations of land and natural resources. Thus, for two centuries have societies, which organized themselves to exploit the innovational stock and flow, fended off Ricardian diminishing returns to land and the Malthusian spectre. Only now have the rate of population increase and threats to the environment cast a shadow over the efficacy of the Newtonian revolution; although science and technology will surely play a part if man succeeds in coming to stable terms with his physical environment. (p. 26)

In searching for an answer to the question of what is to come after the age of high mass-consumption, Rostow (1971) posited the existence of a preliminary "sixth stage," the *search for quality*, which attempted to answer, What will humankind do in a "life in an environment where material scarcity is progressively lifted from him?" (p. 230). It is undeniably the case that federal outlays, in the US case, suggest that the search for a higher quality of life is indicated by a greater desire for such goods as education, health care, travel, and recreation. However, the data also reflect an increase in outlays for economic and vital environmental services (VES), indicating that the latter are also a part of the search for quality (p. 233). The latter 1970s saw Rostow (1979) further recognize that environmental regulations not only could serve the interests of "correcting" the air and water pollution created during the modernization process but also positively contribute to economic growth. Consider the following:

> Now, productivity. The deceleration of productivity increases, in the United States and a number of other advanced industrial countries, is a phenomenon reaching back to the second half of the 1960s. In the United States the major factors accounting for the deceleration are believed to be a disproportionate expansion of women and teenagers in the working force; increased environmental and other social regulation; lowered investment rates, including a reduced proportion of GNP allocated to research and development. In my view, low levels of investment-and, consequently, low growth rates-are the critical factors likely to determine the path of productivity increase in the future. The reason for this judgment is dual. First, a subsidence of the proportion of teenagers in the working force in the 1980s will follow from the subsidence of the baby boom at the end of the 1950s. The demographic factor will begin to operate positively on the rate of productivity increase. Second, the effects of social, environmental, and safety regulations contribute positively to real GNP, although not in ways we now measure; and, in any case, the excessive burden of such regulations, now widely acknowledged, is likely to be gradually reduced by simplification and the weeding out of the less cost-effective forms of regulation. (Rostow, 1979, pp. 183–184)

The foregoing is not in the service of lessening the rightful indictment of modernization theory for its great abuses with respect to natural resource depletion, a reality that Rostow (1971) readily acknowledged in writing about the "bill for prior capital consumption" (p. 239). Moreover, it is certainly not to suggest that Rostow be considered the "father of EM theory." The coverage and goals associated with the Kennedy administration, covered in chapter 4, certainly confirm that *economic rationality*—as opposed to *ecological rationality*—permeated the Rostow conception. *Alternatively, the intent is to show that the overwhelming focus on science and technological innovation as well as the development of political institutions that Rostow had concerned himself with were indeed the foundational basis from which EM theory emerged and subsequently developed.*

Many of the core elements of modernization theory, and political development theory (Leroy and von Tatenhove, 2000; Mol and Sonnenfeld, 2000; Spaargaren, 1997), are firmly entrenched in EM theory. The *belief in progress* as a fundamental core element is essential (Hajer, 1995, p. 33). Related to this belief is an underlying implicit, if not outright, *incorporation of capitalist principles* (McLaughlin, 2012) and blind acceptance of the *human exemptionalist paradigm* (HEP) that posits human superiority vis-à-vis the natural world (Ewing, 2017, p. 130; Foster, 2012, p. 212). Giving birth to the HEP is the idea of *technological optimism*, itself a consequence of the scientific revolution and Age of Enlightenment. In its most naïve form, technological optimism professes a belief in unfettered technological innovation in the face of unrelenting population growth. The net effect is that potential areas of crisis, such as the environment, food production, and energy, among others, will not materialize due to the timely implementation of new technologies (Foster and Clark, 2012; Hannigan, 2006, p. 26; Sezgin, 2013, p. 93).

The increasing technological sophistication accompanying the modernization process certainly enhanced the production proficiency of industrializing countries. Moreover, it also created increased production efficiencies, which governments argue have served to conserve natural resource consumption. Antithetical to this is the argument advanced by the *Jevons paradox* that production efficiencies, relative cost reductions, and subsequent acceleration of economic growth result in both *increased* demand and usage. Jevons (1866) uses technological advances in the steam engine to illustrate the paradoxical outcomes, including *increased* consumption in other aspects of the industrial sector as well.

> It is very commonly urged, that the failing supply of coal will be met by new modes of using it efficiently and economically. The amount of useful work got out of coal may be made to increase manifold, while the amount of coal consumed is stationary or diminishing. . . . *It is wholly a confusion of ideas to suppose that the economical use of fuel is equivalent to a diminished consumption. The very contrary is the truth.* . . . It is the very economy of the use of coal that makes our industry what it is; and the more we render it efficient and economical, the more will our industry thrive, and our works of civilization grow. . . . *[T]he reduction of the consumption of coal, per ton of iron, to less than one-third of its former amount, has been followed, in Scotland, by a ten-fold total consumption,* not to speak of the indirect effect of cheap iron in accelerating other coal consuming branches of industry. (pp. 122–135, in passim)

The modernization mentality of technological optimism may well provide the mechanism by which resource consumption can be lessened, but the EGP largely negates this possibility with its emphasis on climbing the ladder of industrialization, what Huber (1989a) equated with modernization (p. 365). Simply put, an increasing *rebound effect* (i.e., take-back effect) negates the extent to which technological innovation serves to reduce the consumption of environmental resources throughout the modernization process. In essence, *the N-Curve Dilemma* negates the environmental gains that have been made via economic growth (Lambin and Meyfroidt, 2011; Jänicke, 2008).

The realization of the role of technology in the Jevons paradox, while conveniently alien to modernization theorists, was not entirely lost on the first generation of EM theorists. Moreover, the decreasing benefits of technological inputs coupled with the purported movement from heavy to light industries set the stage for Huber's (1982; 1985, p. 174) *ecological switchover*. According to Gibbs's (2006) interpretation of Huber, the ecological switchover "is a logical, necessary, and inevitable stage in the development of the industrial system" (p. 197). Moreover, it refers to the procedural mechanism by which traditional norms of industrial development in modernization theory, and the EGP associated with it, transforms into an increasing focus on ecological considerations in the production process. Huber (1985) refers to this process metaphorically in this oft-quoted line: "Die hässliche IndustrieRaupe werde sich im Zuge ihrer Metamorphosen noch als ökologischer Schmetterling entpuppen." [The ugly industrial caterpillar will turn out to be an ecological butterfly in the course of its metamorphoses.] (p. 20).

Himself a stage theorist, Huber (1982, 1985) maintains that the process of industrial development proceeds through three stages: (1) the *industrial breakthrough*, (2) the *construction of the industrial society*, and (3) *superindustrialization*. It is during this latter stage that Huber maintains that the "butterfly" will materialize. It is arguable that the ecological switchover that occurs during superindustrialization may also occur during the latter years of Rostow's age of high mass-consumption or preliminary "sixth" stage, the search for quality, whereby the aforementioned emphasis is on securing a higher quality of life (i.e., well-being), which would ostensibly include environmental concerns. It is more likely to occur during the search for quality stage, however, if the postmaterialist thesis advanced by Inglehart (1990, 1997) is accurate. Inglehart (1997) maintains that there is a movement to postmaterialist values (i.e., the need for environmental protection) by those industrial countries whose populations have achieved relatively high levels of economic security, resulting in lesser priority being given to materialist values (i.e., economic growth) (p. 31). As such, the ecological switchover is, perhaps, a *natural* (i.e., organic) outgrowth of the industrialization/modernization process.

EM theory reflects the movement from materialist to postmaterialist values via the aforementioned concepts of *economic rationality* and *ecological rationality*. Germane to the current discussion, economic rationality centers on maximizing the potential benefit accruing via industrial production. Moreover, it effectively mirrors the characteristics associated with the economic growth paradigm. For example, both utilize economic growth to evaluate the progress associated with production processes. Similarly, both downplay the importance of overconsumption of resources and related environmental harms stemming from emerging industrial production (Jorgenson, 2016a, p. 3).

The aforementioned ecological switchover is the manner by which the dominance of economic rationality *partially* yields to ecological rationality.

Ecological rationality, as both a construct and application, seeks to reconfigure the dominance of economic rationality and the EGP during the earlier stages of modernization/industrialization (Clark and York, 2005, p. 410). An "ecological awakening" regarding unbridled reliance on VES in industrial production materializes from a variety of societal institutions via a process of Weberian rationalization. As such, the "awakening" is not a violent process but rather one that envisions a permanent ecological *complement* to existing economic structures of production *and* consumption (Huber, 1985; Mol et al., 2009). According to Mol (2006a), "although environment moves up and down the 'issue-attention cycle' of politics, it is strongly embedded in the core institutions and social practices of modern society, which strongly subdues any radical and sudden breakdown of environmental gains" (p. 32). Ecological rationality is in no conception a holistic substitute for economic rationality—that is, an overthrow of the dominant capitalist system of industrialization—although some have conceived of an EM theory whereby "development is made conditional on giving primacy, not equality, to the ecological rationality" (Toke, 2011, p. 23). Mol (2002) speaks to the ecological challenge, its complementary nature to economic processes, and its institutionalized permanence:

> In the economic domain, ecological rationality has started to challenge the dominant economic rationality. And since, according to most scholars, the growing independence of an ecological rationality and perspective from their economic counterparts in the domain of production and consumption is crucial to "the ecological question," this last step is the decisive one. It means that economic processes of production and consumption are increasingly analyzed and judged, as well as designed and organized from both an economic and an ecological point of view. Some profound institutional changes in the economic domain of production and consumption have been discernible from the late 1980s onward. Among these changes were the widespread emergence of environmental management systems, the introduction of an economic valuation of environmental goods via the introduction of eco-taxes, the emergence of environment-inspired liability and insurance arrangements, the increasing importance attached to environmental goals such as natural resource saving and recycling among public and private utility enterprises, and the articulation of environmental considerations in economic supply and demand. The fact that we analyze these transformations as institutional changes indicates their semi-permanent character. Although the process of ecology-induced transformation should not be interpreted as linear and irreversible, as was common in the modernization theories in the 1950s and 1960s, these changes have some permanency and would be difficult to reverse. (p. 94)

Summary of Beliefs

Post–World War II economic growth led to an overabundance of environmental concerns (i.e., degradation) both in the US and internationally by the late 1960s. The dominant EGP associated with modernization/industrialization facilitated great technological innovations, accelerated industrial production, and ever-increasing natural resource withdrawals (Sezgin, 2013, p. 93). Numerous apocalyptic scenarios quickly emerged suggesting that the EGP, coupled with increasing population growth, would have to be effectively addressed for the GSE to survive. Taken together, these scenarios represented the 1970s environmental discourse known as *survivalism* (Dryzek, 1997, p. 26). According to Dryzek (1997), "The basic story line of survivalism is clear enough: human demands on the carrying capacity of ecosystems threaten to explode out of control, and draconian action needs to be taken in order to curb these demands. This story line is in turn constructed from . . . metaphors, other rhetorical devices, assumptions about natural relationships, agents and motives" (p. 34).

Several works are representative of the survivalism discourse. Garrett Hardin, in his 1968 article, *The Tragedy of the Commons*, concerned himself with the Malthusian question of overpopulation, its impact on resource consumption, and its unjust facilitation by the welfare state. He asserted that individuals left to their own conscience, one that is born greatly from the *rational actor model*, will not willingly limit their "freedom to breed" and that "no technical solution can rescue us from the misery of overpopulation" (Hardin, 1968, p. 1248).[6] Also in 1968, Paul and Anne Ehrlich would publish their neo-Malthusian treatise, *The Population Bomb*, arguing that the "birth" side of the *birth/death equation* should be the focus of our attention. Moreover, Ehrlich (1968) would argue for negative population growth facilitated by a variety of tax disincentives, sterilization and monetary incentives, and foreign aid based on a system of *international triage*.[7] A third treatise, *The Limits to Growth*, by Meadows et al. (1972) would also focus attention on the population/environment nexus but seemingly integrated food production, industrialization, resource consumption, and pollution more intentionally into the discussion via computer modeling. Of critical importance was the implementation of the idea of exponential versus constant (i.e., static) resource consumption. Incorporating the former meant that the apocalyptic scenarios purported by the likes of Hardin (1968) and Ehrlich (1968) would occur much sooner than otherwise expected under a constant-use model.[8] Sezgin (2013) provides a rather succinct, but loose, description of the survivalism discourse:

> They depicted doomsday scenarios of a world crumbling in the upcoming 100 years. Furthermore, they shared a common belief that there is a zero-sum game

> between economic growth and environmental protection. Since these works portrayed the environmental problematique as a matter of survival, their proposed solutions were also equally radical, such as zero-growth or demodernization. Nevertheless, the unfeasibility of such solutions for the established economic and political set-up of modern industrial society soon led to the flourishing of more optimistic solutions to environmental problems. (p. 94)

Ecological rationalization was a riposte to the apocalyptic voices of "environmental radicalism" who argued that modernization and entrenched structures of industrial production *and* consumption were the bane of human existence due to a variety of factors, including the blatant disregard for the increasing utilization and precipitous decline of VES (Mol, 1997, p. 138; Mol and Spaargaren, 2000, p. 19). The construction of EM theory, generally speaking, was one such optimistic response to the environmental catastrophe purported by the survivalism discourse.

The tenets associated with EM theory, like those of any newly developing theory, have undergone reconsideration, as the theoretical orientation continues to develop and examines an array of consequential factors (Gibbs, 2006; Mol, 1999). Critical reviews of EM theory have pointed to several concerns, such as the original overemphasis on technological determinism/optimism and production processes while giving virtually no consideration to the importance of political institutions and consumption practices (Carolan, 2004). Moreover, the eventual investigation of power relationships (e.g., inequality) and a Eurocentric bias in the initial research reflects the historical growth of the theory (Mol et al., 2014, pp. 21–22). Mol (1999) speaks directly to the ongoing development of EM theory and its core tenets in response to varied critiques: "Ideas of ecological modernization have been developed in constant debate with more critical evaluations—both within this school of thought and beyond. It gives evidence of the fact that ecological modernization theory is still in full development and has not yet crystallized into a stable set of uniform characteristics. The increasing number of studies on and applications of ecological modernization ideas also contributes to some divergences from the more or less strictly defined core features" (p. 170).

In its first two decades, Mol (1999, p. 169) suggested that EM theory already had three identifiable stages of development. The first decade of EM theory exhibited multiple beliefs but none weighed more important than the idea that applying innovative technology to production processes would procure environmental reform (Huber, 1982, 1985; Jänicke, 1985). The prevalence of capitalism was important, and industrial production processes were specifically to blame for environmental demise. The nation-state level of analysis was typical, as was great disdain for the state—an entity thought to be highly dysfunctional. Moreover, the initial stage largely excluded what would emerge as two key actors in the later development of EM theory—the recognition that increases in human agency/social movements and market actors/system dynamics could also stimulate environmental reforms (Mol, 1999, p. 169).

The second stage, from approximately the late 1980s on, tempered the emphasis on technological determinism/optimism, as the key—if not only—causal determinant of environmental reforms (Spaargaren and Mol, 1992). Continued emphasis was on the nation-state level of analysis via case and comparative studies of the industrial production processes associated primarily with Western developed nations (Hajer, 1995). Moreover, a relatively greater appreciation for the role of the state, the market, and human agency in producing environmental reforms became evident during this stage (Mol, 1999, p. 169; Zahran et al., 2007, pp. 41–42).

Mol's third identifiable stage of EM theory, from the mid-1990s on, still emphasized industrial production but also gave rise to consumption-related processes in the service of environmental reforms (Fudge and Rowe, 2001, pp. 1528–1529; Spaargaren, 1997). Moreover, in response to earlier criticism, there also existed an intentional movement away from a purely Eurocentric focus while paying increased attention to the role that global dimensions of ecological modernization play in the transformational process (Mol, 1999, pp. 169–170).

Several threads within the EM literature enhance the clarity of these stages or simply serve to provide a different nomenclature to an already identifiable evolution of theoretical development. For example, Huber (1985) had earlier provided the basic difference between Mol's (1999) characterization of the first and second stages of EM development in referencing the difference between "technocratic" and "sociocratic" development paths. These paths were born out of Huber's (1985, 1989b, p. 63) differentiation of modern society into three distinct domains: the *technosystem* (i.e., industrial system), which has historically dictated to *human society* (i.e., the living world domain) and *nature* (i.e., the environment). At its foundation, EM theory argues for the relative *emancipation* of human society—and in reality, nature—via the ecological restructuring (i.e., modernization) of the technosystem.[9]

Research during Mol's third stage of EM theory increasingly incorporated the role of human agency and social movements (Zahran et al., 2007, p. 42), while some EM theorists also downplayed the utility of technological innovation in the Huberian "ecological switchover." For example, Hajer (1995) spoke pejoratively of Huber's positive conception of the role of technology, choosing to refer to it as the *techno-corporatism* stage due to its top-down approach to technological innovation and the corollary that the "silhouette of technocracy" would stand "in the way of implementing 'real solutions' for what are very 'real problems'" (Hajer, 1996, p. 253). Hajer (1995) juxtaposed techno-corporatism with a second stage, *reflexive ecological modernization*, which would highlight "the importance of the mobilization of independent opinions versus the respected power of authorities (p. 281). Societal members would transition into the aforementioned ecological rationality exerting pressure on corporations and governments to adopt environmentally sound practices (Islam, 2017). Grounding this stage in the vernacular of *reflexive modernization* and the *risk society* (Beck, 1992; Beck et al., 1994) was, perhaps, an attempt to legitimize the status of EM as a bona fide theory in environmental sociology (Buttel, 2000, p. 62), suggesting the conceptual process for the EM transition from techno-corporatism. According to Beck (1992):

> *Just as modernization dissolved the structure of feudal society in the nineteenth century and produced the industrial society, modernization today is dissolving industrial society and another modernity is coming into being.* . . . Modernization within the horizon of experience of *pre*-modernity is being replaced by *reflexive* modernization. . . . Modernization *within* the paths of industrial society is being replaced by a modernization *of the principles* of industrial society, something not provided for in any of the theoretical scenarios and political recipe books still in use to this day. (p. 11)

Dependent on whether it overemphasized the role of technology innovation or incorporated reflexivity, Hajer's dichotomous perspective provided a basis for furthering the construction of EM as either "weak" or "strong." Christoff (1996) further evinces the importance of reflexivity while emphasizing the role of political pluralism and volition as a determinant:

> I would suggest that different interpretations of what constitutes EM lie along a continuum from weak (one is tempted to write, false) to strong, according to their likely efficacy in promoting enduring ecologically sustainable transformations and outcomes across a range of issues and institutions. . . . The political contest between the environment movement on the one hand and governments and industry on the other is predominantly over which of these types of EM should predominate. (pp. 191–192)

The characterization of "weak" EM involves the view that technology, while an important aspect of the production process, is limited by a *closed system* of economic and political elites (Hajer, 1995) instituting *technological adjustments* that are primarily in the service of cutting production costs and thus maintaining/regaining a competitive position in the marketplace (Christoff, 1996, pp. 182–184). The "policy-oriented" approach incorporates *instrumental rationality* in a top-down manner, assuming an exploitative relationship between industry and nature (Christoff, 1996, p. 195). However, the role of the state in this process is perceived to be minimal (Christoff, 1996, Glynn et al., 2017, p. 29; Huber, 1982, 1985; Jänicke, 1985). Moreover, any significant benefit to the environment is an attendant "positive byproduct" rather than a genuine result of intentionally restructuring production processes with broader national and international ecological objectives in mind. In effect, this *narrow* application of technological innovation focuses on reducing source emissions and increasing efficiencies in resource usage (Zahran et al., 2007, p. 41), reflecting an overly *economic* orientation which "does not necessarily reflect any significant and overwhelming changes in corporate, public or political values in relation to desired ecological outcomes" (Christoff, 1996, pp. 182–183). Compounding the relative ineffectiveness of "weak" EM is the reductionist focus on only industrialized states as well as the incorporation of a *hegemonic/unitary* structure that assumes only industrialized states can formulate sound structural principles (e.g., a unilinear, evolutionary mode of ecological development) by which to acquire EM (Christoff, 1996, p. 189; Glynn et al., 2017, p. 29).

The "strong" end of the continuum maintains that EM "denotes a process of structural change in economic, political, and cultural institutions that directly affect environmental outcomes" (Zahran et al., 2007, p. 40). The transition from an economic orientation to an ecological orientation is intentional and structural, refocusing attention from the *economization of nature* to the *ecologization of the economy*. Jänicke (1988) implies that the latter presupposes a stronger EM with its technological focus on preventive/anticipatory aspects of industrial and societal reform, while the former focuses only on remedial actions. Simonis (1985) maintains that the transition from a *react-and-cure* strategy to an *anticipate-and-prevent* strategy is one from traditional environmental policy to true ecological modernization (pp. 369–370). Moreover, the ecologization of the economy focuses not on treating the symptoms associated with the lack of economic competitiveness but rather on addressing the underlying ecological disease via the implementation of ecologically favorable economic, political, and cultural advances (Gibbs, 2006, p. 197). The latter requires the institution of innovative eco-friendly technologies that decrease resource consumption and environmental decline while concurrently facilitating economic growth (Jänicke, 1988, pp. 15–17). Consequently, the focus of a "stronger" EM must include structural change that addresses both production *and* consumption processes. The *internalization of externalities* is a key mechanism to its success. Moreover, the "instrumental rationality" present in weaker expressions of EM will transition into a more holistic vision of the importance of the environment. According to Christoff (1996),

> The strongest or most radically *ecological* notion of ecological modernisation will often stand in opposition to industrial modernity's predominantly

> instrumental relationship to nature as exploitable resource. Recognition that over-production—the use of material resources beyond regional and global ecological capacities—must cease because of the threat of imminent ecological collapse, does not allow for the self-serving gradualism of the weak forms of ecological modernisation discussed earlier. (p. 195)

"Strong" EM also presupposes "a collaborative, deliberative process, where the state provides markets and civil society actors access to all the necessary information and institutions for achieving the desired environmental outcomes" (Glynn et al., 2017, p. 29). The implementation of a *communicative rationality* and democratic orientation to decision-making facilitates a broader focus *and* deeper integration of societal interests. In an analogous manner, the broadening of the approach includes a greater respect for the role that globalization has played in shaping environmental policy. Recognizing the international flow of natural resources as well as the global integration of manufacturing prompts further realization that successful EM requires focusing on the larger international system of states and the various mechanisms that displace ecological costs from one state to another (Christoff, 1996, pp. 188–189; Howell, 2007, pp. 86–92). Concurrent with this is an enlightened discernment that no one view of EM, especially one singularly rooted in the historical experience of industrialized states, can dictate the "correct" strategy for developed and developing states alike.

In sum, "strong" EM does not take the position that capitalism is inherently evil, requiring its disavowal in any EM strategy (Burns, 2013, p. 11; Mol, 2002; Mol and Spaargaren, 2000, p. 23). However, "strong" EM strategies are tantamount to Hajer's reflexive ecological modernization (Mol and Spaargaren, 2000) and require substantial restructuring of both industrial production *and* consumption processes, and the attendant institutional dimensions of modernity.[10] Moreover, the cultural dispositions of societal members, whether the latter are formal or informal decision-makers with respect to the implementation of EM strategies will need to be effectively addressed (Gibbs, 2006, p. 197; Zahran et al., 2007, p. 39). The ultimate expected result of such interactions is the *decoupling* of economic growth from environmental degradation, pollution, and VES, generally speaking (Foster, 2012, p. 213; Gibbs, 2006, p. 197; Glynn et al., 2017, p. 37; Howes et al., 2010; Islam, 2017; Mol, 2006a, p. 6; Saat and Ali, 2014, p. 119; Sezgin, 2013, pp. 97–99).

As can be seen above, the core tenets of EM theory are numerous and interrelated, and they have evolved over time as different perspectives and assumptions have waxed and waned. Through it all, however, there has been a certain degree of consistency in its general belief system. Underlying EM theory is the dual structural belief in the HEP and the positive forces of the capitalist world economy (CWE), if not industrialization. As mentioned earlier, these foundational beliefs are rooted in, and are a carryover of, the tenets associated with earlier modernization and political development theories. EM theory has always recognized the environmental ills associated with resource extraction, production, and waste disposal inherent in the CWE, precisely what the survivalism discourse maintained as problematic. In its infancy, the foundational beliefs of EM theory extolled the virtues of the CWE to make positive "progress" on both economic and environmental fronts via a somewhat limited perspective that emphasized technological innovation/optimism in all facets of production.

As infancy gave way to adolescence, EM theory recognized the limitations of a solitary emphasis on technological innovation. In so doing, it focused efforts on projecting a broader perspective, an *ecological iron triangle* (EIT) of sorts, to understand the underlying forces that would spur positive, qualitative progress on both the economic *and* ecological fronts. The structural foundational beliefs went largely untarnished even though the immature overemphasis on economic institutions, and their related processes, became readily apparent. Responding to this, the EIT supposed an interrelated set of factors representing economic, political, and social institutions. Although representing a substantial break from the unidimensional focus on technological innovation, the EIT maintained its allegiance to the foundational beliefs while further elevating the prominence of the CWE and its ability to transition itself from "economic rationalization" to "ecological rationalization" (i.e., reflexive modernization). This transition would be facilitated by the structural transformation of entities associated with the EIT: economic institutions—markets; social institutions—human agency; and political institutions—the state. Continued economic growth and development, within the CWE, provide the impetus for these institutional "shifts."

The more reasonable adolescence of EM theory entered early adulthood with the foundational structural beliefs and the EIT largely intact. However, the adolescence of EM theory largely, although not exclusively, equated markets with "production and sellers" while not fully integrating "consumption and buyers" into the equation. Early adulthood would see the full-fledged development of the belief that both production *and* consumption were important facets in attaining positive progress on both the economic *and* ecological fronts (Mol and Spaargaren, 2004).

Beyond the fundamental structural beliefs in the HEP and CWE, and the overwhelming belief that positive progress is possible with respect to both the economy and environment, EM theory has increasingly incorporated the belief that the market and human agency (i.e., attendant public demands) are vital to acquiring positive progress. The role of human agency, however, is largely seen in terms of a natural progression of "wants" out of the market once economic growth has generated a sustained level of economic affluence.

This parallels the findings regarding perceptions related to the economic/environment juxtaposition presented in chapter 2. Ironically, the Marxian dictum that capitalism "sows the seeds of its own destruction" appears to be relevant here, as the successes of the CWE and economic rationality produce the levels of affluence necessary for ecological rationality to emerge![11]

The increasing belief that the state (i.e., government) is a critical change agent fostering a mutually beneficial middle ground between economic and ecological rationalities is also critical to an evolving EM theory. Just as the market facilitates increased human agency at the societal level, the government facilitates the institutionalization of a new policymaking process that is geared toward the effective integration of economic and ecological rationalities (i.e., demands) that are conducive to mutual progress (i.e., sustainable outputs). There remains, however, a qualified belief that a decentralized government is a superior structure in facilitating progress and that limited government interference in the natural working of the market should be emphasized.

Finally, evolutionary EM theory doesn't specifically argue for the decoupling of the environment from the economy, nor does it call for an unqualified increase in production and/or consumption in order to promote progress while concurrently minimizing environmental degradation. Mol and Spaargaren (2004) maintain that the emphasis of EM theory should take into account "the environmental dimensions and performance of production processes, the goods and services they generate and the consumption practices they help constitute (pp. 261–262).

Method of Inquiry

The application of EM theory and associated attempts to validate its conceptual iterations have taken many forms (i.e., qualitative vs. quantitative approaches, policy-oriented vs. conceptual development, etc.) (Gibbs, 2006). The popularity of any one form has largely reflected the time period in which the analysis occurred as well as a European academic bias toward more qualitative-interpretative case studies (Mol, 2006b). Early investigations were largely Eurocentric, involving qualitative case studies of highly specific organizations and institutions within already industrialized countries. These characteristic orientations would engender a good deal of criticism and would revolve around the disease of "particularism" and the inability to discern grand, structural patterns of behavior that are widely generalizable. Indeed, numerous critiques of EM theory, both of the time and yet today, center on the nature of the inquiry and the cases analyzed (Ewing, 2017; Toke, 2011; York, Rosa, and Dietz, 2010, pp. 80–86).

In their review of EM theory, past and future, Mol and Sonnenfeld (2000) conceded that it originally only applied to industrialized, developed countries but maintained that by the mid-1990s, the geographical scope of application included new transitional economies, newly industrializing countries, and developing countries (p. 5): "From the initial contributions onwards, the aim of Ecological Modernisation Theory has been to analyse how contemporary industrialised societies deal with environmental crises. The core of all studies in the tradition of Ecological Modernisation focuses on (existing and programmed) environmental reforms in social practices, institutional designs and societal and policy discourses to safeguard societies' sustenance bases" (Mol and Sonnenfeld, 2000, pp. 5–6). As aforementioned, the initial scope of application was in large part a function of the geographical origins of EM theory and the original research cases being drawn from OECD countries (i.e., those who had experienced industrialization) (Mol and Spaargaren, 2000, p. 42; Spaargaren and Mol, 1992, p. 324). However, the indictment involving Eurocentrism has merit if only looking at the early years of its development, as one can point to a plethora of microlevel EM case studies of entities from countries not generally considered part of the industrialized, developed world. For example, Saat and Ali (2014) examined solid waste management in Malaysia, concluding that multiple factors indicate that a national sustainable policy is still far away. Moreover, Wong (2012) found that both the state and industry in Singapore framed environmental concerns too narrowly and could further benefit from the greater inclusion of civil society (i.e., environmental activists). Still, while there has been an increasing number of non-OECD cases studied, it would be erroneous to suggest that EM research is equitable in its geographical inquiries. While Asian and Southeast Asian countries have been targeted greatly, the least developed countries, especially those on the African continent, have been largely ignored by EM research (Mol et al., 2014, pp. 24–25).

While this criticism is perhaps still warranted, it is also the case that many question whether EM theory is even applicable to select countries/regions due to a variety of peculiarities (Howes et al., 2010). For example, Cohen (1998) questioned the national capacity of some European countries to implement EM based on cultural beliefs pertaining to the environment (pp. 155–163). Moreover, researchers began to question the application of EM theory to non-European countries in general (Blowers, 1997, p. 854; Hannigan, 2006) and developing countries (Fisher and Freudenburg, 2001).

As EM theory becomes more applicable during "late development," it would appear that developing countries must largely complete the transition through Rostow's stages of economic development before the application/testing of EM theory is practical/advisable. Contrary to this, Zahran et al. (2007) maintain that developing countries can "leapfrog" with respect to the development of both technology and institutions (p. 40), thus bypassing this concern. Regardless of which view is correct, there still lies the problem that most EM research into the economic/environment nexus is of a qualitative-interpretative case study approach, which may limit the ability to generalize results to other countries and paint a more global picture of the reality.

Ecological Unequal Exchange Theory

Historical and Intellectual Roots

On a cursory level, EUE theory has its origins in the economic principles of *division of labor*, *unequal exchange*, and the political/economic concepts of *core*, *periphery*, *and semiperiphery.* More intrusively, EUE derives from the endeavors of a variety of neo-Marxist adherents—born out of the twentieth-century school of structuralism—to explain the lack of "development" and persistence of "underdevelopment" in developing countries. As a theory of development, *structuralism* premised its philosophy on the dual notion that there exist overarching structures within systems and that these structures underlie (i.e., inform) the perceptions, beliefs, and behaviors of humans. Consequently, the attempt to explain the relations between individuals, groups, nations, and other entities is one that must focus on the identification of these larger, overarching structures and how they "direct" the associated behaviors of those being studied. In discussing the study of social change, Wallerstein (1974a) spoke to the importance of these structures:

> And in the present we are all irremediably the products of our background, our training, our personality and social role, and the structured pressures within which we operate. That is not to say there are no options. Quite the contrary. A social system and all its constituent institutions, including the sovereign states of the modern world, are the loci of a wide range of social groups—in contact, in collusion, and above all, in conflict with each other. . . . Man's ability to participate intelligently in the evolution of his own system is dependent on his ability to perceive the whole. (pp. 9–10)

The school of structuralism[12] spawned both *dependency theory* and *world-systems analysis*,[13] given its argument that the lack of economic development, via unequal exchange, was a result of weak domestic structures that disadvantaged developing countries in domestic production *and* international trade. Consequently, inter alia, structuralism supported "statism" whereby the state would play an enlarged role in facilitating changes to weak domestic structures in an effort to enhance development prospects. Increased targeted state investment and ISI policies were common government responses by which to overcome domestic-oriented structural disadvantages. While ISI policies enhanced optimism among state leaders regarding prospects for greater *economic* development, they were also a strategy closely tied to tenets related to the aforementioned modernization theory—an affinity that would create rifts among dependency theorists.

Structuralism also supported the belief that *periphery* countries were disadvantaged in their international trade with *center* countries, as disproportionate (i.e., unequal) levels of development would accrue to the center. This recognition served to enhance the call for ISI policies, increasing regional trade with other periphery countries, and forgoing trade with nations of the industrialized "center" (O'Toole, 2007, p. 426). The Prebisch-Singer thesis—that historically the price of primary commodities declines relative to the price of manufactured goods resulting in declining terms of trade for primary commodities-based economies—underlined the necessity of the aforementioned ISI policies among other state-facilitated initiatives.

The Prebisch-Singer thesis provided a foundational basis for the repudiation of modernization theory and the introduction of a plethora of research generally known as dependency theory. Raúl Prebisch (1950), Hans Singer (1950), and Celso Furtado (1963), inter alia, would epitomize Latin American structuralism albeit while endorsing ISI policies that would result in a new dependency arrangement involving access to technology, export markets, foreign sources of capital, and the like (dos Santos, 1970). Conversely, others such as Fernando Henrique Cardoso and Enzo Faletto (1979), while loosely attached to structuralism, saw opportunities for development via "associated dependent development/capitalism" (pp. 172–173). Still another cohort of dependency theorists—while concurring that the nature of the problem centered on structural inequalities—chose to conceptualize the problem and responses in neo-Marxist class analysis at the international level of analysis. The common denominator was a belief in the concept of "unequal exchange"[14] between classes at the international level (i.e., center and periphery).

The work of Paul Baran, Paul Sweezy, Samir Amin, Arrighi Emmanuel, and André Gunder Frank set the stage for world-systems analysis by elaborating on the variable manifestations of unequal exchange between the center and periphery. The much maligned, Ukrainian-born Baran (1957), for example, sketched the outline of this relationship, not based on the terms-of-trade facet but with respect to economic surplus—defined as the difference between output and consumption in a given economy—being transferred from "underdeveloped" countries to advanced countries.[15] Baran and Sweezy (1966) applied Baran's three forms of economic surplus—*actual*, *potential*, and *planned*—to the US in illustrating how a monopolistic, capitalist economy and monopoly capital may dominate the economies of peripheral countries. The Egyptian-born Amin (1970, 1974, 1976, p. 193), alongside Emmanuel (1972), maintained that "unequal exchange" was primarily facilitated by wage differentials between center and periphery countries but that productivity differentials also played a role. Moreover, Amin (1976) posited that the three distortions inherent in the development of peripheral capitalism—bias favoring export activities financed by foreign capital, preference toward tertiary activities, and an orientation toward light industry—reflected the power and economic asymmetries between the center and periphery countries (p. 288).

While numerous variants of "dependency theory" exist (O'Toole, 2007, p. 434) perhaps the most notable (i.e., recognizable) is that of the German-born Frank, who formulated the concept of "satellitization" to refer to the overarching structural framework of underdevelopment. According to Frank (1966):

> When we examine this metropolis-satellite structure, we find that each of the satellites, including now-underdeveloped Spain and Portugal, serves as an instrument to suck capital or economic surplus out of its own satellites and to channel part of this surplus to the world metropolis of which all are satellites. Moreover, each national and local metropolis serves to impose and maintain the monopolistic structure and exploitative relationship of this system . . . as long as it serves the interests of the metropoles which take advantage of this global, national, and local structure to promote their own development and the enrichment of their ruling classes. (p. 21)

Frank dismissed the Prebisch-Singer thesis—which advocated domestic restructuring, ISI, state-sponsored, sector-targeted investment, and an export orientation to facilitate industrialization—instead focusing attention on the perceived externalities that negatively impact periphery development. Working within the doctrine of internationalism (i.e., globalism) would only further disproportionately benefit the metropole to the *relative* detriment of the periphery. Alternatively, the emphasis was on identifying how externalities, such as monopolies (i.e., monopoly capitalism à la Baran and Sweezy) and multinational corporations (MNCs), encouraged unequal exchange, especially via profit repatriation (Brolin, 2007, pp. 178–179). Moreover, like several dependency theorists, Frank advocated reform of the CWE and socialist revolution in the periphery as the only means by which to sever dependency, unequal exchange, and underdevelopment[16] (Frank, 1978, p. 346: O'Toole 2007, pp. 437–438).

Frank's conception of dependency was the basis for world-systems analysis as advanced by Immanuel Wallerstein. In fact, some submit that there is slight difference between the two types of analysis. Chirot and Hall (1982), for example, not only maintain that little separates the two "theories" but that they also ironically represent the essence of the core/periphery relationship.

> Because world-system theory is in most ways merely a North American adaptation of dependency theory, there is little to distinguish them from each other as theoretical constructs. To understand dependency theory, and to know its literature is to hold a firm grasp of its latter-day little Yankee brother. Of course, cultural imperialism being what it is, the world-system theorists from the North are now being used by the Southern dependency theorists to legitimize their ideas. No more ironic illustration could exist of core domination and the use of peripheral resources. The periphery can now reimport the product it originally exported, and leave behind a surplus of cultural prestige and strength in the core. (p. 91)

The similarities of both theories are easily recognizable, as Wallerstein's conceptualization of world-systems analysis (1) also borrowed from Marxist theory, (2) was a response to the inadequacies of modernization theory and neoclassical economic approaches, (3) was influenced by Raúl Prebisch and the UNECLA, (4) incorporated the dependency terminology of core and periphery, and (5) posited the existence of a structure of "unequal exchange" (Goldfrank, 2000, p. 164; Noble, 2017, p. 243).

Contrary to this point of view is the reality that world-systems analysis was more than a restatement of dependency theory or "the little Yankee brother" of said theory. It was, in effect, the next generation of a radical family orientation that spurned modernization theory—especially stage theorists such as Walt Rostow—and its inability to spark economic growth and development in developing countries. Perhaps the most general of distinctions is the reality that dependency theorists didn't offer a detailed analysis of the CWE and place it in proper historical perspective (Palma, 1978, p. 900). In his rebuke of modernization theory, Wallerstein (1974b) offered "totalities" (i.e., social systems) to illustrate historic *mini-systems* that no longer exist, and three different world-systems: *world empire*, *world economies*, and *socialist world government*:[17]

> If we are to talk of stages, then, and we should talk of stages, it must be stages of social systems, that is, of totalities. And the only totalities that exist or have historically existed are mini-systems and world-systems, and in the nineteenth and twentieth centuries there has been only one world-system in existence, the capitalist world-economy. We take the defining characteristic of a social system to be the existence within it of a division of labor, such that the various sectors or areas within are dependent upon economic exchange with others for the smooth and continuous provisioning of the needs of the area. Such economic exchange can clearly exist without a common political structure and even more obviously without sharing the same culture. (p. 390)

The international axial division of labor is integral to Wallerstein's characterization of the modern CWE, as it not only defines the boundaries of the social system but also allows for greater development of the bimodal center/periphery dependency theory characterization of labor. Wallerstein (1974a) proscribed a division of labor in the modern CWE as *international* in scope and providing not just a functional aspect—who holds what occupations—but a geographical component as well (p. 349). The division of labor is exemplified by borrowing the core/periphery characterization of Prebisch and adding to it a necessary structure, the "semi-periphery" (Wallerstein, 2004, pp. 17, 104). Production in the core and production in the periphery represent different ends of the continuum with respect to technology, wages, exploitation, surplus value, and capital accumulation, with the core utilizing capital intensive technologies and relatively higher paid, less exploited labor who are generating greater surplus value and consequently greater capital accumulation via unequal exchange (Chase-Dunn, 1998, pp. 346–347). Arrighi and Drangel (1986) succinctly summarize the bimodal division of labor when stating that

> core activities are those that command a large share of total surplus produced within a commodity chain and peripheral activities are those that command little or no such surplus. All states enclose within their boundaries both core and peripheral activities. Some (core states) enclose predominantly core activities and some (peripheral states) enclose predominantly peripheral activities. As a consequence, the former tend to be the locus of world accumulation and the latter the locus of exploitation and powerlessness. (pp. 12–13)

The addition of the semiperiphery is an important addition to dependency theory as it provides a necessary "layer" that helps preserve the stability of the modern CWE via its economic *and* political benefits (Wallerstein, 1976). Some research appears to emphasize the economic aspect between the core and periphery by referring to the search for lower production costs to enhance profit making (Arrighi and Drangel, 1986, pp. 26–27; Grell-Brisk, 2017) or for a more suitable environment—relative to the periphery—for capital investment (i.e., intensity) (Goldfrank, 2000, pp. 169–170).[18] Given that a world-economy presumes multiple political systems (i.e., national states) and cultures, the horizontal structuring of the international economy is not feasible. Consequently, the result is a vertical structure that aides in providing system stability. Ceteris paribus, the political benefits of the semiperiphery are more important given the focus on world-system stability in order to avoid disintegration. Indeed, Dunaway and Clelland (2017) argue that the economic status of the semiperiphery in the modern era, relative to core states, necessitates greater attention paid to the role of the semiperiphery (p. 403). Wallerstein presumed that a polarized system—defined as a world-economic system with only a core and periphery—would have the unintended consequence of disintegration due to the periphery mounting a unified opposition to their exploitation by the core via unequal exchange mechanisms. According to Wallerstein (1974b),

> Besides the upper stratum of core-states and the lower stratum of peripheral states, there is a middle stratum of semi-peripheral ones. This semi-periphery is then assigned as it were a specific economic role, but the reason is less economic than political. That is to say, one might make a good case that the world-economy as an economy would function every bit as well without a semi-periphery. But it would be far less politically stable, for it would mean a polarized world-system. The existence of the third category means precisely that the upper stratum is not faced with the unified opposition of all the others because the middle stratum is both exploited and exploiter. (p. 405)

If not yet realized, world-systems analysis significantly departs from earlier approaches by not focusing on the nation-state as the crucial unit of analysis in research. Rather, Wallerstein maintained that the world-system (i.e., historical social system) is the appropriate unit of analysis for purposes of comparison. Wallerstein was critical of modernization theorists on this point but also suggested that while Sweezy and Frank appeared to be in line with the proposition, they were not explicit on their acceptance (Wallerstein, 1974b, p. 393). Born out of several beliefs, the proposition was integrally related to the argument that world-systems analysis was a "unidisciplinary" field—not recognizing interdisciplinary, multidisciplinary, or transdisciplinary attempts at understanding—and is more accurately reflected in the title of "historical social science." According to Wallerstein (2004),

> World-systems analysis was an attempt to combine coherently concern with the unit of analysis, concern with social temporalities, and concern with the barriers that had been erected between different social science disciplines. World-systems analysis meant first of all the substitution of a unit of analysis called the "world-system" for the standard unit of analysis, which was the national state. On the whole, historians had been analyzing national histories, economists national economies, political scientists national political structures, and sociologists national societies. World-systems analysts raised a skeptical eyebrow, questioning whether any of these objects of study really existed, and in any case whether they were the most useful loci of analysis. Instead of national states as the object of study, they substituted "historical systems" which, it was argued, had existed up to now in only three variants: minisystems; and "world-systems" of two kinds—world-economies and world-empires. (p. 16)

A final idea setting world-systems analysis apart from dependency theorists, and which may have importance for later EUE studies, is the notion of "tightness" of the world-system. Disowning the nation-state as the appropriate unit of analysis did not mean that Wallerstein believed it to have no importance. World-systems analysis stipulated that the modern CWE consisted of an integrated system of both cultures *and* states. Furthermore, it was thought that these "lesser" structures would evolve either in support of the current CWE or present a structural crisis. The built-in assumption here is that states have unequal power and that they will pursue (i.e., compete) in the CWE in order to disproportionately benefit from the vertically structured system. Moreover, states might well ally in order to facilitate this objective. Of key importance is the underlying belief that no one state is powerful enough to outright control the whole of the CWE. However, as Wallerstein (1974b) states,

> We shall find on closer inspection that there are periods where one state is relatively quite powerful and other periods where power is more diffuse and contested, permitting weaker states broader ranges of action. We can talk then of the relative tightness or looseness of the world-system as an important variable and seek to analyze why this dimension tends to be cyclical in nature, as it seems to have been for several hundred years. (pp. 406–407)

Summary of Beliefs

Highlighting the transition from world-systems analysis to EUE theory is not arduous. The fact that the seminal works of Wallerstein and others in the dependency/world-systems milieu focused on sociohistorical aspects of the world-system is readily apparent, as the focus has been on economics (i.e., unequal exchange), political economy (i.e., class analysis), history (i.e., mini-systems), sociology (i.e., status relationships), and similar contexts. What appears to be missing, however, is any emphasis on the importance of the GSE. Wallis (2010) notes this when stating that capitalism "abuses the soil as much as it exploits the worker" (p. 32). The *Annales School*, in particular the seminal work of Fernand Braudel, greatly influenced Wallerstein's construction of world-systems analysis. Braudel's (1949/1972; 1949/1973) stipulation of three levels of time (i.e., history)—*geological*, *economic and social*, and *political and diplomatic*—loosely reflected thousands (*longue durée*), hundreds (*moyenne durée*), and decades (*courte durée*) of years. Wallerstein was greatly influenced by the periods of short and average duration but discounted the period of long duration that dealt almost exclusively with the environmental structure of history. Chew (1997) decries the omission of the "human-nature nexis" as a fundamental flaw in world-systems analysis given the importance of the GSE to the process of capital accumulation by core states:

> World-systems analysis has focused only on the macro-level relations within the human social organization instead of also analyzing the relations between social and the natural worlds. Yet this relation is the very basis of the reproduction of human societies. It is underscored in the early civilizations of Egypt, Mesopotamia, Indus, and the Hwang Ho, whose social reproductions were contingent on economic (production of surplus) and ecological relations. These societies' reproductive and expansionary capacities were conditioned by their specific ecological surroundings coupled with the needed search/exchange in other ecological landscapes for the natural resources (timber, metals and certain stone) they lacked and/or had already exhausted by unsustainable exploitation and "accumulation." Thus, the ecological relation is as primary as the economic relation in the self-expansionary process of these societies. . . . The core-periphery dynamic as exemplified through core-sponsored developmental strategies (such as export-oriented manufacturing) further exacerbates ecological degradation in peripheral areas. Whether this core-periphery relation is within a specific territorial boundary or between territorial boundaries this core-periphery dynamic with its impact on Nature, over the long term establishes limits to the reproduction of accumulation processes or the reproduction of life for that matter. . . . The continued ecological depletive effects in core and peripheral areas as a consequence of the process of accumulation and core-periphery dynamic also force the relocation of production depending on the exigencies of the accumulation processes. . . . Hegemonic rivalries via economic and trade competition have also resulted in ecological degradation where the search for cheap natural resources as well as low labor costs has led to penetration of fragile ecological environments to enhance and facilitate the accumulation process. (pp. 385–386)

In stark contrast to this view is the assertion by Moore (2003, p. 310) that a closer look at Wallerstein's account of the transition from feudalism to capitalism reveals a moderate level of attention paid to ecological concerns. Both sugar plantations and silver mines played a role in facilitating the transition to the modern CWE—concurrently impacting the GSE through increased grazing, soil deterioration, deforestation via increased timber requirements, and so on. Moreover, the "widening and deepening" of the newly forming capitalist structure was enhanced by the increasing quest for land and raw materials, effectively serving to refashion the structured provision of environmental goods. It is perhaps ironic that a population decline during the period of capitalist transition (due to the Black Death), coupled with financial retrenchment, resulted in a "perfect storm" whereby state actions facilitated the search for additional labor and greater markets and revenues. Inter alia, production sectors that required less labor, such as animal husbandry, increased, even though it meant the depletion of another aspect of the GSE—for example, sheep farming, which resulted in the trampling of agricultural producing fields (Moore, 2003, pp. 308–315 in passim).

It is perhaps surprising to note the extent to which Wallerstein discussed, albeit on the periphery of other more core topics (pun intended), the importance of the GSE in the transition from feudalism to capitalism. It is nonetheless the case that world-systems analysis paid a considerable amount of attention to ecological forces in the conditioning of diverse forms of labor. Perhaps more surprising than this, however, is the extent to which Wallerstein himself was surprised in reflecting on the extent that ecological forces played in the construction of world-systems analysis. In 2013, University of Connecticut professor Gregory Williams asked Wallerstein if he thought Moore's (2003) assertion that his work is to be read as a volume of environmental history is fair. As stated in Williams (2013), Wallerstein responded,

> Well, actually, his article startled me because I hadn't realized how much I had done that in volume one. But I don't think he's wrong. I don't think he's wrong at all. I thought what he was trying to do was defend me against all those people who say I ignore these issues. He said no, not at all, they are central to what I was doing, and he's right. But I have to say that in 1971 when I was actually writing the book, I didn't think of it as environmental history. Nobody was doing environmental history at that time. It wasn't a concept that I was utilizing. But I was utilizing the concept of holism, right? And so it seemed to me perfectly natural to include all of these elements. (pp. 205–206)

The origination of modern EUE theory rests in the work of Bunker (1985, 1984) and Bunker and Ciccantell (2005). While maintaining that the world-systems analysis emphasis on an international division of labor is important, it mistakenly does so at the neglect of including "commodities whose values are primarily extracted from nature rather than produced by labor and capital, from the periphery to the core" (Bunker, 1984, p. 1055). It is through the same mechanism—unequal exchange—that the ecological dimension of world-systems analysis becomes increasingly magnified. As such, the tenets of EUE theory are closely born out of a world-systems conception of development and its associated environmental harms in such areas as biodiversity loss, various forms of pollution, waste disposal, and CO_2 emissions (Givens et al., 2019, p. 9). While the vast majority of EUE research originally focused on the impact of structural processes on deforestation, Noble (2017) has called for research to continue to move beyond this traditional emphasis to a broader orientation that would also include "the unequal use of natural resources, overutilization of environmental space, and the displacement of environmental risks to poor nations" (p. 246).

Similar to its EM counterpart, the general belief system associated with EUE theory has remained relatively consistent, perhaps even more so than EM, throughout its existence. In large part, this is a function of the underlying tenet related to the structure of the international system.[19] Underlying EUE theory is the dual structural belief in the New Ecological Paradigm[20] (NEP) debate of the 1980s (Catton and Dunlap, 1980, 1978) and the negative forces associated with a highly structured international system that fosters the continual inequitable distribution of power, broadly defined. These foundational beliefs are rooted in and are a carryover of the major tenets of world-systems analysis. Central to the NEP is the belief that there is *critical interdependence* between humans and nature. As such, human-conditioned political and economic choices *and* the GSE inform the relationship within and between states in the modern CWE. The NEP further assumes that environmental goods and services are not finite and that human volition operates within the confines of a zero-sum game at all levels of analysis. Given this, EUE theory believes that the orientation of political units (i.e., states) is vigorous competition for scarce environmental goods and services (Hornborg, 2003, pp. 209–211).

The second foundational belief involves the world-system structure in which political units operate and the structures (i.e., mechanisms) by which interactions take place. In accordance with world-system analysis, EUE theory assumes the existence of a highly structured system within which the major political units, states, hold different political, economic, *and* ecological statuses. Characteristically speaking, these state-level statuses, *core*, *periphery*, and *semi-periphery*, evince power inequities (i.e., asymmetries) that are manifest in their relations with one another. It is important to note that the semiperiphery also has the potential to exercise its relative power via "recursive exploitation" with weaker states in both the semiperiphery and periphery (Burns et al. 2003, p. 362; Jorgenson, 2016b). Moreover, these power asymmetries may also occur within the domestic structure of states (Oulu, 2016, p. 447).

As aforementioned, the exercise of asymmetrical power initially focused on the parallel concerns of labor and capital accumulation in the CWE. This focus would evolve into an understanding of how labor and capital accumulation are not only a function of the *ecological position* of the competing political units in the CWE but a facilitator of said position as well. In overly simplistic terms, EUE theory believes that core states utilize various inequitable power mechanisms to elevate their ecological status relative to other competing states. A nonexhaustive list of the asymmetrical structures utilized include international trade, foreign direct investment, technological competence, and military prowess (Jorgenson, 2016b). Due to their greater status with respect to these mechanisms, EUE theory posits that core states have *disproportionate* access to scarce VES, such as mineral deposits and waste depositories, in both the semiperiphery and periphery. In essence, the latter states provide both the "tap" for VES to be withdrawn and the "sink" for pollution and wastes to be deposited (Rice, 2009, p. 16).

EUE theory also posits that the appropriation of VES from the periphery, as well as the displacement of environmental loads to the periphery, occur on two distinct levels (Foster and Holleman, 2014; Hornborg, 2009). The aforementioned focus on asymmetrical structures confers an understanding of the *spatial* dimension, or the transfer of VES from one state to another. Coupled with this is the belief that such transfers also occur on a *temporal* dimension, from one generation to another. Perhaps most concerning of all is the EUE belief that all aspects of global commodity chains[21] (i.e., extraction, production, consumption, and disposal) are impacted by the asymmetrical power structures (Givens et al., 2019, p. 5). In general, EUE theory believes that the unequal distribution of environmental harms to those in the periphery not only impacts more greatly their prospect for development and the GSE but also produces *second-order effects* related to individual well-being (i.e., education, health care, human rights, the lack of economic development, etc.).

Method of Inquiry

The continued qualified influence/acceptance of world-systems *analysis* to EUE is because it is not a rigid theory but rather a relatively "looser" frame of reference. Testing world-systems *theory* would be considerably difficult given impediments imposed by the core beliefs of said theory. A case analysis evaluating the theory would be tantamount to a narrative accounting of historical events construed as plausibly lending support to the theory. A comparative analysis is obviously exceedingly difficult due to the world-system *unit of analysis* affording few historical or present-day cases to compare. According to Wallerstein (1974a),

> This was of course enormously simplifying. I had one type of unit rather than units within units. I could explain changes in the sovereign states as consequent upon the evolution and interaction of the world-system. But it was also enormously complicating. I probably only had one instance of this unit in the modern era. Suppose indeed that I was right, that the correct unit of analysis was the world-system, and that sovereign states were to be seen as one kind of organizational structure among others within this single social system. Could I then do anything more than write its history? I was not interested in writing its history, nor did I begin to have the empirical knowledge necessary for such a task. . . . But can there be laws about the unique? In a rigorous sense, there of course cannot be. A statement of causality or probability is made in terms of a series of like phenomena or like instances. . . . There had only been one "modern world." Maybe one day there would be discovered to be comparable phenomena on other planets, or additional modern world-systems on this one. But here and now, the reality was clear—only one. . . . I was looking to describe the world-system at a certain level of abstraction, that of the evolution of

> structures of the whole system. I was interested in describing particular events only insofar as they threw light upon the system as typical instances of some mechanism, or as they were the crucial turning points in some major institutional change. (pp. 7–8)

Moreover, quantitative studies seeking to evaluate the "theory" would likewise meet with their own devilish obstacles. Wallerstein recognized the limitations in the method of investigation given the emphasis on the world-system rather than the nation-state as the unit of analysis. According to Wallerstein (2004),

> World-systems analysts are not against quantification per se (they would quantify what can usefully be quantified), but (as the old joke about the drunk teaches us) they feel that one should not look for the lost key only under the street lamp just because the light is better (where there are more quantifiable data). One searches for the most appropriate data in function of the intellectual problem; one doesn't choose the problem because hard, quantitative data are available. This debate can be what the French call a dialogue of the deaf. In the end, the issue is not an abstract issue about correct methodology but is about whether world-systems analysts or rather nomothetic positivists can offer more plausible explanations of historical reality and therefore throw more light on long-term, large-scale social change. (pp. 19–20)

Emerging from world-systems analysis, EUE *theory* has this same problem. It would be better to speak in terms of EUE *analysis* given the acceptance of the world-system as the basic unit of analysis. In essence, EUE researchers should not seek to "prove or disprove" the highly structured *theory* but rather take as their starting point the tenets related to EUE theory. In concert with Wallenstein, subsequent analyses should then analyze how the unfettered competition of states operating within the world-system of the modern CWE, and their associated structures, produces ecological "winners and losers" as Western development exploits weaker states via numerous presumed "superior-inferior" relationships (e.g., trade, colonialism, investment).

Somewhat paradoxically, EUE research has consisted of both qualitative and quantitative approaches. Ironically, qualitative studies into specific aspects (e.g., deforestation, fisheries, CO_2 emissions, coffee production, water scarcity, and water pollution)[22] of single countries have the same potential problem for which EUE theorists often indict EM case research—the Netherlands fallacy (Ehrlich and Holdren, 1971, p. 1214). EM research is predominantly qualitative, case specific to one particular country, operating at a single level of analysis (i.e., local, regional, and/or national in scope), and thus limited in its conception and incorporation of relevant externalities of either a *cause and/or effect* nature (Givens et al., 2019; Jorgenson and Clark, 2012; Thombs, 2018, p. 4).

Most EUE research has incorporated a cross-national, quantitative orientation that serves to "extend" the national foci of EM research (Jorgenson, 2016b). Such an international approach is more system level yet focused on responding to the aforementioned concerns related to world-systems analysis. Problematic within this orientation, however, is the fact that much EUE research appears driven by concerns related to the availability of quality data (Givens et al., 2019, p. 9). In effect, EUE research often does concentrate on those structures and problems that are indeed "under the streetlamp," where the light is brightest!

THE INTERSECTION OF EM AND EUE, AND THE GSE NEXUS

The "survivalism narrative" certainly prompted great focus on explaining the omnipresent dilemmas with respect to the development/environment nexus. In a rather long breath, one can identify various schools that have, with their own assumptions and peculiarities, attempted to inform/persuade researchers, societies, and governments alike: counterproductivity/deindustrialization, various *neo-Marxist* conceptions, and neo-Malthusians, among others. During a time when EM theory was perhaps the most "notable" of these theories, Mol, Sonnenfeld, and Spaargaren (2009) identified several orientations that they viewed as EM rivals, suggesting that a good many of them are overly negative and pessimistic about the economic/environment juxtaposition, certainly when compared to those aligned with EM theory. In brief, they identified "neo-Marxist" theories (such as Schnaiberg's Treadmill of Production [TOP], various world-systems–based theories such as EUE, structural Marxists such as Foster's Metabolic Rift, etc.), "*Deep Ecology*" perspectives (such as those associated with ecofeminists, postmodernists, and anarchists), and "*Structural Human Ecology/Neo-Malthusian*" orientations. While the authors are somewhat optimistic about the contributions of the neo-Marxists to EM theory, they are relatively more critical of what the Deep Ecology perspective offers while finding the Structural Human Ecology/neo-Malthusians unbearable. The authors contend that the latter orientation is radically different from EM theory (i.e., overly abstract, structurally rigid, and extremely pessimistic), implicitly messaging that there isn't room for conversation (pp. 15–19 in passim). It is interesting to note that the rather pessimistic and structural orientation of most neo-Marxist orientations appears to be inconsequential to the prospect of future dialogue/understanding of EM theory.

At first glance, it appears that EM and EUE theories represent polar opposites with no apparent significant overlap, conceptually or in reality. The empirical research of each also appears greatly polarized along two competing worldviews regarding the nature of the relationship between humans and the larger environment. In fact, the proponents of each are quite adamant as to the virtue of their respective theories, the approach taken to evaluate hypotheses born from theory, and the results generated. However, the competition of ideas is a hallmark of scientific research that, in a Kuhnian world, will lead to greater understanding of the issue(s) under study (i.e., the dilemmas surrounding the intersection of economics and the environment, and the GSE nexus). Jorgenson (2016a) evinces this orientation with respect to theoretical development and practical realities. While complementing the "rich sociological frameworks for understanding" that both EM and TOP represent, he goes on to state that

> future sociological work on environment and development would benefit from stronger integrations of ecological unequal exchange and other related approaches with treadmill of production theory and ecological modernization theory. As important, future integrative work needs to move beyond zero-sum characterizations of these various perspectives and conduct rich environment and development comparative analyses at multiple scales that employ a plurality of methods. (p. 12)

It is exactly this view that has led many proponents of EUE theory to suggest that EM theory needs to incorporate components of EUE theory to more fully understand the domestic *and* global structures of *intermestic action* that impact the GSE so negatively. For example, Jorgenson and Clark (2012) state that both EM theory and TOP need to include the structured international relationships that inform our understanding of "environmental harms and economic development" (p. 30). Thombs (2018) has illustrated how market forces are not having the desired decoupling effect with respect to economic growth and carbon emissions. In contemplating the findings, he argues that a world-systems approach could better inform the beliefs of those aligned with a market orientation (p. 18). Givens et al. (2009) also maintain the need for more qualitative *and* quantitative research that involves meshing EUE theory with the "core" theories of EM and TOP (p. 17).

To be fair, EM researchers have also proposed greater interaction between EM theory and some of its rivals. The debates with neo-Malthusians and neo-Marxists orientations did have proven utility in the development of the EM school. Moreover, the rise of TOP theory spurred intense debate between itself and EM theory resulting in the additional "maturation" of the latter, theoretically speaking. Mol and Sonnenfeld (2000) reflect on the importance of looking outward in order for EM to "grow" when stating that

> Ecological Modernisation Theory is very much a living and growing school-of-thought. Although reared in the context of political and policy debates in north-western Europe, its intellectual "stock" becomes more heterodox as its scope and influence expands. Old demarcations, such as with certain forms of neo-Marxism and green politics in the western European context are tested again in new contexts and encounters with similar but different intellectual traditions from other parts of the world, with challenging outcomes. Ecological Modernisation Theory's accommodation with concerns about global and local inequality illustrate this dynamic, as are efforts to "stretch" it to address or explain dynamics in the vastly different political contexts of transitional societies, both in Europe and Asia. (p. 11)

Notwithstanding the foregoing, there does appear to be a certain reluctance to entertain existing environmental theory such as the insights offered by ecological unequal exchange. Perhaps this reluctance is born out of Buttel's (2000) recommendation that the future of EM "is not to emphasize empirical debates over the potentials and limits of environmental engineering and industrial ecology, but rather to deepen the links to political-sociological literatures which will suggest new research problems and hypotheses" (p. 64). Indeed, the main proponents of EM theory appear to be heeding this advice rather than encouraging further the examination/application of EUE theory to the existing precepts of ecological modernization. Earlier it was noted that EM theory adapted/matured by utilizing Beck's (1992) "reflexive modernization" and "risk society" rather than focusing its efforts on examining/incorporating useful insights from neo-Marxist schools. In the wake of Buttel's advice, it appears that instead of further examining the utility of EUE in addressing the shortcomings of EM theory (e.g., geographical scope, global versus national emphasis, vertical flows, etc.) that the major proponents of EM (Spaargaren et al., 2006) are "moving" the school toward a reconceptualization of "society" based on "global networks and flows" à la Urry (2000). As stated by Mol et al. (2014),

> Spaargaren et al. (2006) have related ecological modernization theory to the new sociology of networks and flows (Urry 2000) and, as such, have opened up a new field for research on environmental reform. Instead of the conventional notion of place-based environmental reform, the emphasis shifts to environmental reform in the 'space of flows' related to globalized, deterritorialized, and de-nationalized mobilities and flows. This shift has started to inspire a range of

empirical studies on the environmental reform of all kinds of global environmental issues and transnational flows. (p. 26)

Irreconcilable Differences?

There are undoubtedly many "irreconcilable differences" between EM theory and EUE theory. One of the most notable points of disagreement is with respect to the conceptual level of analysis employed. EM theorists primarily conceive of the environmental harms produced by the CWE at either the local, regional, and/or national level. In contrast, EUE theorists primarily conceive of the ills created at the system level. This conceptual difference, however, is somewhat "masked" when evaluating the empirical research of each orientation. As aforementioned, Wallerstein made clear the inherent problems related to cases and the like that make explicitly evaluating the merit of world-systems theory a virtual impossibility. The same commentary applies to EUE theory, itself an extension of world-systems analysis.

Empirically, however, the research evaluating both EM and EUE employ hypotheses and variables that most often allow only a nation-state level of analysis. Moreover, the apparent emphasis of EUE inquiries, and that which the vast majority of research illustrates, is on developing subsystem level, "piecemeal" hypotheses that are born out of the system level conceptualization. This realization, to a limited extent, is perhaps more a point of tacit agreement than an irreconcilable difference.

A second difference revolves around the associated beliefs of the HEP/NEP debate of the 1970s into the 1990s, generally speaking. There are those in environmental sociology who see the dismissal of the HEP, disciplinarily speaking, as sacrilegious. The resurgence of EUE theory, coupled with the newfound EM interest in international flows, might be construed as a further radicalization of the NEP (Mol and Spaargaren, 2005, p. 98). That is only to the extent that looking at environmental flows (i.e., material flows) is equated with one of many EUE emphases. Many other points of disagreement would also appear, in part, to be a function of what many regard to be a HEP/NEP debate that was put to bed long ago.

Third, there is seemingly no common ground with respect to the nature of resource availability. EM theory posits the *cornucopian belief* embedded in the HEP paradigm (i.e., the separateness of humans and nature with the latter reigning superior in its relations with nature). In essence, there is no need to worry about the impact that population has on resource availability, for example, as technological and economic advances will impede the realization of scarcity, making the idea of a finite world folly. Simply put, EUE theorists disavow the cornucopian belief in *critical interdependence* between humans and nature, the idea of finite resources, and that the GSE is a vital component to how states act in the CWE (Hornborg, 1998, 2003, 2013).

Beyond these concerns, there are major debates between EM and EUE theorists, inter alia, regarding whether there is a need for structural change in the modern CWE, whether extractive activities result in a disproportional use of ecological resources, and as to the appropriate level of analysis for research endeavors (York et al., 2003, pp. 287–289). While not an exhaustive list of "irreconcilable differences," the foregoing speaks to some issues where there is considerable disagreement between EM and EUE with respect to assumptions made, resultant beliefs, and policies to implement.

Tacit Parallels?

It is not possible to take these disagreements lightly. However, there are several aspects of EM and EUE theory where tacit parallels appear to exist. These points of commonality represent potential inroads that the schools can take to understand better the relationship between economic development and environmental harms. Perhaps the most notable point of tacit agreement between EM and EUE is the understanding that the CWE is the underlying "structure" giving rise to environmental harms. Moreover, human behavior within the confines of the structure have historically served to increase environmental harms (Gellert, 2019, pp. 110, 113–114). EM theory has matured with respect to its view of the CWE and industrialization, however, as a more "nuanced" revision has taken place. According to Mol and Spaargaren (2002):

> Consequently, mainstream ecological modernisation theorists interpret capitalism neither as an essential precondition for, nor as the key obstruction to, stringent or radical environmental reform. They rather focus on redirecting and transforming "free market capitalism" in such a way that it less and less obstructs, and increasingly contributes to, the preservation of society's sustenance base in a fundamental/structural way. (p. 23)

Second, both EM and EUE emphasize the role of political and cultural concerns in responding effectively to environmental harms and promoting further the discourse on the GSE. EM theory has evolved from a position of technological optimism to an enlightened understanding that political units, primarily states, and "civil society" (e.g., environmental interest groups, etc.) are necessarily components in promoting positive change. Moreover, EUE theorists speak of the asymmetries related to the structure of the international system that maintain the unequal distribution of power in its many manifestations (e.g., labor relations, human rights, trade, foreign direct investment, etc.).

Third, both believe that technology has played a role in the historical enlargement of environmental harms, albeit in separate ways. Huber's (1985) insistence on the need to transition the "techno-system" underlies EM theory. From an EUE perspective it is relatively easy to see how technology differences in, for example, extractive activities can lead to an unequal distribution of resources among countries. Likewise, they both believe that technology also has a role to play in an effective, more holistic response to environmental harms (Gellert, 2019, p. 113). Moreover, both theories appear to harbor a belief that *uncritical devotion* to technology fosters a negative result vis-à-vis the GSE.

Fourth, both are centrally concerned with the processes and institutions related to production and consumption and that the concept of "unequal exchange" is applicable to more than just international labor concerns; that the concept is applicable to ecological concerns. The processes related to production and consumption, whether investigated at the local, regional, national, or international level of analysis, are critical in uncovering the entire impact that development efforts have on the GSE. Moreover, the focus on institutions also provides a more holistic appraisal of how environmental harms are the result of political and social forces.

Similar to Christoff's (1996) "shading" of EM theory, there are certain "shades" with respect to the extent to which some of these points of tacit agreement exist. What is necessary is for proponents of EM and EUE theory to realize that these areas of tacit agreement exist and that further investigation into them will only result in furthering research, understanding, theoretical development, well-being, and policymaking and implementation regarding economic development and the GSE. In so doing, however, it will be necessary for the proponents of the various theoretical orientations to put down their personal and profession predilections and forge a path where "different" theories are used to further greater understanding based on those areas where tacit agreement exist. In agreeing with London's (1987, p. 30) exhortation that analyses evaluating only international *or* intra-national dynamics are but "partial explanations," Sommer et al. (2019) stated it best:

> There must be a willingness by sociologists to self-consciously rid themselves of the sort of "theoretical blinders" that lead to the categorical analysis of how international factors (e.g., mining export flows) and intranational factors (e.g., repression) affect the natural environment. . . . It is only by considering possible interactions among internal and external characteristics of a nation that we will arrive at the most comprehensive understanding of the factors shaping the natural environment and be able to refine theory accordingly. (p. 185)

NOTES

1. EM theory does not suggest that capitalism, as defined by Giddens (1990, pp. 11–12, 55–63), is inherently evil and as such the sole underlying cause for environment degradation. As such, the emphasis of EM theory is not on capitalism per se but on Giddens concept of *industrialization*. Given the dislike that some have when EM theory is linked to modernization theory, perhaps a better name for it would have been *Ecological Industrialization Theory*.

2. The importance of the political realm is reflected in EM theory, as government institutions and social movements give rise to increased importance being attached to the global sustainable environment.

3. "Symptoms" is used to convey the sense that Rostow attaches a certain backwardness, almost illness-like condition, to those who are at this stage of economic growth.

4. Rostow refers to this growth as "compound interest" as a way of facilitating the conceptualization of geometric growth versus arithmetic "simple interest" growth.

5. In particular, the establishment of the railroad has been the primary impetus giving rise to the take-off in such countries as the US, Germany, France, Canada, Russia, Japan, Sweden, and others. This is in large part due to the impact that railroads have on lowering domestic transportation costs, establishing/enlarging the export sector, and facilitating the growth of industrial sectors (Rostow, 1960, p. 55).

6. Hardin's thesis would be severely criticized on several counts, including his endorsement of abortion rights, eugenics, and the cessation of non-Western immigration into the United States. 2009 Nobel laureate Elinor Ostrom would debunk Hardin's main conclusion concerning the inability of humans to successfully manage common environmental resources without government intrusion and/or privatization strategies.

7. Ehrlich would also come under fire for the methods that he felt governments should use to effectively coerce populations into accepting/implementing a plethora of programs designed to address the "birth" side of the birth/death equation. The use of "international triage," based on population control program effectiveness, was first suggested by Paddock and Paddock (1967).

8. Ironically, the sanctioning body of this report, the Club of Rome, would later come to support the approach outlined in EM theory (see Dryzek, 1997).

9. An EM focus on the social development route was present in Huber, but as Mol and Spaargaren (2000) make clear, Huber's primary focus was on the restructuring of the industrial system (p. 20).

10. It would appear that this is an area of EM theory where an unfortunate level of reductionism occurs. Traditionally, EM theorists believe it only to be related to the industrialism dimension of modernity as defined by Giddens (1990). Spaargaren and Mol (1992, p. 341) identified the fact that Giddens's other dimensions, in particular capitalism and surveillance, are neglected in the literature and may prove productive to EM theory. While they exclude the fourth dimension, military power, Giddens (1990, pp. 58–63) makes abundantly clear the linkages between the four dimensions.

It would appear prudent that, at a minimum, future EM research should attend to how the industrialization of war plays a role with respect to the GSE.

11. Obviously, it is not "labor" that is the primary focus here. Rather, it is the impact that both individual and national wealth have on the increasing wants associated with luxury goods, such as environmental quality.

12. Latin American Structuralist School is a more accurate designation.

13. World-systems "analysis," as opposed to world-systems "theory," is utilized as it is more in alignment with the conceptual orientation of the approach as well as how it was intended and constructed by its chief architect, Immanuel Wallerstein. As stated by Wallerstein (2002):

> It became not the search for the eternal truths of comparative organizational analysis, which was the norm in post-1945 sociology (including in political sociology), but rather the story of a singular phenomenon, the modern world-system, informed by a mode of explanation I was calling world-systems analysis. (p. 363)

Moreover, it has been suggested that dependency "theory" has greater utility not as theory but as a concept that may be applied to "concrete situations of dependency" (Palma, 1978, p. 882).

14. The Greek-born Arghiri Emmanuel originated the concept "unequal exchange" while maintaining that the Prebisch-Singer thesis was "on the fringe of unequal exchange" (Emmanuel, 1972, p. 80). However, several theorists before them spoke specifically to the "non-equivalent" exchange between "centre" and "periphery" nations, but by different terms. For an excellent review of the various precursors to Emmanuel and Prebisch as well as the application of unequal exchange to ecological theory, see Brolin (2007).

15. The calculation of economic surplus, based on both producer surplus and consumer surplus, is obviously more involved than what the cursory definition used here would suggest.

16. In the late 1990s, Frank would dismiss the idea that "actual capitalism" and "actual socialism" existed, thus questioning the worth in further discussing how the CWE affects the periphery. Moreover, he became contrite upon realizing that even self-professed socialist nations cannot break from dependence and that the recommendations that some dependency "theorists," including himself, made were not pragmatic:

> The short answer is that we were right and we were wrong in the main questions we addressed and that we completely failed to address some other relevant questions. YES there is dependence of the kinds we identified, denounced, and combated. Those who denounced us on this issue did and still do not have an empirical leg to stand on. . . . The simple truth is that none of us found a way out of dependence. . . . The question we did not adequately address was how to eliminate dependence. True there were different schools that offered in part similar and in important respects different anti-dependence theory, policy and praxis. They reigned from the most social democratic reformist "dependent development" of Fernando Henrique Cardoso to the most "revolutionary socialist" "Underdevelopment or Revolution" of Frank, Rui Mauro Marini, and Theotonio dos Santos and others in between. Samir Amin and I saw delinking or deconnexion from the

world capitalist economy externally and socialism internally as the only paths to salvation. In retrospect our positions were not nearly as different as we claimed at the time, and on the question of what to do to eliminate dependence we were all wrong [all of us and altogether]. . . . Where we failed completely was in the policy of delinking, which proved to be impossible, even by the so called "socialist" countries. (Frank, n.d.)

17. Wallerstein (2004, p. 17) credited Karl Polanyi (1944, pp. 43–55) for providing a basis for the conception of the three concrete types of social systems. Polanyi identified three economic systems—*reciprocity*, *redistribution*, and *market*—that Wallerstein borrowed and later identified as mini-systems, world-empires, and world-economies, respectively.

18. Babones (2015) argues that the political aspect is most important to semiperiphery inclusion in world-systems analysis.

19. While there exist multiple "kissing cousins" of EUE theory, such as Foster's (1999) elaboration of Marxian Metabolic Rift and Moore's (2003, 2000) World Ecology, they are all based on an interpretation of Wallerstein's well-structured, world-systems analysis, albeit with various similarities and differences. The current lack of focus on metabolic rift and world ecology is not dismissive of their importance in theorizing but only a reflection of the extent to which both are in part a product of the emergence and development of EUE itself.

20. Catton and Dunlap would change their original presentation of the "New Environmental Paradigm" in 1978 to the "New Ecological Paradigm" in 1980.

21. Or global supply/value chains, if you prefer.

22. For example, see Austin (2017), Clelland (2014), and Swamy (2017).

PART III

A Test of Two Theories in the Post–Great Recession Era

Chapter 6

Essential Issues in the Study of EM and EUE

Part of chapter 5 presented the historical background, summary of beliefs, and methods of inquiry for two distinctive schools of thought in environmental sociology. The EM and EUE orientations each have unique approaches informed by an entirely distinct set of important characteristics (i.e., assumptions, beliefs, variables, measurements, conclusions, etc.). For example, EM is in large part concerned with the impact that a goodly number of domestic-oriented variables such as development, economic productivity, economic system, government commitment to the environment, societal "pressure," and technology inputs have on determining the impact of anthropocentric actions on the global sustainable environment. In particular, the contention is that companies/countries, in conjunction with "civil society," and low-level state involvement will reach *turning points* (Jorgenson, 2016a, p. 2; Spaargaren and Mol, 1992, p. 340) whereby ecological rationality will emerge and "ecologize the economy." While often pointing to the *Environmental Kuznets Curve* (EKC) as evidence, EM theory maintains that economic growth, utilizing capitalist principles, is preserved while concurrently lessening environmental harms (Roberts and Grimes, 1997, pp. 191–195).

Conversely, EUE is concerned with the structure of the international system and its impact on countries. By definition, EUE requires an *intermestic* approach, emphasizing the interplay of both domestic and international factors. Consequently, while factors such as affluence, development, economic expansion, and technology, among others, are important, the greater concern is with the structure of international trade and the inequalities between countries in such areas as the production and consumption of energy, vertical trade, and foreign direct investment, and their impact on the GSE.

Chapter 5 also contends that EM proponents have not fully explored the significance of EUE in the further development of EM theory, as the major proponents of the latter orientation have suggested "moving on" to new areas of concern (e.g., looking at EM within the context of networks and flows in the wake of redefining the concept of "society"). The fact that each school has pursued a variety of research questions, factors, and models for investigation is incontrovertible. Moreover, the resurgence of EUE in the second decade of the twenty-first century has been accompanied by a respectable level of research examining it within the context of EM theory (Jorgenson, 2016a; Jorgenson and Clark, 2012; Thombs, 2018). By no means, however, do these good works suggest that the "exploratory linkages" between the two orientations have been exhausted. Moreover, the move to "network flows" and reconstructing the meaning of "society" seems to preclude any further investigation regarding the utility of EM and EUE with respect to major international events that reflect both the domestic and intermestic nature of their respective approaches. The application of both EM and EUE in the immediate aftermath of an international recession is one such area that has been neglected by the literature. Moreover, examining how different subsets of developing countries experience recession, in relation to the GSE, is a critical area that has been largely neglected. Examining EM and EUE within these contexts is surely a worthwhile endeavor that will provide greater understanding to those working toward a world where economic and ecological rationality may complement one another.

EM AND EUE IN THE WAKE OF THE GREAT RECESSION

The subjective perceptions presented in chapter 2 indicate, inter alia, a distinctive pattern suggesting that people perceive the economy and environment as polar opposites playing within the confines of a zero-sum game. The polling data strongly suggest that having both a strong economy *and* a flourishing environment are not possible (i.e., that there is a fundamental choice to be made between them). The polling results constitute prima facie evidence contradicting the EM contention that you can have both a strong economy *and* environment, as is reflected in "reflexive modernization." Moreover, the data in both figures 2.1 and 2.2 (immediately after the 2001 and 2007–2009 recessions) suggest that economic recessions appear to significantly bolster this subjective individual-level belief. Conceptually, economic downturns should have a negative impact on the effective pressure that "civil society" can exert on a government to effect positive environmental changes. This also begs the question as to how companies and countries will respond to a downturn in the capitalist world economy. Does an economic downturn necessarily mean that "turning points" will not emerge, as ecological rationality is sidelined in favor of a quick return to economic growth and profit making? Does it necessarily mean that if indeed there is a reversion to "weaker EM" and economic rationality, it will entail greater transfer of environmental harms to developing countries? Does it mean that *tipping points* (Intergovernmental Panel on Climate Change, 2021) will likely occur much sooner as a consequence? The data presented in chapter 3 on the "objective" state of vital environmental services (VES) is important to comprehend when responding to these inquiries. Does the existence of a recessionary period mean that the time is opportune for a redefinition of what is meant by "development," in essence, reconstructing the processes associated with both economic production and consumption in order to speed up the advent of ecological rationality and a "stronger" conception of EM? Does it mean that this reflection might then result in greater emphasis on the Aristotelian conception of *eudaimonia* (i.e., well-being), a conception that would enhance the development of both humans and the natural environment alike?

These are undoubtedly tough questions to answer. However, an inquiry into this arena, facilitated by principles associated with both EM and EUE, can help us better understand human behavior *and* its effects on the GSE in the aftermath of a global recession. Moreover, it will illustrate how there is much more to be learned by entertaining two vastly different orientations in theorizing about the economic/environment nexus. Ultimately, understanding the economic/environmental nexus in the aftermath of a global economic recession is important to governmental policymaking processes that seek to enhance the idea of "well-being" as it relates to both economic development and the GSE. The present evaluation of EM and EUE is primarily in the service of this end.

DATA AND METHODS

The present analysis is based on a balanced cross-sectional longitudinal dataset comprised of eight annual observations of 136 countries, further broken down by country subset (see below), for the 2010–2017 period. Admittedly, the temporal period covered is relatively short when compared to recent studies (Bradford and Stoner, 2017; Thombs, 2018; Wang et al., 2019) that utilize lustrum periods. Contrary to the use of five- or ten-year point estimates, however, one-year point measures aren't as prone to "masking" short-term effects, are less likely to have measurement bias, and are less likely to reflect additional idiosyncrasies (Muller, 1985, p. 52; Weisskopf, 1972). Moreover, the immediate aftermath of a major global economic downturn is typically associated with a considerable rate of increase in the demand for product (i.e., consumption). These type of immediate changes in demand are better reflected in annual point measurements as opposed to longer periods (Noble, 2017, p. 251).

The EM and EUE schools elaborated upon in chapter 5 identify several propositions that can be effectively translated into testable research hypotheses that relate to both EM and EUE theory, identify the key variables therein, expound on measurement considerations, state the relevant hypotheses, and present the overall design of the research. Prior to that presentation, however, is an overview of case selection in terms of identification of the country subsets as well as the temporal period under study.

Country Subset Delineation and the Role of Network Analyses

EM Country Subsets

Appendix A contains a listing of all country subsets utilized in this analysis.[1] Given the assumptions of both EM and EUE theory, it is necessary to define several country subsets that are instrumental in further understanding the interplay of EM and EUE as they pertain to the GSE. One set of country subsets reflects the richest and poorest countries of the world. EM suggest that *turning points* are likely to happen first in developed countries, due to advantages associated with technological advances and economic development (Mol, 2003, pp. 68–69). Consequently, both OECD and LDC subsets are included in the analysis. Membership in these subsets is institutionally defined by the OECD and the UN Office of the High Representative for the LDCs, LLDCs and SIDS (UN-OHRLLS), respectively. Three country subsets, all constituted by developing countries, are identified by specialty concerns and are included in the analysis. As mentioned in chapter 3, LLDCs and SIDS represent two different geographical concerns, while LIFDCs represent food-dependent countries. Like LDCs, LLDC and SIDS membership are institutionally defined by UN-OHRLLS. LIFDC membership is defined by the Food and Agriculture Organization of the United Nations (UNFAO).

EUE Country Subsets

Given the EUE emphasis on the CWE and the power inequalities that it inherently produces (Frank, 1967; Galtung, 1971; Wallerstein, 1974a), the present analysis also identifies and evaluates the role of CORE, SEMI, and PERI country subsets. Unlike the aforementioned country subsets, the definitions of CORE, SEMI, and PERI are not institutionally derived, hence leading to a good deal of debate among researchers and policymakers alike as to their composition. Not surprisingly, definition as to what constitutes the core has been variable over time. What is not up for debate, however, is the conceptual understanding that these three country subsets are defined in relation to one another.

A variety of emphases have been utilized to derive the associated lists. Some researchers have focused on the extent to which "periphery" trade relations are reliant (i.e., dependent) on a "core" group of countries (Rice, 2007a, p. 1377) or on the basis of whether a country was a net recipient of official development assistance (ODA) (York et al., 2003, pp. 289–290). Others have utilized a weighted index that is in part based on GDP per capita (GDPPC) (Jorgenson, 2009, pp. 33–34; Jorgenson et al., 2009, pp. 272–273; Shandra et al., 2009, p. 57). Still others have relied upon a relatively more sophisticated measure of "core" created by *network analyses* of international commodity trade patterns. For example, Rice (2007a) borrowed from the work of Smith and White (1992) by defining the core as a set of eleven countries "occupying the central or dominant position in the structure of the global economy" (p. 1377).

The seemingly constant refinement of problems associated with network analyses of international commodity trade flows produces resultant lists of "core" countries that can be quite different dependent on the types of "networks" that are incorporated to determine country subsets. For example, Snyder and Kick (1979) incorporated a four-network block model that included data on "trade flows, military interventions, diplomatic exchanges, and conjoint treaty memberships" (p. 1105) to determine a list of core countries for the year 1965. Their analysis resulted in a list of twenty-one core countries, including Australia, Austria, Belgium, Canada, Denmark, France, Italy, Greece, Japan, Luxembourg, Netherlands, Norway, Portugal, South Africa, Spain, Sweden, Switzerland, the United Kingdom, the United States, West Germany, and Yugoslavia. Kick et al. (2011) incorporated a similar set of criteria as Snyder and Kick (1979), resulting in a similar list of "core" countries but with notable outliers, such as "India, Indonesia, Malaysia, Pakistan, the Philippines, Thailand, and possibly even China," that the authors dismiss due to the rules of structural equivalence modeling (pp. 316–317).

In contrast to these studies, Smith and White (1992) focused exclusively on trade flows by incorporating fifteen traded commodities (p. 866). The result was a more concise listing of four "core" countries—Canada, the United Kingdom, the United States, and West Germany—for the year 1965 (p. 872). A more recent network analysis by Mahutga (2006) incorporated twelve commodity groups and further reduced the number of "core" countries in 1965 to just Germany, the United Kingdom, and the United States (pp. 1868–1874).

Network analysis can yield remarkably similar results with respect to the identification of the core countries, as has been illustrated by several studies. Kick and McKinney (2014) utilized a four-dimensional measure, resulting in like results as Kick et al. (2011) for the 1995–1999 period. Moreover, studies by Smith and White (1992) and Nemeth and Smith (1985) yielded very similar results, as a comparison of the results for 1980 yielded a list of ten core countries while Nemeth and Smith also added Switzerland to the core (p. 871). The extent to which the results of network analyses parallel one another is summarized by Mahutga's (2006) conclusion that the list of core countries has remained exceptionally stable throughout the 1965–2000 period (p. 1880), potentially suggesting that the enhanced integration of the international trading system has only reinforced the position of core powers throughout the period.

Remarkable about these attempts to define a core, as is noted by Clark and Beckfield (2009), is that they fail to impose a true "trichotomous" distinction (that world-systems analysis calls for) that can be applied in the form of a core, semiperiphery, and periphery. In their own analysis, however, they reference the somewhat common belief (even held by Wallerstein) that a listing of three discrete categories for country inclusion may not "fit the data" and that a "continuous" orientation may be preferable (pp. 10–11, in passim). Nonetheless, exclusively based on trade data, Clark and Beckfield (2009) derived a new trichotomous measure to better fit the strict, conceptual intention of Wallerstein. While they find that twenty countries make up the core, they ultimately state that "the pattern of ties between our core, semiperipheral, and peripheral countries is quite similar to Mahutga's (2006) commodity specific network analysis" (p. 12).

It appears that the attempt to skillfully place countries into CORE, SEMI, and PERI categories is, to a certain extent, an exercise in academic futility. The membership of these discrete country subsets seemingly have some continuity at times, dependent on the studies evaluated. However, it appears that the argument suggesting that the world-system "placement" is best achieved via a "continuous" orientation has merit. Perhaps more important than delineating the definitive membership of each of these subsets at any point in time (which may not be feasible in reality) is to recognize the limitations of the subset as it is constituted.

Moving forward from this realization, this study utilizes the information in Mahutga (2006) with an assumption that there is continuous movement in and out of the core and semiperiphery, and less so for the periphery, over time. This fluidity is in alignment with many who note that country placement in the world-system should not be forced into discrete categories but be seen in a more continuous manner. The comments of Chase-Dunn (1998) are relevant here:

> For myself, the vocabulary of zones is simply shorthand. I don't see any advantage in spending a lot of time trying to define and empirically locate the boundaries between zones because I understand the core/periphery hierarchy

> as a complex continuum. Since there is upward and downward mobility in the system there must be cases of countries or areas which are in between zones, at least temporarily. For me it doesn't matter whether there are "really" three zones, four zones or twenty zones. (p. 214)

Mahutga (2006) presents both a continuous measure of country placement at any one point in time as well as a temporal/spatial comparison recognizing the fact that countries routinely enter and leave a particular subset over time. This is evident for several countries over the 1965–2000 period. For example, Sweden is cast as a SEMI in 1965, a CORE in 1970 and 1980, and a SEMI in both 1990 and 2000. Similarly, Belgium is cast a SEMI in 1965, a CORE in 1970 and 1980, a SEMI in 1990, and a CORE in 2000. In essence, having been a CORE once in your history doesn't mean that you will ever have that status again.

For purposes of this analysis, the CORE is defined in terms of its continuity over time as a CORE subset. Those countries that Mahutga has determined to be a CORE in two or more successive time periods constitute the CORE in this analysis. The result is a group of ten CORE countries: Belgium, Canada, France, Germany, Italy, Japan, the Netherlands, Sweden, the United Kingdom, and the United States. Somewhat coincidentally, these ten countries are the same ten that Mahutga (2006) identifies as constituting the CORE in 1980 (p. 1874). These ten countries routinely appear as part of the CORE designation of countries (Clark and Beckfield, 2009; Kick et al., 2011; Rice, 2007a; Snyder and Kick, 1979), regardless of the basis upon which the group of core countries is determined.

This analysis defines the SEMI subset in a much "looser" sense than the defining criteria utilized for CORE. Relatively speaking, the semiperiphery has been studied greatly while generating, perhaps, even less consistency with respect to identifiable membership at any one point in time. Multiple attempts to define the semiperiphery, based either on network analyses, income levels, or "continuum" analyses (Babones, 2005, p. 34), have resulted in diverse listings for different time periods, as the earlier studies attest. Ruvalcaba (2020) provides a summary of multiple studies that illustrate this point beyond controversy (pp. 43–46). Beyond these "criterion-based" attempts are those, including Wallerstein (1979, p. 100) himself, who don't appear to use any underlying basis for classification (Arrighi and Drangel, 1986, p. 14).

The rise of the "discrete/continuous" debate has led to even less clarity as to what constitutes the semiperiphery as it has prompted the rise of "affiliated" categories of the semiperiphery. To cite some examples, Babones (2005, pp. 50–51) speaks of "organic" semiperipheral countries, Mahutga (2006, pp. 1874–1875) of the "strong" and "weak" semiperiphery, Arrighi and Drangel (1986, pp. 40–44) of the "core perimeter" and "periphery perimeter," Clark and Beckfield (2009, pp. 25–28) of an "orthodox position" and "trade position" semiperiphery, Kick et al. (2011, pp. 316–321) of the possibility of both an "upper" and "lower" semiperiphery; Nemeth and Smith (1985, p. 535) conceive of a "first" and "second" semiperiphery, Smith and White (1992, pp. 874–885) of "semiperiphery 1" and "semiperiphery 2"; and Mahutga and Smith (2011, pp. 262–264) define the semiperiphery as constituted by the "core contenders" and the "upper-tier semi-periphery."

Simply put, there is no common understanding of how to measure (i.e., identify) the semiperiphery even if one can conceive of it being constituted by either a discrete or continuous representation. Moreover, these analyses have been criticized for the lack of cases used in the analysis (Clark and Beckfield, 2009, p. 12), and for "aberrational" placements such as the Snyder and Kick (1979) study, whose method of determination resulted in Cyprus and Burma listed as semiperiphery countries while Brazil and Chile were identified as periphery countries (pp. 1109–1116). For purposes of this analysis, SEMI is defined in terms of the extent to which there appears to be a common understanding (i.e., prima facie validity) as to what constitutes the semiperiphery circa 2000. Countries that are included no fewer than four times in the aforementioned studies will constitute the SEMI subset, with the understanding that criticism based on perceived errors of both omission and commission will be forthcoming. The result is the group of twenty-one SEMI countries listed in appendix A. By default, PERI is constituted by those countries not included in either CORE or SEMI.

Temporal Analysis

Four global economic recessions are identifiable in the modern era (i.e., since 1950): 1975, 1982, 1991, and 2009. In every case the world average GDPPC, when controlling for inflation, declined significantly. Without argument, however, the Great Recession of 2007–2009 was the most impactful on the capitalist world economy. According to Kose et al. (2020): "The global recessions were highly synchronized internationally, with severe economic and financial disruptions in many countries around the world. The 2009 global recession, set off by the global financial crisis, was by far the deepest and most synchronized of the four recessions. As the epicenter of the crisis, advanced economies felt the brunt of the recession. The subsequent expansion has been the weakest in the post-war period in advanced economies, as many of them have struggled to overcome the legacies of the crisis" (preface).

This analysis focuses on the post-2009 recession for a variety of reasons, among them: (1) the 2007–2009 recession has been the most damaging to the CWE, (2) the postrecession expansion has been the slowest of the four for developed countries, and (3) much research that has been done on EM and

EUE has occurred during the first three global recessions. Virtually none of that research, however, directly focuses on the impact that global economic recession has on the GSE via human behavior in government, companies, and civil society. Moreover, relatively little EM and EUE research in the post-2009 period directly focuses on the impact of global economic recession. Perhaps the most notable is Huang (2018) who investigated the relationship between developing country exports to the US and CO_2 emissions from 2000 to 2010.

VARIABLE CONCEPTUALIZATION, MEASUREMENT, AND ASSOCIATED HYPOTHESES

Dependent Variable

GSE Impact

Appendix B contains a summary of all variables, measures, and sources utilized in this analysis. The selection of the most appropriate measure to gauge how the GSE has been impacted has been greatly contested in the literature. Some studies have utilized measures emphasizing one or two particular aspects of the GSE, among them, deforestation (Ehrhardt-Martinez et al., 2002; Jorgenson et al., 2009; Noble, 2017) and carbon emissions (Bradford and Stoner, 2017; Dean, 2002; Grant et al., 2018; Huang, 2018; Thombs, 2018; Wang et al., 2019). Others have utilized one of several composite indexes, such as the Environmental Sustainability Index (Whitford and Wong, 2009), the Index of Sustainable Economic Welfare (Daly and Cobb, 1994), and/or the Human Appropriation of Net Primary Production (Vitousek et al., 1986). While the former are limited by their one-dimensional measure of impact, the latter utilize multiple measures that incorporate a broader range of GSE impact and then reduce these various measures into one, often arbitrarily weighted, index value (York, 2009, pp. 205–206). Sometimes the component measures are given equal weight for no apparent logical reason. Moreover, Pillarisetti and van den Bergh (2010, p. 50) maintain that arbitrarily derived, equal weighted index measures are fundamentally flawed in that the dimensions of GSE impact are not truly valued equally.

The Ecological Footprint (EF) is also an additive, multidimensional measure (i.e., index) that combines a variety of ecoservice indicators (see below), and their associated measures, into one convenient number known simply as the *ecological footprint* of a country. While admittedly an oversimplification, the EF consists of quantifying the supply (i.e., production—biocapacity) and demand (i.e., consumption—ecological footprint) of ecosystem services *and* renewable resources. In essence, it is the sum of human activity (i.e., demand) with respect to the pressure (i.e., impact) that is placed upon the GSE.[2]

Although the use of an index remains suspect, it is laudable that the methodology utilized in producing an EF for countries has continued to be refined to produce a more accurate conception and subsequent measurement of variables. For example, the 2011 edition of the National Footprint Accounts included several improvements including the use of *constant global hectares* to facilitate more accurate comparisons of annual data. Refinements since have included the creation of an "environmentally extended multiregional input–output (EE-MRIO) model" to better track EF by "economic sectors and final-demand categories," improvements in the accuracy of key equation factors, such as *equivalence factors*, in the determination of the ecological footprint, and improvements in the calculation of the carbon footprint, to mention but a few (Lin et al., 2018).[3]

The EF is conveniently measured by incorporating the totality of six land-use dimensions of human activity:

- *Cropland Footprint*, which "consist[s] of the area required to grow all crop products, including livestock feeds, fish meals, oil crops and rubber."
- *Grazing Land Footprint*, which "measures the area of grassland used in addition to crop feeds to support livestock [and] . . . comprises all grasslands used to provide feed for animals, including cultivated pastures as well as wild grasslands and prairies."
- *Fishing Grounds Footprint*, "calculated based on the annual primary production to sustain a harvested aquatic species . . . the mass ratio of harvested fish to annual primary production needed to sustain that species, based on its average trophic value."
- *Forest Land Footprint*, which "measures the annual harvests of fuelwood and timber to supply forest products."
- *Carbon Footprint*, "the only land use type . . . which is exclusively dedicated to tracking a waste product: carbon dioxide."
- *Built-Up Land Footprint*, "calculated based on the area of land covered by human infrastructure: transportation, housing, industrial structures and reservoirs for hydroelectric power generation." (Borucke et al., 2013, pp. 524–525)

The EF revises and incorporates *yield factors* and *equivalence factors* for different countries, to ensure comparability in the various standardized EF formulae. In essence, these factors account for differences between countries in terms of the extent of their different land-use component behaviors so that the unstandardized measure, average hectares, can be transformed into a standardized measure, constant global hectares. All six land-use components of the EF are given equal weight in the EF aggregate measure (Borucke et al., 2013, p. 526).

The dependent variable measure in this study is the aggregate measure of EF, expressed in constant global hectares per person. Data transformation by incorporation of the natural logarithm is performed to normalize what are a highly skewed set of dependent variable data regardless of the country subset examined.[4] Various iterations of this measure have been utilized in a good deal of research evaluating harm to the GSE (Bagliani et al., 2008; Jorgenson, 2009, p. 33; Jorgenson, 2016a; Jorgenson and Clark, 2011, p. 232; Jorgenson et al., 2010, pp. 14–15; Kick and McKinney, 2014; Rice, 2007a, p. 1377; York et al., 2003, p. 289).

Independent Variables

Development: Well-Being and Relative Affluence

EM theory posits that while greater development results in a greater negative impact on the GSE in the short term, it ultimately will result in "decoupling," or a lesser impact, in the long term. EM maintains that the positives that accrue to the GSE will in large part result due to increasing development of political institutions and state regulation (Huber, 1982; Mol, 1995; Vlachou, 2004). Moreover, the evolution of the market and social structures will result in greater eco-efficiencies, resulting in less impact on the GSE (Ehrhardt-Martinez et al., 2002, p. 228; Jorgenson and Clark, 2011, pp. 227–228).

The driving force leading to improvement in the GSE is an economy that is reflexively modernizing via the incorporation of ecological rationality. Conceptually, this transition is clear. While the reality appears to be somewhat more nebulous, the driving force is an ever-developing economy that transforms itself to be more in alignment with more ecologically sound outcomes. How researchers have conceived of this "development," however, has resulted in a great oversimplification of what true development entails. As has been noted earlier in the text, most of the research revolving around EM and EUE construes "development" as exclusively economic in its orientation (Jorgenson et al., 2009, p. 273; Jorgenson and Clark, 2011, p. 233; Jorgenson et al., 2010, p. 16; Jorgenson and Clark, 2009, p. 631; Rice, 2007a, p. 1378; York et al., 2003, pp. 288–290). This construction, however, is shortsighted inasmuch as the benefits of elevated levels of "economic development" are maximized when the proceeds from said development are invested back into the country and its people via support for the various components of *human well-being*, such as education and health care. Soubbotina (2004) explicitly states the underlying importance of economic development in funding relative *affluence*:

> It is somewhat easier to say which countries are richer and which are poorer. But indicators of wealth, which reflect the quantity of resources available to a society, provide no information about the allocation of those resources—for instance, about more or less equitable distribution of income among social groups, about the shares of resources used to provide free health and education services, and about the effects of production and consumption on people's environment. . . . In a broader sense the notion of human development incorporates all aspects of individuals' well-being, from their health status to their economic and political freedom . . . human development is the end—economic growth a means. (pp. 7–8)

In brief, to conceptualize development in purely economic terms is to dismiss its importance in producing greater relative affluence. While some research speaks of *affluence*, it is largely conceptualized as synonymous with *economic development* (Bradford and Stoner, 2017, p. 304; Kick and McKinney, 2014, p. 265) and measured purely in economic terms, most often as GDPPC (Dietz et al., 2007, p. 13; Jorgenson and Clark, 2009, p. 631).

The importance of economic growth and development to EM theory is of obvious importance, but economic development is not distributed equally in societies and consequently glosses over inequalities related to *well-being* such as the need for (and subsequent consumption of) education, health, and other more socioeconomic conditions (i.e., relative affluence) for which people consume ecosystem services and renewable resources alike. In effect, economic development is a country-level measure that by itself (1) does not consider the extent to which it results in equitable distribution, and consumption, among societies members who continuously place "pressure" on ecosystem services, and (2) is relatively limited in its ability to provide acceptable levels of relative affluence barring very high levels of government involvement. This research includes two variables, and associated measures, which are conceptually different but treated as if they are the same: a broader development variable, the level of *well-being*, and the level of *relative affluence*.

The Human Development Index (HDI) is a multidimensional measure incorporating variables that represent a more holistic conception of development as well-being. At its very foundation is the belief that human development is a better measure of the development of a country than is solely economic development.[5] Similar to EF, HDI has also witnessed a series of changes seeking to improve upon the original measurement. For example, the HDI formula was revised for the 2010 (twentieth anniversary) edition of the Human Development Report. Changes included substituting mean years of schooling and expected years of schooling for the education index, changing how the goalposts were derived, and reconfiguring the formula itself (United Nations Development Programme, 2011, pp. 216–217). The UNDP measures HDI by incorporating:

- *Life Expectancy Index*, measured as: "Life expectancy at birth: Number of years a newborn infant could expect to live if prevailing patterns of age-specific mortality rates at the time of birth stay the same throughout the infant's life."
- *Education Index*, measured as: (1) "Expected years of schooling: Number of years of schooling that a child of school entrance age can expect to receive if prevailing patterns of age-specific enrolment rates persist throughout the child's life," and (2) "Mean years of schooling: Average number of years of education received by people ages 25 and older, converted from education attainment levels using official durations of each level."
- *GNI Index*, measured by: "Gross national income (GNI) per capita: Aggregate income of an economy generated by its production and its ownership of factors of production, less the incomes paid for the use of factors of production owned by the rest of the world, converted to international dollars using purchasing power parity (PPP) rates, divided by midyear population." (UNDP, 2020, p. 346)

The 2020 life expectancy index has changed to incorporate goalposts of twenty and eighty-five years for the evaluation of a country. The index is derived by taking the actual value for life expectancy minus the low goalpost and dividing it by the range of the low and high goalposts. Both education subindices have a minimum goalpost of 0, while 18 is the maximum goalpost for "expected years of education" and 15 the maximum goalpost for "mean years of schooling." Both education subindices utilize the same generic formula for the life expectancy index before meshing the two subindices by calculating the arithmetic mean. The GNI index is constructed the same as the life expectancy index except that the goalposts of $100 and $75,000, reported in constant 2017 PPP, are logarithmically transformed prior to their inclusion in the equation. Finally, the HDI is calculated by taking the geometric mean, as opposed to arithmetic mean, of the three indices (UNDP, 2020, p. 335; see "technical notes"). The novel incorporation of the geometric mean is more appropriate, given that HDI data exhibit a high degree of correlation and because the geometric mean reduces the extreme impact of outliers. The resulting value ranges from 0 through 1, with higher numbers reflecting higher human development.

Relative affluence is conceptualized differently from the mainstream understanding of affluence. Traditionally, to be affluent is to have an overabundance of desired goods, income, and wealth. What is conveyed is an asymmetrical relationship between individuals and countries, and the various measures (e.g., income shares) that delineate and impose strata among groups of individuals (e.g., elite and nonelite) and groupings of countries (e.g., core, semiperiphery, and periphery). The affluent are not defined in relation to each stratum but rather amassed only at the very top of any level of analysis.

Alternatively, *relative affluence* conveys a broader understanding, one born of the recognition that "affluence" occurs on numerous levels and is multidimensional and that the identification of "affluent" individuals and countries is dependent upon what measure of affluence is considered (Peichl and Pestel, 2011, p. 2). In effect, one can also posit that affluence is relative to different societal strata and countries, dependent upon one's conceptualization. Moreover, identifying relative affluence involves understanding that at its core is a foundational basis (i.e., resources) with which to work, and the ability to put that foundation to work for the individual and/or country, given the current state of existence. Sahlins's (1972) proposition that economics is "the application of scarce means against alternative ends to derive the most satisfaction possible under the circumstances" (p. 4) is instructive here. The foundational basis may be predicated on income, wealth, culture, material resources in general, the existence of "super-affluent consumers," and capitalist marketing, to name a few examples (Wiedmann et al., 2020). However, key is that a sufficient resource base, ability to employ that resource base, and desire to employ it are present and can be transformed into acquiring whatever the relative perception of affluence is—not in the whole, but at a particular stratum.

It is possible to acquire relative affluence at any given stratum when the aforementioned prerequisites are present. Moreover, any measure of the potential for relative affluence must reflect these prerequisites. It must also reflect the idea that there is a definable "cutoff" whereby these prerequisites are perceived to be nonexistent. Imposing such a demarcation is problematic, as some countries—the US, for one—impose an absolute dollar value, which is often revised over time, to determine such institutionalized concepts as "poverty line," among others. Alternatively, other countries implement relative percentage distinctions to derive this and similar concepts. For example, multiple European countries define poverty, a concept measured in relation to the wealth/affluence of a country, as "the bottom 40 percent of median family income" (Besharov, 2007, p. 7). Consequently, the percentage share of pretax national income held by the bottom 40 percent of adults (age twenty and older) is the measure for the potential level of relative affluence used presently. Conceptually, a higher percentage of national income held by this segment represents a lesser potential for relative affluence among the other 60 percent of the population, presumably meeting the prerequisites for acquiring relative affluence. As such, EM theory suggests a positive, short-term relationship between relative affluence and the GSE. Akin to economic development, EM adherents believe that this deleterious short-term relationship will decrease over time (i.e., the EKC hypothesis) due to the incorporation of technological advances, democratic norms, and capitalism's ecological response to environmental decline, generally speaking.

Democratic Orientation

Proponents of EM theory argue that the political orientation of governments can have a noteworthy influence on ecological "modernization" by introducing reforms that speak directly to improving environmental conditions (Lengefeld and Smith, 2013, p. 13; York et al., 2003, p. 285; Zahran et al., 2007, pp. 41–42). Moreover, the freedoms associated with the institutions of democracy are said to lay the foundation for the emergence of a citizenry (i.e., civil society) that is more informed about environmental issues, more able to express their demands for reform (as individuals and in groups), and more able to exact change via different forms of environmental activism (Ehrhardt-Martinez et al., 2002, p. 230; Neumayer, 2002, p. 140).

It is typically presumed by EM theorists that a greater democratic orientation will result in less harm to the GSE, as leadership is assumed to be responsive to the demands placed upon it (Shandra et al., 2009). On the other side of the same coin, others maintain that a lesser democratic orientation will lead to greater environmental impact, as leadership is more able to thwart the freedoms that allow for environmental demands to flourish, and greater incentive to limit these freedoms due to the uncertain nature of their political tenure (Congleton, 1992, pp. 413–417). Relatedly, expensive policies that would benefit the GSE, such as pollution abatement policies, would, ceteris paribus, impede the ability of authoritarian leaders to maximize their personal wealth.

In assessing EM arguments pertaining to democracy, it is important to utilize a measure that addresses not only the extent of democratic orientation but the extent to which it has become institutionalized in a country. Moreover, EM theory highlights the role of a participatory citizenry in the transition to ecological rationality. The conceptualization and measurement of democratic orientation in the literature have been quite variable but have largely favored either the incorporation of civil rights and political freedom data from Freedom House (Barrett and Graddy, 2000; Congleton, 1992; Lv, 2017; Midlarsky, 1998; York et al., 2003) or data from the Polity IV Project dataset (Neumayer, 2002; Zahran et al., 2007; Kuhn and Bernauer, 2006). While Bradford and Stoner (2017, p. 306) argue for the appropriateness of using Polity IV data, Noble (2017, p. 254) argues that the Bollen Liberal Democracy Series I Indicator is superior to those measures commonly used because it controls for measurement error.[6]

Seemingly unexplainable is the relative lack of a literature that utilizes a "participatory" measure of democracy, in conjunction with a democratic orientation measure, in explaining the variation in environmental impact. The Polity IV Project database does include, in its additive measures of democracy and polity, a subscale that focuses on the "competitiveness of political participation," but even its authors maintain that in certain situations, it is not practical or wise to utilize it and effectively recommend its nonuse.[7] An interval-level measurement of democratic orientation and the extent to which it is characterized as "participatory" is necessary given that there "is no 'necessary condition' for characterizing a political system as democratic, rather democracy is treated as a variable" (Marshall et al., 2011, p. 15).

The present study incorporates an interval variable measure from the Varieties of Democracy Institute (V-Dem) Project database. The authors of V-Dem maintain that it

> is a new approach to conceptualizing and measuring democracy. We provide a multidimensional and disaggregated dataset that reflects the complexity of the concept of democracy as a system of rule that goes beyond the simple presence of elections. The V-Dem project distinguishes between five high-level principles of democracy: electoral, liberal, participatory, deliberative, and egalitarian, and collects data to measure these principles. (V-Dem, 2021b)

Of the five disaggregated components of "democracy" listed, the electoral and participatory dimensions of democracy are of greatest utility in the current study. It is particularly noteworthy that the construction of these five indices involves taking both the weighted averages of various subscales *and* the multiplicative interaction of the subscale indices. As the authors note, the resultant measure represents "a compromise between the two most well-known aggregation formulas in the literature, both allowing partial 'compensation' in one sub-component for lack of polyarchy in the others, but also punishing countries not strong enough in one sub-component according to the 'weakest link' argument" (V-Dem, 2021a, p. 43). The "electoral democracy index" subscale emphasizes competitive elections, open and free civil society involvement, and responsiveness of a government to its people. As stated in the V-Dem codebook:

> The electoral principle of democracy seeks to embody the core value of making rulers responsive to citizens, achieved through electoral competition for the electorate's approval under circumstances when suffrage is extensive; political and civil society organizations can operate freely; elections are clean and not marred by fraud or systematic irregularities; and elections affect the composition of the chief executive of the country. In between elections, there is freedom of expression and an independent media capable of presenting alternative views on matters of political relevance. (V-Dem, 2021a, p. 43)

The "participatory democracy" index, also a subscale of "big D" democracy, pertains to electoral and nonelectoral involvement in the electoral democracy. As stated in the V-Dem codebook:

> The participatory principle of democracy emphasizes active participation by citizens in all political processes, electoral and non-electoral. It is motivated by uneasiness about a bedrock practice of electoral democracy: delegating authority to representatives. Thus, direct rule by citizens is preferred, wherever practicable. This model of democracy thus takes suffrage for granted, emphasizing engagement in civil society organizations, direct democracy, and subnational elected bodies. To make it a measure of participatory democracy, the index also takes the level of electoral democracy into account. (V-Dem, 2021a, p. 44)

The measure of democratic orientation (i.e., electoral plus participatory components) is the V-Dem Participatory Democracy Index (PDI). This measure reflects participatory democracy within variable levels of electoral democracy. Like the HDI, the PDI is measured on a 0–1 interval scale.

Capitalist Orientation

Proponents of EM theory also contend that the economic orientation of governments can have a significant impact on the GSE. Specifically, one strand of the literature has argued that the presence of capitalism can result in a significant decrease in environmental impact via the discovery and implementation of environmental technologies. Moreover, capitalism will spur the restructuring of industry and lead it to a more rational, ecologically friendly state. While some studies support this conclusion (Mol and Spaargaren, 2000; York et al., 2003, p. 292), others suggest that the impact of capitalism is at best insignificant (Congleton, 1992, pp. 419–420; Rice, 2007a, pp. 1381–1382).

The conceptualization and measurement as to the role of "capitalism" has often taken the form of a simple dummy variable born out of a simple perception as to whether a country evinces relatively higher degrees of "economic freedom" (i.e., capitalist, state-capitalist, mixed-capitalist, mixed-socialist, socialist, etc.) (Congleton, 1992, p. 418; York et al., 2003, p. 289). Gastil (1987, pp. 72–78) further defines the aforementioned types by whether a majority of the population utilizes the structured form of economic freedom in their daily lives (i.e., inclusive) or not (i.e., noninclusive). Like the measurement for democratic orientation, however, it is preferable to utilize an interval level measure based on the underlying principles/dimensions associated with an economy that is operating somewhere on a "capitalist" continuum. While undoubtedly requiring yet another "index" measure, the resultant measure would increase meaning and be more reflective of the actual differences between countries operating under different varieties of capitalism.

Since 2017, the Heritage Foundation has produced the annual Index of Economic Freedom (IEF), an additive index of twelve quantitative and qualitative factors/dimensions related to various aspects of the foundation of capitalism: economic freedom.[8] Each of the twelve dimensions range from 0 through 100, allowing for an additive IEF, with the equal weighting of dimensions, ranging between 0 and 100 with 100 representing the greatest level of economic freedom (i.e., the greatest capitalist orientation) on that dimension. The twelve dimensions are combined into four aggregate indices representing the "rule of law," "government size," "regulatory efficiency," and "open markets." Rice (2007a) utilized the entirety of the IEF to measure "the degree of supportive institutional structures and policies in supporting free market economic activity" but found that it had no significant impact on ecological footprint per capita (p. 1378). It can be argued, however, that the latter two aggregates are more instrumental in the evaluation of the capitalist orientation of EM theory, as they pertain to factors that are more instrumental in the decision of firms to transition their current production processes to those more in sync with ecological rationality. The *regulatory efficiency* aggregate combines the following three dimensions:

- *Business Freedom*, which "measures the extent to which the regulatory and infrastructure environments constrain the efficient operation of businesses. The quantitative score is derived from an array of factors that affect the ease of starting, operating, and closing a business."
- *Labor Freedom*, "a quantitative measure that considers various aspects of the legal and regulatory framework of a country's labor market, including regulations concerning minimum wages, laws inhibiting layoffs, severance requirements, and measurable regulatory restraints on hiring and hours worked, plus the labor force participation rate as an indicative measure of employment opportunities in the labor market."
- *Monetary Freedom*, which "combines a measure of inflation with an assessment of various government activities that distort prices. Price stability without microeconomic intervention is the ideal state for the free market."

The *open markets* aggregate reflects the following three dimensions:

- *Trade Freedom*, "a composite measure of the extent of tariff and nontariff barriers that affect imports and exports of goods and services."
- *Investment Freedom*, which "evaluates a variety of regulatory restrictions that typically are imposed on investment. Points, as indicated below, are deducted from the ideal score of 100 for each of the restrictions found in a country's investment regime. It is not necessary for a government to impose all of the listed restrictions at the maximum level to eliminate investment freedom."
- *Financial Freedom*, "an indicator of banking efficiency as well as a measure of independence from government control and interference in the financial sector." (The Heritage Foundation, 2021, pp. 458–463)

For purposes of this study, the simple average of an equally weighted additive index of the six dimensions is used, resulting in a 0–100 interval level measure that most closely reflects the capitalist orientation of the country and the potential ease with which production entities may incorporate an ecological rationality if desired.

Structure of Economic Activity

Integral to EM theory is the idea that economies more highly reliant on industry and manufacturing will have a much larger impact on the GSE than those countries whose economies are primarily nonextractive and dominated by the service sector (Dietz et al., 2007, pp. 13–14; Ehrhardt-Martinez et al., 2002, pp. 229–230; York et al., 2003, p. 286). More specifically, relative "dematerialization" of a manufacturing economy in its transition to a service-based economy is said to reduce the absolute requirements placed upon the GSE. Indeed, several studies have produced results indicating that higher reliance on the service sector doesn't significantly increase environmental impact (Jorgenson and Clark, 2011, pp. 233–234; Shandra et al., 2009; Wang et al., 2019, p. 15), while greater reliance on the manufacturing sector does (Huang, 2018, pp. 6–8; Jorgenson et al., 2010, pp. 20–23).

The conceptualization and measurement of the impact that a service-based economy has on the GSE is easily achieved, as one only needs to procure a measure that reflects the extent to which the GDP of an economy is based on the service sector. While an economy may not be service dominated (i.e., defined as a simple *majority* of GDP derived from one sector), it is really the relative extent to which the service sector plays a role in producing GDP that is of importance. Consequently, a continuous variable is preferable to a discrete variable, especially when the latter may only represent a plurality rather than a majority with respect to generating growth. For example, an economy that is 33 percent agriculture based, 33 percent manufacturing based, and 34 percent service based would take on the same discrete value as an economy that is 100 percent service based, although one could hardly say that the economy of the former is dominated by the service sector. The measure used in the current study is services, value-added, as a percentage of gross domestic product.

Technological Sophistication

Related closely to the argument concerning the role of capitalism is the early EM debate as to whether technological sophistication will result in significant reductions in environmental impact. Mol and Spaargaren (2000, pp. 18–25) provide an overview of the debates pertaining to the role of technology in abating environmental decline. Like its stance on capitalist orientation, early EM proponents maintained that technological advances pertinent to the GSE are a consequence of capitalist industry becoming more ecologically rational in its production processes (i.e., internalizing environmental values) and/or as a result of increasing market pressure by civil society and, to a lesser extent, government implementation of more strict environmental regulations. Moreover, change is presumed to be holistic, affecting societies at both the macroeconomic and microeconomic levels (Buttel, 2000, p. 61; Gibbs, 2006, pp. 196–197; Jorgenson and Clark, 2011, p. 228; York et al., p. 284).

The conceptualization of the role of technological sophistication (i.e., advancement) pertains to the potential capability of countries, and private enterprise, to discover and implement sophisticated technologies. For example, inter alia, Borlu and Glenna (2021) found a significant relationship between a dichotomous technology adoption variable and prioritization on water availability and cost (p. 206) among US specialty-crop producers while noting an insignificant relationship when the "threat" was climate change. While not entirely the most satisfying manner by which to capture this conceptualization, one can incorporate a continuous measure that evaluates the extent to which sophisticated (i.e., high) technology is currently infused into the economy. Such a measure infers the extent to which countries possess the technological capabilities to exact change but does not, however, get at whether countries (and private enterprise) intentionally incorporate ecological rationality (i.e., make choices resulting in low environmental impact) even if possessing the requisite technological level of sophistication.

Technological sophistication is measured by the percentage of total exports constituted by manufactures with high skill and technology intensity, according to the Standard International Trade Classification, revision 3 (SITC, rev. 3) (UNCTADstat, 2021a). More specifically, according to SITC, rev. 3, manufactures with high skill and technology intensity exports are constituted by such products as, inter alia, pharmaceuticals, explosives, chemical products, television and radio receivers, aircraft equipment, optical instruments, and telecommunication equipment (UNCTADstat, 2021b).

Global Economic Integration

The EUE orientation posits that developing countries are negatively entrenched in the global economic system and that this entrenchment, while a positive for developed countries, is quite negative for the GSE of developing countries. Implicit in this conceptualization is the idea that "unequal exchange" occurs in the context of global environmental power politics. The Netherlands fallacy maintains that the reason why developed countries appear to have less impact to their GSE than their counterparts in the developing world is that they now rely greatly on the transfer of material production inputs from other countries (Rice, 2007b, p. 63). In essence, their impact on the GSE is not limited to their national borders and is facilitated via global economic integration. Consequently, developing countries that are more globally integrated, economically speaking, are likely to experience a greater negative impact to their GSE due to this transfer of material goods. Moreover, economic development, and well-being, is stalled due to the consumption of these goods taking place primarily in developed countries. The potential importance of global economic integration is condensed by Howell (2007) in the following passage:

> The ecological footprint data and geographical location of environmental degradation unequivocally demonstrate that the North's development path (albeit unsustainable ecologically) relies on the South exporting its bio-capacity to the North. Thus, the North's development path is dialectically responsible for environmental degradation in the South. (p. 81)

Conceptually, global economic integration is a very general variable that primarily assesses the extent to which an economy is integrated with all other economies. It doesn't make a distinction as to whether the integration linkage is with a developing versus developed country, a capitalist versus a socialist economy, and so forth. As such, this conceptualization doesn't speak as specifically to the tenets of EUE as a variable that breaks down the level of economic integration between developing and developed countries. However, this conceptualization does provide a general "benchmark" of sorts by which the more focused conceptualizations and measures of "economic integration and dependence" can be developed and evaluated, as is done below. Moreover, one could make the argument that *any* external linkage, regardless of whether it fits within the EUE orientation or not, is potentially reflective of a transfer of VES from the source to the destination country and as injurious to the former as what EUE maintains linkages with developed countries are to developing countries.

The measure for global economic integration is total exports as a percentage of GDP. This measure has been routinely accepted as a valid means to gauge the extent to which national economies are globally integrated, generally speaking (Huang, 2018; Jorgenson et al., 2010, p. 17; Rice, 2007a, p. 1378). The identification as to where specifically exports are flowing is also critical to EUE and is covered below.

Trade Inequality

The EUE school posits that developing countries are negatively entrenched in the global economic system via inherent inequalities, primarily in the structure of trade relations with developed countries. Rooted in dependency theory, Howell (2007) describes this structured relationship as obligatory on the part of the developing countries, though detrimental to their GSE.

> These countries are in fact "locked-in" to a path of ecological destruction to supply the voracious consumption of the richer segments of the capitalist world economy. A power discourse analysis highlights the importance of bargaining power differentials between economically powerful states and economically disempowered states. (p. 81)

One aspect of this structurally disadvantageous relationship involves trade inequality. As a concept, trade inequality conveys the extent to which countries asymmetrically benefit, or lose, from their trade relations with other countries. Conceptually, EUE assumes trade inequality reflects a zero-sum game whereby there exist relative winners and losers. The obvious counter is the argument that while trade inequalities exist, the bottom line is that total trade increases serve to benefit all at a relatively higher level than would have existed otherwise. As it applies to environmental impact, however, relative asymmetrical trade relations are said to follow the tenets of a zero-sum game serving to favor developed countries. As Jorgenson (2009) maintains:

> More generally, the populations of higher-income countries are positioned advantageously in the contemporary world economy, and thus are more likely to secure and maintain favorable terms of trade allowing for greater access to the natural resources and sink capacity of bio-productive areas within lower-income countries. This greater access facilitates the externalization of environmental and human well-being costs of resource extraction to lower-income countries, which contributes to heightened resource depletion and environmental degradation within their borders. (p. 29)

Others have attempted a more intrusive analysis of "environmental terms of trade" by estimating the pollution content of imports and exports to derive a terms-of-trade measure that more closely approximates the environmental impact of trade inequalities (Giljum and Eisenmenger, 2004; Muradian et al., 2002; Rice, 2009, p. 228). While an environmental terms-of-trade measure would be advantageous, data constraints would restrict such an analysis to a relatively small number of countries.

The measure for trade inequality is the annual terms-of-trade index from 2010 through 2017. The base year of the index, whereby terms of trade are indexed at 100 for all countries, is 2010. Simply put, "net barter" with regard to terms of trade is "defined as the ratio of the export unit value index to the import unit value index" (UNCTADstat, 2021a). While not as "environmentally intrusive" as the environmental terms-of-trade indicator, the terms-of-trade index is less reliant on "estimated" data and can still speak to trade asymmetries and their potential environmental impact.

Core/Periphery Dependence

Consistent with the idea that greater trade inequalities and global economic integration serve to have a greater environmental impact in developing countries (i.e., PERI countries) is the idea that asymmetrical trade linkages with specific developed countries (i.e., CORE countries) may further exacerbate environmental impact in developing countries. More specifically, the extent to which PERI countries are dependent on CORE countries for their trade relations can greatly impact their GSEs. The EUE school specifically posits that the greatest environmental harm to developing countries comes from their unequal ecological exchange with *CORE* countries. Moreover, Rice (2009) maintains that this detrimental set of trade relations occurs with respect to both "withdrawals" from, and "additions" to, developing countries:

> We define ecological unequal exchange as the environmentally damaging withdraw of energy and other natural resource assets from the periphery and the addition or externalization of environmentally damaging production and disposal activities within the periphery of the world-system. It constitutes both the obtainment of natural capital or the stocks of natural resources that yield important goods and services and the usurpation of sink-capacity or waste assimilation properties of ecological systems in a manner enlarging the domestic carrying capacity of industrialized countries to the detriment of peripheral societies. (p. 221)

Conceptually, for purposes of the present analysis, the most important aspect of core/periphery dependence is the extent to which developing countries are integrated into the global economy and whether relative increases in integration (i.e., dependence) with CORE countries serves to increase the ecological deterioration of countries in the periphery. Moreover, it is entirely plausible that a process of core/semiperiphery and semiperiphery/periphery dependence is also present and having a deleterious ecological impact in relatively lesser developed countries. While this "recursive exploitation" (Jorgenson, 2009, p. 30; Rice, 2009, p. 223) is an important conceptual and practical idea to study, the present focus is exclusively on core/periphery dependence.

The second part of the core/periphery equation dictating that the level of dependence of the latter on the former also be evaluated as "dependence" is conceptualized as a two-way street (i.e., withdrawals and additions). Consequently, with respect to trade flows, for example, it would be important to include both "import dependence" and "export dependence" on CORE countries. Accordingly, the measure of core/periphery dependence utilized in this study is the total trade with CORE countries as a percentage of total trade to all countries. Trade data is drawn from UNCTADstat (2021a).[9]

Core/Periphery Primary Export Dependence

The EUE school posits that developing countries are negatively entrenched in the CWE with greater integration resulting in greater destruction to the GSE of developing countries. The theory also maintains that the structure of international economic production, from a world-systems theoretical viewpoint, is to blame for the ecological decline that many PERI countries experience. The fact that CORE countries are dominant in both the production and consumption of goods is by itself problematic but becomes increasingly so when one understands that CORE country production is increasingly reliant upon the extraction of primary goods (i.e., withdrawals) from PERI countries concurrent with utilizing PERI countries as a repository for waste generated (i.e., additions). Furthermore, EUE argues that one cannot simply look at any one country and conclude that its production/consumption structures have no impact on ecological deterioration outside of its borders. As stated earlier, the Netherlands fallacy maintains that the total deleterious ecological impact of any country is in no way restricted to its national borders. Those who coined the fallacy, Ehrlich and Holdren (1971), specifically applied the concept to the inequitable distribution/utilization of *natural resources*, its ramifications for increased trade, and increased ecological destruction outside of one's own borders:

> It cannot be stated too forcefully that the developed countries (or, more accurately, the overdeveloped countries) are the principal culprits in the consumption and dispersion of the world's nonrenewable resources as well as in appropriating much more than their share of the world's protein. Because of this consumption, and because of the enormous negative impact on the global environment accompanying it, the population growth in these countries must be regarded as the most serious in the world today. . . . One of the common errors made by the uninitiated is to assume that population density (people per square mile) is the critical measure of overpopulation or underpopulation. For instance, Wattenberg states that the United States is not very crowded by "international standards" because Holland has 18 times the population density. . . . We call this notion "the Netherlands fallacy." The Netherlands actually requires large chunks of the earth's resources and vast areas of land not within its borders to maintain itself. For example, it is the second largest importer of protein in the world, and it imports 63 percent of its cereals, including 100 percent of its corn and rice. It also imports all of its cotton, 77 percent of its wool, and all of its iron ore, antimony, bauxite, chromium, copper, gold, lead, magnesite, manganese, mercury, molybdenum, nickel, silver, tin, tungsten, vanadium, zinc, phosphate rock (fertilizer), potash (fertilizer), asbestos, and diamonds. It produces energy equivalent to some 20 million metric tons of coal and consumes the equivalent of over 47 million metric tons. (p. 1214)

Conceptually, the ability to spare one's own core country from the perils of ecological decline is dependent upon the ability of said country to import those items that it consumes, thereby distancing itself from the locale that its overconsumption directly impacts (Rothman, 1998). The needs of CORE countries, for example, would need to be met largely through the invasive extraction of mineral resources and various food imports from PERI countries. Moreover, the ability to structure and accomplish this task would be accentuated to the extent that the generated waste of CORE countries could be "absorbed" by the GSE of PERI countries. Such a two-way process of displacing the true environmental costs of both production and consumption onto PERI countries has been referenced in several ways, including "withdrawals and additions" (Rice, 2009, pp. 223–229), the creation of "environmental space" (Jorgenson and Clark, 2009, p. 628; Rice, 2007a, pp. 1372–1376), and "environmental cost shifting" (Ehrhardt-Martinez et al., 2002, p. 231; Howell, 2007, pp. 86–87; Jorgenson, 2009, p. 30; Rice, 2007b, p. 54; Rice, 2009, p. 223; Shandra et al., 2009, p. 55). Regardless of the wording used, the EUE posits that this two-way process leads to a resource *consumption/environmental degradation paradox* whereby the displacement of true environmental costs by CORE countries results in greater resource extraction as well as lower consumption in the PERI (Jorgenson, 2009, p. 30; Jorgenson and Clark, 2009, p. 627; Rice, 2007a, pp. 1374–1375).

The measure of core/periphery primary export dependence is total primary sector exports to CORE countries as a percentage of total primary sector exports to all countries. For purposes of this analysis, primary sector exports include primary commodities, precious stones, and non-monetary gold (Group A11 of SITC, rev. 3). As such, it includes the following categories: (0) food and live animals, (1) beverages and tobacco, (2) crude materials, inedible, except fuels, (3) mineral fuels, lubricants, and related materials, (4) animal and vegetable oils, fats, and waxes, (68) non-ferrous metals, (667) pearls, precious and semi-precious stones, and (971) gold, non-monetary (UNCTADstat, 2021c). Trade data is drawn from UNCTADstat (2021a).

Climate

While EM and EUE propositions are the focus of this inquiry, the effects of climate are important to model. Born out of the Human Ecology school, the effect of geographic location is instrumental to the depletion of VES, especially as it relates to the production of energy, heat, and food. Research has incorporated various measures, incorporating latitude, to gauge the effect of climate. Kick and McKinney (2014, pp. 265–266), York et al. (2003, p. 289), and Jorgenson and Clark (2011, pp. 236–238) all utilized a dummy variable defining three climate zones: (1) arctic, latitude greater than 55 degrees, (2) temperate, latitude between 30 and 55 degrees, and (3) tropical, latitude between 0 and 30 degrees. Unsurprisingly, all three studies found a significantly higher use of VES (as measured by ecological footprint) as you move from the tropical to the arctic. Using the same measure, McKinney et al. (2009) found a significant decrease in the percentage of threatened bird species when moving from the tropical to arctic zone (p. 109).

While having no countries located in the arctic region, Jorgenson (2009) also found a significant increase in ecological footprint when moving from the tropical to temperate zone (pp. 38–39). Given the existence of Norway, Sweden, and Finland in their dataset, it is presumed that Lengefeld and Smith (2013) reduced the traditional trichotomous dummy variable to a dichotomous one (tropical and temperate) in showing that countries in the tropical zone have significantly less carbon emissions (pp. 18–20). While these measures of the impact of climate on VES may suffice, Kick and McKinney (2014) indicate that "the coding of our latitude measure is crude, even if it does follow convention" (p. 268). Although also crude, the current study incorporates a continuous, time-invariant measure for climate: latitude coordinate reported by the CIA World Factbook.[10]

Model Estimation and Descriptive Data

STATA 16.0 software is utilized to estimate time-series cross-sectional Prais-Winsten (PW) regression models with panel-corrected standard errors (PCSEs). This is a short (i.e., micro) panel whereby the number of countries is larger than the number of time periods. While the models presented are statistically robust, reflecting many propositions associated with both EM and EUE theory, they do not control for all variables that may provide additional insight. The construction of parsimonious models, however, served to enhance the sample size while retaining balanced panels (i.e., no missing data). A conscious choice was made to utilize balanced panels for two reasons. First, the nature of unbalanced panels is such that they can sometimes produce computation and estimation issues, although most software packages today are able to work effectively with unbalanced panels even if in a somewhat convoluted manner. Second, the following analysis utilizes 136 cases for which there is complete data. This is a considerably larger number of cases than is incorporated by most all research studies to date. When considered together, the decision was made to forgo a larger number of cases in favor of the greater "simplicity" of balanced panels. Time was also taken to ensure that the operational definitions (i.e., measurements) of the variables in the current study were consistent over the 2010–2017 period. It was mentioned earlier that the HDI formula was revised for the 2010 anniversary year. However, the calculation of the index has been consistent since (United Nations Development Programme, 2011, pp. 216–217).

Other potential issues with the data were also addressed. Greater reliability of results was enhanced by ensuring consistency in the measurement level (i.e., unit of analysis). As such, the 1,088 total observations in the dataset are weighted equally. Since the cases are countries (i.e., nation-states, to be more exact), time was spent ensuring that there were no differences in the status of a case during the 2010–2017 period under study, thus ensuring that "dual observations" don't occur. For example, one might notice that both Sudan and South Sudan are incorporated in the analysis even though South Sudan's formal independence was not achieved until July 9, 2011. However, its inclusion is warranted given the long period of autonomy from the Sudan (since July 2005) and the fact that the data sources utilized in this study have been tracking "South Sudan" data prior to 2011.

Table 6.1 presents the descriptive summary statistics of the logged, continuous variables in the subsequent analyses. One will note that while skewness is minimal and within acceptable range, kurtosis is greater than three for many variables. In lay terms, this suggests a greater propensity for outliers, as the combined data in the tails of the leptokurtic distribution are "heavier" (i.e., greater) than is found in the tails of a normal distribution of data. Outlier checks were subsequently performed and no significant outliers were identified in the analysis. Table 6.2 presents the pairwise correlation statistics and associated significance of all the logged, continuous variables. Finally, it should be noted that all variables, except for the country subsets, are measured in a continuous fashion to avoid use of random effects modeling and the inability to effectively compare the relative significance of a time invariant factor to that of time varying independent variables (Wooldridge, 2010).

Table 6.1. Descriptive Summary Statistics for Continuous, Logged Variables

	Mean	*Median*	*N*	*Min*	*Max*	*SD*	*Skewness*	*Kurtosis*
GSEIMPACT	.977	1.005	1088	−.554	2.761	.697	.038	2.147
WELL-BEING	−.356	−.288	1088	−1.106	−.047	.236	−.761	2.585
AFFLUENCE	2.179	2.206	1088	.464	2.848	.350	−1.036	6.125
SERVICES	4.048	4.077	1088	2.875	4.476	.246	−1.084	5.630
DEMOCRACY	−1.207	−1.023	1088	−3.912	−.218	.766	−1.174	3.988
CAPITALISM	4.149	4.178	1088	2.959	4.501	.203	−1.320	6.794
TECHNOLOGY	1.930	2.920	1088	−2.300	3.300	2.110	−1.490	3.255
GEI	3.578	3.547	1088	1.841	5.399	.595	.146	3.417
TRADEINEQ	4.593	4.605	1088	3.930	4.955	.112	−1.118	7.899
CPDEPEND	−1.194	−1.120	1088	−3.220	−.233	.515	−.921	4.193
CPPDEPEND	3.237	3.398	1088	−.570	4.455	.850	−1.450	5.432
CLIMATE	2.994	3.264	1088	0	4.159	.978	−1.285	4.342

Sources: Raw data drawn from sources in appendix B.

Table 6.2. Pairwise Correlations for Continuous, Logged Variables

Variables	*(1)*	*(2)*	*(3)*	*(4)*	*(5)*	*(6)*	*(7)*	*(8)*	*(9)*	*(10)*	*(11)*	*(12)*
(1) GSEIMPACT	1.000											
(2) WELL-BEING	0.832	1.000										
	(0.000)											
(3) AFFLUENCE	0.229	0.306	1.000									
	(0.000)	(0.000)										
(4) SERVICES	0.443	0.587	0.244	1.000								
	(0.000)	(0.000)	(0.000)									
(5) DEMOCRACY	0.164	0.281	0.264	0.528	1.000							
	(0.000)	(0.000)	(0.000)	(0.000)								
(6) CAPITALISM	0.562	0.590	0.197	0.533	0.422	1.000						
	(0.000)	(0.000)	(0.000)	(0.000)	(0.000)							
(7) TECHNOLOGY	0.270	0.422	0.252	0.426	0.353	0.359	1.000					
	(0.000)	(0.000)	(0.000)	(0.000)	(0.000)	(0.000)						
(8) GEI	0.530	0.418	0.124	0.205	0.021	0.392	0.083	1.000				
	(0.000)	(0.000)	(0.000)	(0.000)	(0.490)	(0.000)	(0.006)					
(9) TRADEINEQ	0.017	0.008	−0.012	−0.067	−0.013	0.028	0.072	0.097	1.000			
	(0.567)	(0.787)	(0.701)	(0.028)	(0.680)	(0.364)	(0.017)	(0.001)				
(10) CPDEPEND	0.389	0.450	0.260	0.345	0.396	0.449	0.268	0.217	0.039	1.000		
	(0.000)	(0.000)	(0.000)	(0.000)	(0.000)	(0.000)	(0.000)	(0.000)	(0.195)			
(11) CPPDEPEND	0.277	0.345	0.111	0.212	0.290	0.321	0.202	0.115	0.053	0.777	1.000	
	(0.000)	(0.000)	(0.000)	(0.000)	(0.000)	(0.000)	(0.000)	(0.000)	(0.080)	(0.000)		
(12) CLIMATE	0.555	0.552	0.345	0.417	0.199	0.364	0.300	0.231	0.023	0.210	0.106	1.000
	(0.000)	(0.000)	(0.000)	(0.000)	(0.000)	(0.000)	(0.000)	(0.000)	(0.453)	(0.000)	(0.000)	

Sources: Raw data drawn from sources in appendix B.

NOTES

1. Country subset membership is determined as of the end of 2018. All countries listed in appendix A are counted in the data presented for VES in chapter 3. However, due to data constraints, not all countries listed in these subsets are included in the data analysis presented later in this chapter. Those countries that are italicized were utilized in the forthcoming analyses.

2. The concept of "pressure," while important, does not measure the consequences of said pressure being placed on ecosystem services. Also noteworthy is the fact that there is no index measure to date (or that the author is aware of) that comprises all aspects of environmental impact (York et al., 2003) or that accurately weights these respective impacts. Consequently, the present use of an index comes with an acceptance of the proposition that indexes do not adequately separate out the relative importance of any one specific ecoservice of the GSE and that an attempt to "assign" such relative importance is dubious at best.

3. See Ewing et al. (2010) for the methodology calculus prior to 2011.

4. Additionally, all continuous variables in the analysis are logarithmically transformed.

5. Dietz et al. (2007) found that life expectancy and educational achievement were not significantly related to environmental impact. While the findings were counterintuitive, they went on to suggest that improvements in these two areas may go on to improve human well-being with no negative environmental impact (p. 16). However, a quick check of the correlations between the life expectancy index, the education index, and ecological footprint revealed very significant and positive results. This casts doubt on the finding reported by Dietz and his colleagues and also lends support for the more holistic measure of HDI to be incorporated in this study.

6. This may well be accurate, but the updated series data to which Noble refers does not appear to be readily accessible. A quick Google search only returns series I references (whose data is quite old and not suitable for the present study).

7. Marshall et al. (2011) state: "The simple combination of the original DEMOC and AUTOC index values in a unitary POLITY scale, in many ways, runs contrary to the original theory stated by Eckstein and Gurr in *Patterns of Authority* (1975) and, so, should be treated and interpreted with due caution. Its primary utility is in investigative research which should be augmented by more detailed analysis. The original theory posits that autocratic and democratic authority are distinct patterns of authority, elements of which may co-exist in any particular regime context. The inclusion of this variable in the data series should not be seen as an acceptance of the counter-proposal that autocracy and democracy are alternatives or opposites in a unified authority spectrum. . . . Investigations involving hypotheses of varying effects of democracy and/or autocracy should employ the original Polity scheme and test DEMOC and AUTOC separately" (pp. 16–17).

8. The IEF incorporated ten indicators of economic freedom in its reporting during the 2010–2017 period of this study. The two additional indicators added in 2017 altered the makeup of the "rule of law" and "government size" aggregates and thus do not impact the consistency of the measure used here.

9. This measure obviously has the potential to mask the independent effects of import dependence versus those derived from export dependence.

10. The data is the rounded latitude figure "for the centroid or center point of a country expressed in degrees and minutes" (CIA World Factbook, 2021), irrespective of being north or south of the equator.

Chapter 7

An Examination and Evaluation of EM and EUE

RESULTS AND ANALYSIS

EM "Baseline" Models

Table 7.1 reports the results of the analysis of seven models that estimate the importance of variables pertaining to a variety of propositions related to EM theory during the 2010–2017 postrecession period. Models 1 and 1A present the "baseline" results for all 136 countries in the analysis. These two models illustrate a comparable set of results for the linear effects of well-being (WELL-BEING), relative affluence (AFFLUENCE), democratic orientation (DEMOCRACY), capitalist orientation (CAPITALISM), structure of economic activity (SERVICES), technological sophistication (TECHNOLOGY), and climate (CLIMATE) on the global sustainable environment (GSEIMPACT). The impact of WELL-BEING on GSEIMPACT is positive and, in terms of magnitude, extremely significant, indicating that increases in this dimension of "development" are, as early EM theory suggested, responsible for greater vital environmental services (VES) consumption.

Model 1A also provides the estimated coefficients for the potential curvilinear effects of the interaction between WELL-BEING and GSEIMPACT in the immediate aftermath of the Great Recession, 2010–2017. The estimated coefficients are positive, with the magnitude of the relationship being extremely significant in all years. Moreover, in relation to 2010, these coefficients continually increase over time, suggesting a considerable lack of support for the "decoupling" argument of EM theory.[1] Reflected visually in figures 7.1 and 7.2, this is a finding applicable to all subsets evaluated and debunks the existence of an EKC as well as the proposition that reflexive

Table 7.1 Unstandardized Coefficients of GSEIMPACT Regressed on Selected EM Variables and over Time, 2010–2017. Prais-Winsten Regression Model Estimates with PCSE and an AR(1) Correction

	Model 1	Model 1A	Model 2 OECD	Model 3 LDC	Model 4 LLDC	Model 5 SIDS	Model 6 LIFDC
WELL-BEING	2.18****	2.07****	2.92****	–.084	1.16****	4.886****	.380****
	(33.68)	(26.09)	(7.03)	(–0.80)	(10.32)	(7.72)	(6.10)
AFFLUENCE	–.028	–.021	–.015	.076	–.010	–.151	–.039
	(–1.39)	(–0.99)	(–0.42)	(0.82)	(–0.15)	(–1.28)	(–0.50)
DEMOCRACY	–.049***	–.055****	–.219**	–.039	.082**	–.066	–.018
	(–2.85)	(–3.48)	(–2.76)	(–1.02)	(2.73)	(–0.66)	(–0.83)
CAPITALISM	.482****	.506****	.255	.102	.159*	.157	.203****
	(4.29)	(4.67)	(1.51)	(0.87)	(1.91)	(0.37)	(3.45)
SERVICES	–.163*	–.155*	.632****	.019	–.141	–1.948****	–.036
	(–2.17)	(–2.16)	(6.04)	(0.32)	(–0.82)	(–4.04)	(–0.71)
TECHNOLOGY	–.031****	–.033****	–.879****	–.010	–.045****	–.102****	–.027****
	(–6.34)	(–7.06)	(–6.63)	(–1.81)	(–4.85)	(–3.52)	(–7.44)
CLIMATE	.123****	.114****	.171***	.128****	.197****	.014	.104****
	(10.98)	(11.23)	(2.89)	(8.06)	(14.62)	(0.34)	(11.71)
Well-Being X 2011		.037****	.108****	–.012****	.010*	.072****	.005*
		(12.48)	(5.89)	(–3.24)	(1.94)	(4.90)	(2.23)
Well-Being X 2012		.105****	.455****	–.007	.085****	.007	.028****
		(30.81)	(16.23)	(–1.15)	(11.11)	(0.17)	(8.11)
Well-Being X 2013		.148****	.737****	–.043****	.087****	.189****	.024****
		(33.47)	(13.40)	(–6.05)	(10.47)	(3.59)	(4.75)

Well-Being X 2014		.204****	.914****	−.062****	.124****	.337****	.041****
		(37.63)	(12.25)	(−5.95)	(12.06)	(14.10)	(5.27)
Well-Being X 2015		.255****	1.03****	−.033**	.172****	.528****	.053****
		(31.08)	(11.18)	(−2.67)	(13.04)	(16.47)	(6.15)
Well-Being X 2016		.302****	1.19****	−.004	.197****	.465****	.076****
		(37.23)	(10.44)	(−0.27)	(15.03)	(12.34)	(8.26)
Well-Being X 2017		.352****	1.11****	.001	.214****	.584****	.079****
		(42.76)	(7.41)	(0.05)	(12.13)	(12.52)	(6.16)
R^2	0.746	0.756	0.879	0.128	0.594	0.881	0.191
N (countries)	136	136	35	27	24	8	34
N (obs)	1088	1088	280	216	192	64	272
Rho	.750	.738	.677	.700	.812	.478	.703

Note: Unstandardized coefficients are reported. Absolute values of *z*-ratios in parentheses.

* $p < 0.05$ ** $p < 0.01$ *** $p < 0.005$ **** $p < 0.001$

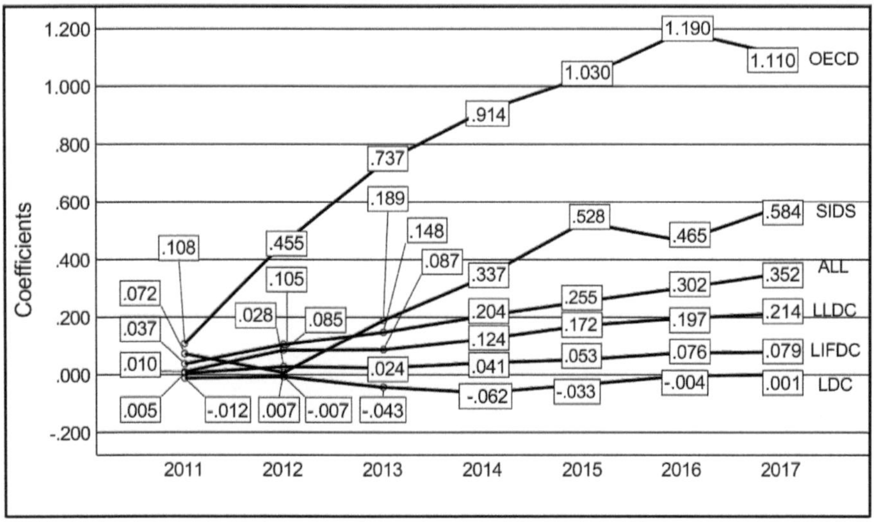

Figure 7.1. Estimated Coefficients for *All*, OECD, LDC, LLDC, SIDS, and LIFDCs, 2011–2017

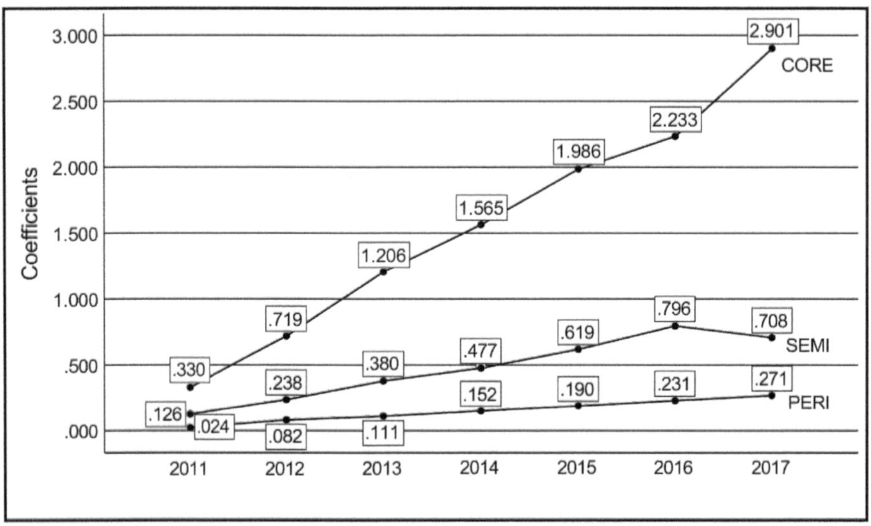

Figure 7.2. Estimated Coefficients for CORE, SEMI, and PERI, 2011–2017

modernization (i.e., a concurrent strong economy and strong environment) can occur.

Models 1 and 1A also evince an insignificant, negative relationship between AFFLUENCE and GSEIMPACT. Conceptually, it was thought that the level of relative affluence would mirror the EM argument pertaining to

WELL-BEING, but the arguments and measures pertaining to how relative affluence relates to the potential for overall well-being will need to be reexamined. The impact of DEMOCRACY on GSEIMPACT is negative and of extreme significance in both models, indicating that greater levels of participatory and electoral democracy are associated with lower VES consumption. This finding parallels the EM proposition that a greater democratic orientation may provide for the emergence of a civil society that has greater potential to promote "ecological rationality" within governmental institutions.

The findings in models 1 and 1A suggest a contrary finding with respect to the impact of CAPITALISM on the GSE. The EM proposition that greater economic freedom will best promote positive technological innovation and reconfiguration of production structures with respect to VES, that "ecological rationality" would supplant the dominant "economic rationality," is unfounded. In both models, the impact of CAPITALISM on GSEIMPACT is positive and extremely significant, reflecting the continued dominance of "economic rationality" in the postrecession period. However, the results for SERVICES and TECHNOLOGY indicate a goodly amount of support for the propositions that the structure of economic activity and technological sophistication have an overall positive impact on VES consumption. Although of moderate significance, the negative relationship between SERVICES and GSEIMPACT indicates that countries whose economic development is more reliant on the service sector have lower VES consumption, thus providing credence to the idea that the structure of economic activity is an important consideration. Moreover, countries with greater technological sophistication also experience significantly less GSEIMPACT in the postrecession period, as the negative and extremely significant TECHNOLOGY coefficient reflects. The latter lends support for early EM theory suggesting that technological innovation is vital to the GSE. However, this finding doesn't mesh well with the findings pertaining to CAPITALISM. Finally, the positive and extremely significant CLIMATE coefficient affirms the results of many earlier mentioned studies from the Human Ecology school.

EM Models and Country Subsets

Table 7.1 also presents the results of several distinct country subsets, including the OECD, LDC, LLDC, SIDS, and LIFDC. The basis for such an investigation pertained to potential masking effects as well as to greater understanding of how the GSE is impacted by anthropocentric forces in the immediate aftermath of a major economic recession.[2] The results for the OECD subset, presented in model 2, largely mirrors the results of the baseline models with respect to the impact of WELL-BEING, AFFLUENCE, DEMOCRACY, TECHNOLOGY, and CLIMATE on GSEIMPACT. Moreover, the temporal interaction effects for the impact of WELL-BEING are positive and significant throughout the entire 2011–2017 period, indicating a lack of "decoupling." The OECD subset differs from the baseline, however, with respect to the role of capitalism and the structure of economic activity. The impact of CAPITALISM was positive, but *insignificant*, while the impact of SERVICES was *positive* and of extreme significance, suggesting that OECD countries whose economic development is more reliant on the service sector are also greater VES consumers. Lastly, the temporal-based coefficients for the potential curvilinear effects of the 2011–2017 interactions between WELL-BEING and GSEIMPACT are virtually identical to those found in model 1A.

Model 3 presents the estimated coefficients for the LDC subset. Most noteworthy is the *lack of any significant linear effects for any EM theory-related variables*. CLIMATE, however, remained positive and incredibly significant in explaining VES consumption. Of considerably greater interest are the temporal interaction effects of WELL-BEING. The impact of WELL-BEING on GSEIMPACT was *negative* for all years except 2017. Moreover, this relationship was extremely significant for 2011, 2013, and 2014 while remaining moderately significant in 2015. In concrete terms, increases in WELL-BEING in these years resulted in a significantly lower GSEIMPACT in four of the first five years following the Great Recession. One might make an argument that these findings reflect a modicum of support for the notion of "reflexive modernization." One should also note, however, that 2015–2017 illustrates a considerable weakening of this relationship, with it turning positive by 2017. In either event, the temporal results of the LDC subset warrant further exploration.

Model 4 presents the findings for the LLDC subset. The results somewhat mirror the baseline models while providing some stark differences with the LDC subset. The results pertaining to WELL-BEING, AFFLUENCE, TECHNOLOGY, and CLIMATE precisely replicate the findings of the baseline models. Moreover, CAPITALISM also followed the baseline models, albeit at a considerably weaker level of statistical significance. Entirely different from both the baseline models and other subsets is the *significant positive sign* for the impact of DEMOCRACY on GSEIMPACT. While the baseline models provided support for EM propositions related to the impact of participatory democracy and "civil society" on VES consumption, the LLDC findings suggest that greater levels of participatory democracy facilitate *greater* VES consumption. The impact of SERVICES on GSEIMPACT, like the finding for the LDC subset, remained insignificant. The results of the temporal interaction effects of WELL-BEING on GSEIMPACT largely parallel the results of baseline model 1A and the OECD experience while standing in stark contrast to the LDC findings in model 3. An extremely significant positive relationship exists in every year but 2011 (which was positive and of weaker significance), indicating that increases in the level of WELL-BEING resulted in greater VES consumption in the posteconomic recession period and a lack of support for the EKC argument.

Model 5 presents the results for the SIDS subset. The findings for the linear effects of WELL-BEING, AFFLUENCE, and TECHNOLOGY mirror the findings of the baseline models. The impact of both DEMOCRACY and CAPITALISM were *insignificant*, paralleling the findings for the LDC subset. Perhaps the most interesting main effects result is the *insignificant* impact of CLIMATE on VES consumption. One might argue that this result is a function of the relatively smaller level of variation among the SIDS countries in the analysis. The temporal interaction effects of WELL-BEING on GSEIMPACT largely mirrored the findings of the temporal baseline and OECD models. An extremely significant positive relationship was found in all years save 2012, suggesting that greater levels of WELL-BEING largely result in greater VES consumption. The isolated insignificance of the 2012 condition, in the context of other years, is left to future investigation.

Model 6 presents the findings for the LIFDC subset. The linear effects of WELL-BEING, AFFLUENCE, CAPITALISM, TECHNOLOGY, and CLIMATE again mirror the baseline models. The noteworthy results here are the *insignificant* results with respect to the impact of DEMOCRACY and SERVICES on GSEIMPACT. The former is more akin to the experience of other developing countries than it is to the temporal baseline or OECD models. Moreover, the effect of SERVICES again parallels the LDC and LLDC results more than the results of either the temporal baseline model or the contradictory findings of the OECD subset. The temporal interaction effects of WELL-BEING on GSEIMPACT substantially mirror model 1A but *precisely* mirror the LLDC experience, suggesting once more a lack of support for "decoupling."

EUE "Baseline" Models

Table 7.2 reports the results of the analysis of eight models that estimate the importance of variables pertaining to a variety of propositions espoused by EUE theory, applied to the post–Great Recession period, 2010–2017. Models 7 and 7A present the "baseline" results for 126 non-CORE countries in the analysis. They illustrate a comparable set of results for the linear effects of global economic integration (GEI), trade inequality (TRADEINEQ), core/periphery dependence (CPDEPEND), core/periphery primary dependence (CPPDEPEND), and climate (CLIMATE) on the GSE (GSEIMPACT).

Both models evince an extremely significant positive relationship between GEI and GSEIMPACT, indicating that deeper global economic integration does result in greater VES consumption by non-CORE countries. Thus

Table 7.2. Unstandardized Coefficients of GSEIMPACT Regressed on Selected EUE Variables and over Time, 2010–2017. Prais-Winsten Regression Model Estimates with PCSE and an AR(1) Correction.

	Model 7	Model 7A	Model 8 SEMI	Model 9 PERI	Model 10 LDC	Model 11 LLDC	Model 12 SIDS	Model 13 LIFDC
GEI	.448****	.451****	.361****	.474****	.180****	.377****	.922****	.258****
	(11.85)	(11.97)	(9.52)	(9.45)	(4.82)	(6.63)	(5.29)	(6.86)
TRADEINEQ	–.178	–.156	.159	–.212	.117	–.309	.532	–.133
	(–1.31)	(–1.07)	(0.85)	(–1.09)	(0.97)	(–1.79)	(1.33)	(–0.99)
CPDEPEND	.128****	.128****	.269	.080**	.036	.148****	.638***	.035
	(3.64)	(3.56)	(1.84)	(2.58)	(0.93)	(3.80)	(2.99)	(1.03)
CPPDEPEND	.059***	.059***	–.230*	.055***	–.052**	.037	–.336****	–.032
	(3.10)	(3.06)	(–2.02)	(3.00)	(–2.48)	(1.58)	(–3.22)	(–1.71)
CLIMATE	.289****	.288****	.238****	.239****	.092****	.259***	.375****	.080****
	(19.54)	(19.41)	(9.20)	(16.40)	(5.23)	(10.78)	(3.94)	(7.36)
GEI X 2011		–.002	–.008****	–.000	–.001	.010****	–.004	–.003
		(–0.90)	(–8.05)	(–0.16)	(–0.50)	(3.55)	(–1.21)	(–1.64)
GEI X 2012		–.004*	–.014****	–.001	–.002	.009****	–.006	–.005*
		(–2.05)	(–9.97)	(–0.23)	(–1.02)	(4.62)	(–1.87)	(–1.98)
GEI X 2013		–.003	–.019****	.001	.007**	.011****	–.004	–.000
		(–1.46)	(–9.13)	(0.25)	(2.71)	(4.38)	(–0.67)	(–0.07)
GEI X 2014		.000	–.021****	.004	.013****	.012****	–.006	–.002
		(0.03)	(–10.16)	(1.67)	(3.82)	(4.18)	(–1.16)	(–0.47)
GEI X 2015		.006*	–.017****	.010**	.015****	.016****	–.017****	.006
		(1.99)	(–7.35)	(2.37)	(4.60)	(3.97)	(–4.46)	(1.84)

GEI X 2016		.007**	−.021****	.012***	.007*	.014****	−.006*	.007**
		(2.35)	(−11.45)	(2.78)	(2.33)	(3.85)	(−1.94)	(2.45)
GEI X 2017		.006**	−.018****	.009***	.002	.023****	−.013****	.003
		(2.53)	(−7.97)	(2.91)	(0.59)	(7.25)	(−4.02)	(0.83)
R^2	0.575	0.576	0.748	0.483	0.270	0.577	0.711	0.330
N (countries)	126	126	21	93	27	24	8	34
N (obs)	1008	1008	168	744	216	192	64	272
Rho	.769	.768	.748	.759	.688	.685	.635	.681

Note: Unstandardized coefficients are reported. Absolute values of *z*-ratios in parentheses.

* $p < 0.05$ ** $p < 0.01$ *** $p < 0.005$ **** $p < 0.001$

there is prima facie evidence for the EUE proposition of ecological unequal exchange. While negative, the impact of TRADEINEQ is insignificant and does not lend support to the EUE proposition that asymmetrical trade relations necessarily benefit developed countries with respect to VES consumption. CPDEPEND and CPPDEPEND are both positively related to GSEIMPACT with the magnitude of the relationships being strong in the latter and extreme in the former. Both findings indicate considerable support for the EUE contention that the specific asymmetrical trade relationship between CORE and non-CORE countries is relatively disadvantageous to the GSE of the developing world. Moreover, the type of trade, in this case primary exports, also matters considerably more in terms of greater VES consumption than when looking at the totality of exports. Indistinguishable from most EM model findings, the continuous, time-invariant CLIMATE variable remains an extremely strong predictor of GSEIMPACT.

The temporal interactive effects of WELL-BEING were included in models 1A–6 to assess a key proposition of EM theory, "decoupling," or the EKC effect. The temporal interactive effects of GEI are included in models 7A–13 but to evaluate a proposition related to EUE theory. EUE theory maintains that PERI countries are caught up in the omnipresent web of globalization and that it is this *ongoing* relationship that disproportionately serves to benefit both the economic and ecological interests of CORE countries while artificially increasing GSEIMPACT in PERI countries. Consequently, evaluating the annual temporal interaction effects of the linear relationship between GEI and GSEIMPACT, in the post–Great Recession years, appears warranted. Moreover, the potential for masking effects also legitimizes this part of the investigation.

Model 7A presents the temporal interaction effects of GEI on GSEIMPACT between 2010 and 2017. Two items attract attention. First, in the immediate years following the recession a negative relationship exists, with it reaching statistical significance in 2012. Second, beginning with an insignificant positive result in 2014, 2015–2017 evinces a positive relationship that grows increasingly significant. Although most likely a "natural" response to the improvement of the international economic system, it is a finding deserving of future research.

EUE Models and Country Subsets

Table 7.2 also presents the results of several distinct country subsets, including SEMI, PERI, LDC, LLDC, SIDS, and LIFDC. The basis for such an investigation again pertains to potential masking effects as well as to greater understanding as to how the GSE is impacted by increasing GEI in the immediate aftermath of a major economic recession.[3] The results for the SEMI subset are presented in model 8. The findings pertaining to the effects of GEI, TRADEINEQ, and CLIMATE largely mirror the results of baseline models 7 and 7A. However, the impact of CPDEPEND, while positive, was not statistically significant. This stands *in contrast* to the baseline models. Moreover, the relationship between CPPDEPEND and GSEIMPACT was *negative and moderately significant*, suggesting that greater primary export dependence by SEMI countries was associated with lower VES consumption. This poses an interesting question for future EUE research given the relative increased "development" that SEMI represents within the larger developing world. It may well be the case that further delineation as to the types of primary goods is necessary to understand this apparent disconnect as primary goods are not created equal in terms of their GSEIMPACT.

The temporal interaction effects regarding the impact of GEI on GSEIMPACT are considerably different for SEMI countries than for the baseline model. The impact of GEI is *negative and extremely significant* throughout the entire 2011–2017 period, indicating the somewhat counterintuitive idea that greater economic integration facilitated lower VES consumption in SEMI countries. Again, this is a finding that deserves greater attention in future EUE research.

Model 9 presents the estimated coefficients for the PERI subset. One will first note that the results for the impact of GEI, TRADEINEQ, CPPDEPEND, and CLIMATE on GSEIMPACT are precisely the same as seen in baseline model 7A. Moreover, while the impact of CPDEPEND is positive, akin to the baseline result, the magnitude of the relationship is less significant. The more notable concern for the PERI subset, however, is with respect to how the CPDEPEND and CPPDEPEND results stand in stark contrast to that found for the SEMI subset. While CPDEPEND was insignificant for the SEMI subset, it was positive and of strong significance for the PERI subset. The latter finding tracks the baseline models and is in line with EUE propositions. Moreover, and perhaps still more noteworthy, was the extraordinarily strong positive relationship between CPPDEPEND and GSEIMPACT for the PERI subset, a finding diametrically different from the significant negative result for the SEMI subset but precisely tracking the baseline result. The temporal interactive effects of GEI for PERI countries closely follow baseline model 7A in that a positive, significant trend occurred over the 2015–2017 period while the immediate years following the recession provided no significant results.

Unlike the SEMI and PERI models, models 10, 11, 12, and 13 provide results for developing country subsets that are largely not identified (i.e., studied) in the EUE literature as they represent subsets of the larger theoretical derived PERI subset. They are presented here to provide similar categorization, and thus comparison, to the EM models investigated earlier.

Moreover, it is important to identify whether the overall EUE focus on PERI countries is masking effects that might well be related to more specific country attributes (i.e., the least developed, the landlocked, the small islands, and the low-income food dependent countries).

Model 10 presents the estimated coefficients for the LDC subset. The results are remarkably similar to the baseline models with respect to GEI, TRADEINEQ, and CLIMATE. In contrast to the baseline, however, is the insignificant finding for CPDEPEND and the significant *negative* finding for CPPDEPEND. Remarkably, this subset is very similar to the results found for the SEMI subset with respect to all variables in the analysis. Noteworthy is the significant negative finding for the impact of CPPDEPEND on GSEIMPACT already mentioned, suggesting that the LDC subset saw lesser VES consumption associated with *greater* global economic integration. What is considerably different between the SEMI and LDC subsets, however, are the temporal interaction effects of GEI on GSEIMPACT. While a negative relationship existed between GEI and GSEIMPACT throughout 2011–2017, the complete opposite was found for the LDC subset. While insignificant in 2011 and 2012, the LDC subset revealed positive and strong significant findings over the 2013–2016 period. While the LDC subset is just one part of the larger PERI, this finding suggest that it is considerably "in tune" with the EUE proposition regarding the disproportionate effect that greater GEI has on VES consumption in PERI countries. Moreover, these findings may speak to the potential for recursive exploitation between SEMI and PERI, or at least the LDC subset of PERI.

Model 11 presents the estimated coefficients for the LLDC subset. The results pertaining to GEI, TRADEINEQ, CPDEPEND, and CLIMATE mimic the baseline models with respect to their effect on GSEIMPACT. Of considerable difference here is one peculiarity regarding EUE theory. While CPDEPEND was found to be positive and extremely significant, the impact of CPPDEPEND on GSEIMPACT was negative and resoundingly insignificant, representing a rather large discrepancy with the associated EUE hypothesis pertaining to the export of primary goods. With respect to the temporal interactive effects, the results lined up in accordance with EUE propositions evincing a positive relationship of extreme significance throughout the entirety of the 2011–2017 period. This finding is more spectacular than those found for either the LDC or PERI subsets and is diametrically opposite to the temporal interactive results for the SEMI subset.

Model 12 presents the estimated coefficients for the SIDS subset. The results pertaining to GEI, CPDEPEND, and CLIMATE mimic the baseline models with respect to their effect on GSEIMPACT. The impact of TRADEINEQ was positive but insignificant. Most noteworthy of the linear effects is the negative and significant coefficient for CPPDEPEND. This result stands in opposition to the baseline models and EUE propositions but is consistent with the results from the SEMI and LDC subsets, indicating that greater CORE/PERI primary export dependence results in less VES consumption. From an EUE perspective, this oddity will need to be addressed in future research. The temporal interactive effects of GEI were negative and insignificant in the immediate postrecession years (i.e., 2011, 2012, 2013, and 2014), but were of great significance in 2015 and 2017 while moderately significant in 2016. In effect, greater global economic integration resulted in less VES consumption. Like the LDC results for CPPDEPEND, this finding is in stark contrast to the larger PERI subset.

Model 13 contains the results for the LIFDC subset. Analogous to many subset findings already presented, the results for GEI, TRADEINEQ, and CLIMATE are in sync with the baseline models. The results for both CPDEPEND and CPPDEPEND, however, were of *no statistical significance*. These results more closely paralleled the results of the SEMI subset, as CPPDEPEND was negative and neared significance. The temporal linear effects of GEI were inconsistent, as the 2011–2014 period evinced a negative relationship with significance in 2012, while the 2015–2017 period revealed a consistent positive relationship with significance in 2016. This finding loosely resembles the baseline models, PERI, and LDC subsets.

DISCUSSION

The foregoing analysis evaluated several propositions related to both EM and EUE theory for a variety of country subsets during the immediate aftermath of a major global economic downturn, the Great Recession of 2007–2009. Underlying the evaluation of hypotheses associated with these theories was the contention that it is too early for EM theory, and its proponents, to move its research agenda to interpreting the merit of the associated propositions on "networks and flows" in the wake of redefining the concept of "society." Moreover, we still have much to learn with respect to how certain intermestic events, such as major economic downturns, impact the well-being/GSE nexus. For example, do major global recessions provide an artificial "turning point" whereby "economic rationality" gives way to "ecological rationality" or at least becomes more harmonious with it?

The results of the EM models suggest that broadening the traditional conception of "development," one that alternatively defines it in terms of Aristotelian *eudaimonian well-being*, is justifiable. The impact of well-being on VES in all country subsets, save the LDC subset, was positive, meaning that the broader conception of well-being was found to be as damaging to the GSE as studies utilizing the traditional, solely economic-based, measure of development. While these findings support the EM proposition that increasing development increasingly damages the GSE in the short term, there is virtually no evidence of an EKC materializing during the 2011–2017 period. Moreover, none of the findings suggests that "ecological rationality" has taken hold, let alone evidence for it occurring first in developed countries. The plausible appearance of reflexive modernization would appear nonexistent in this environment. Conversely, the associated focus on relative affluence as a component part of well-being revealed no significant findings for any of the subsets evaluated. Upon reflection, the validity of the measure utilized is suspect and probably should have focused more on a traditional measure (e.g., GENI Index), although doing so would have resulted in a substantially smaller dataset for analysis.

That countries with a greater orientation toward participatory and electoral democracy also witnessed decreases in their consumption of VES reflects positively the EM proposition pertaining thereto. However, this finding was only significant for the baseline models and the OECD subset. The contrary significant finding for the LLDC subset presents an interesting question as to why greater democracy resulted in increased consumption of VES and why it was peculiar only to this subset in the post–Great Recession period. What happens in the process of creating greater "civil society," articulating and aggregating proenvironmental demand on government, that leads to this result in the LLDC subset? Might the answer perhaps lie in further investigation as to the role of government responsiveness?

Also begging for greater explanation within the context of the economic downturn are the relatively consistent, significant results that greater economic freedom (i.e., capitalist orientation) had on the consumption of VES. While mostly associated with early EM theory, these significant contrarian results for the baseline models as well as the LLDC and LIFDC subsets suggest the need for greater consideration of the differentiating characteristics associated with the LLDC and LIFDC subsets. Even the insignificant coefficients revealed a positive sign. These results stand firm in maintaining that the immediate post–Great Recession period is awash in "economic rationality."

The structure of economic activity variable utilized in this analysis, and its measure reflecting the extent to which countries are reliant on the service sector for growth, certainly affirms what proponents of different environmental theories have long thought: that a service economy has either no impact or a lesser impact on VES consumption. Indeed, the current results—at least as they pertain to the baseline models and the SIDS subset—affirm this belief. However, the results for the OECD subset beg the question as to whether qualitative differences in the type of "services" lead to different impacts on VES. What is it about the OECD subset that makes for such a formidable retort to the dominant belief pertaining to the impact of a services-based economy?

Perhaps most supportive of EM theory, whether the early iteration or otherwise, is the role that technological sophistication plays in reducing the consumption of VES. A significant negative finding for the baseline models and the LLDC, SIDS, and LIFDC subsets lends considerable credence to the importance that EM proponents have attached to the role of technological innovation and implementation. Yet two concerns remain present. First, the LDC subset doesn't reveal significant support for this EM proposition—similar to the findings regarding the impact of well-being. Second, there appears to be a disconnect regarding the present findings pertaining to the related roles of capitalist orientation and technological sophistication. EM theory expects greater synchronization between these two concerns as well as the related democratic and capitalist orientations. However, the findings are consistently incongruent with this expectation.

EUE theory posits that greater global economic integration is a net negative for developing countries, as "withdrawals" of VES and "additions" of environmental wastes accrue in accordance with structural processes implied in the Netherlands fallacy. The results of the present investigation support many EUE propositions. In all cases, from the full model to SEMI, PERI, LDC, LLDC, SIDS, and LIFDC subsets, the result is the same: greater global economic integration results in greater consumption of VES. It is important to note, however, that these findings only reflect global economic integration in general terms. They do not speak directly to the structural impact that greater developing country integration with the CORE subset may have. What is perhaps most noteworthy is that the general GEI results for the SEMI and PERI subsets are near identical. This suggests a prima facie case against the existence of "recursive exploitation" between the SEMI and PERI subsets. Alternatively, one might conclude from an assessment of models 7A and 8 that the temporal findings for SEMI in the immediate post–Great Recession years is suggestive of a displacement of environmental harms onto other countries, specifically the PERI, LDC, and LLDC subsets.

The trade inequality variable utilized in this analysis does not lend support for that aspect of EUE theory that points to structural inequities in trade relations having a deleterious impact on the VES of developing countries. Alongside inconsistent directional results are the consistent insignificant findings across all country subsets. These findings, coupled with the zero-sum game assumption by EUE theory, beg the question as to the validity of the measure utilized. One will recall that the measure presently utilized was the terms-of-trade index in its absolute sense. One might make the argument that what is needed is a measure that *reflects percentage yearly changes* in the terms of trade, something akin to the average annual percentage growth in [environmental] terms of trade.

Contrary to the global economic integration variable, the CORE-PERI dependence variable specifically expounds on the EUE proposition that increases in this linkage result in greater consumption of VES in developing countries. The full model certainly provides ample evidence for this proposition based on the combined import/export measure of dependence. Particularly intriguing are the results for the SEMI and PERI subsets. SEMI dependence on the CORE has a statistically insignificant impact on VES, while greater PERI dependence on the CORE has a significant negative impact on VES consumption. In terms of the GSE, the SEMI subset appears to be in a relatively advantageous position vis-à-vis that of the PERI subset. One might suggest that future research focus on the role that technology transfers from the CORE to the SEMI and PERI subsets, respectively, play in reducing the impact on VES in developing countries. Finally, it is noteworthy that the CORE-PERI dependence variable significantly impacted the LLDC and SIDS subsets but not the LDC or LIFDC subsets.

The sector-specific CORE-PERI primary export dependence variable elaborates more extensively on the structural relationship posited by EUE theory, in the post–Great Recession period. The results for the full model provide significant evidence for EUE theory: greater primary export dependence on the CORE results in greater consumption of vital environmental services. In alignment with EUE theory, and to the CORE-PERI dependence variable, this significant relationship to VES was present for the PERI subset as well. This, however, is where the similarities to the CORE-PERI dependence variable end. The significant negative finding for the SEMI subset, indicating that greater primary export dependence on the CORE results in lower VES consumption, runs counter to EUE theory. A disaggregation of what is meant by "primary" goods might provide further insight into this seemingly counterintuitive result. Additionally, the same significant relationship was found for the LDC and SIDS subsets. This begs the question as to what is different about these two developing country subsets that the findings stand opposed to EUE theory and to the present results of the full model and PERI subset.

Although utilized as a control variable in the present analysis, the focus on climate (i.e., geographical latitude) is worthy of a brief note. Consistent with prior dummy variable research, the results of the continuous, time-invariant measure utilized here further confirm the significant importance of climate to the consumption of VES. A significant relationship exists irrespective of its inclusion in the EM or EUE models. The sole exception to this, the SIDS EM model, may well be a function of extremely low variance among the small number of SIDS cases and subsequent observations. Were this the case, however, one would have expected a similar insignificant outcome for the SIDS EUE model.

NOTES

1. These results better support the ideas associated with the Treadmill of Production theory pertaining to the impact of "development" on VES consumption.

2. Moreover, an interaction term testing for whether OECD countries significantly differed from non-OECD countries in the analysis resulted in a positive finding of extreme significance, indicating the need to look more at non-OECD countries in general (which is usually what has been done in the literature) and subsets of non-OECD countries based on peculiar characteristics (which is usually not done in the literature).

3. An interaction term testing for whether CORE and SEMI countries significantly differed from PERI countries revealed in both cases a positive finding of extreme significance, indicating a need to look at PERI separately (which the literature has largely done) and perhaps with greater focus on subsets (which the literature has largely neglected).

Conclusion

THE JOURNEY EXAMINED

This book has primarily been about investigating the utility of two economic-based environmental theories, EM and EUE, in explaining the consumption of vital environmental services (VES) in the post–Great Recession period. Setting the stage for this investigation was an overview of *subjective* societal perceptions regarding the importance of the global sustainable environment (GSE), and specific environmental concerns, juxtaposed with perceptions related to energy needs and the economy. It was argued that the concepts of *psychological distance* and *the issue-attention cycle* provide a sound explanatory basis for the historical patterns of behavior uncovered. Moreover, these results greatly paralleled the EM concepts of "ecological rationality" and "economic rationality," when applied to the individual level of analysis. For example, US public opinion evinces greater ecological rationality when the economy is perceived to be thriving and/or when the specific environmental issue of concern is one that is in closer *tangible proximity* to their person, that is, to members of the US public. Conversely, global data for the populations of Organisation for Economic Co-operation and Development countries and non-OECD countries alike indicate that the majority in those countries view global warming as a major threat, even though global warming is not in close tangible proximity to their person. However, the data for Israel and the US indicate that their populations' perceptions are especially antithetical to that of most other OECD countries, especially in the post–Great Recession period.

While public opinion data can provide a subjective, coarse measure of the relative importance of the economy and energy concerns when juxtaposed with the GSE, they cannot inform about the *objective* rate of VES consumption. Consequently, a more objective assessment of the patterns of historical consumption of VES by country subset further set the stage for the investigation. VES included the assessment of data for cropland, grazing, forestry, fisheries and aquaculture services, and CO_2 emissions, and were presented in lustra for 1966–2016. Due to the related limitations of much research on EM and EUE with regard to major characteristic differences between developing countries, select subsets were introduced to acquire more specific knowledge pertaining to VES consumption patterns and would further be utilized in the larger investigation pertaining to the overall utility of EM and EUE theory.

From a Human Ecology perspective, the population increases documented earlier and their consequent impact on VES consumption, require increased attention. Early EM theory, certainly implicitly if not explicitly, realized the impact of population growth, as the latter would necessarily lead to greater environmental deterioration via greater production and consumption unless appropriate technologies were developed and implemented. It would certainly appear that the population increases associated with many of the country subsets necessitate the technological innovation that early EM theorists routinely advocated for investigation. The *intensity measures* of VES consumption presented in chapter 3 convey an increasingly problematic state of affairs with respect to the intersectional dynamic of population, technology, economic growth, and the GSE. For example, the decline of VES consumption in the post–Great Recession period in cropland, grazing, and forestry services, coupled with population growth, resulted in downward pressure on their intensity measures, continuing a pattern long existent before the Great Recession of 2007–2009.

Beyond the population-related intensity concerns is the EUE proposition that the structure of international trade significantly disadvantages developing countries in their structural relations with developed countries. The *objective* data for cropland, grazing, and fisheries and aquaculture VES over the 1966–2016 period are unambiguous on this point, as total CORE VES in these areas has radically declined, while total SEMI and PERI VES has dramatically increased. Moreover, cropland and fisheries and aquacultural VES data in the post–Great Recession period indicate great consistency in the structured behavior.

Having considered subjective perceptions and objective realities, we moved into a discussion of the utility of certain concepts that have long been utilized by EM and EUE theorists to denote what is meant by "development." It was argued that the *traditional view of development*, delineated in exclusively economic growth and economic development terms, was particularly limiting when exploring the explanatory efficacy of EM and EUE theory in the post–Great Recession period. It was further argued that usage of the Aristotelian concept of *eudaimonia* (i.e., well-being) both enriches and clarifies the multidimensional nature attributed to the *modern view of development*.

However, the subjective and objective data presented earlier indicate a lack of any real appreciation of GSE being an integral part of any conception of "development." Perhaps Nussbaum's (2011, pp. 33–34) conception of a capabilities approach, *respect for human dignity*, of which control over one's environment was considered a necessity, comes closest to the Aristotelian idea of development as *well-being*. Utilizing the broader conception of Aristotelian well-being as a measure of the modern view of development, while clearly more expansive, has not impeded the present investigation as to the utility of EM and EUE theory in explaining that which impacts the consumption of VES in the post–Great Recession period. It is also highly probable that its use will not preclude further politicization of the concept of "development" and the competition between environmental theories that this politicization has spawned. However, its use provides us with a more intrusive understanding of why continued respect for human dignity, or "ecological rationality," at any level of analysis, is necessary regardless of whether the engines of economic growth are operating at maximum capacity or have temporarily stalled.

Flowing from the adoption of this enhanced, multidimensional understanding of "development" and the politicized emergence of EM and EUE was a more detailed comparative exposition regarding the historical and intellectual roots, tenets, and predominant methods of inquiry associated with each theory. It was argued that a good deal of research is overly particularistic in that the whole of EM and EUE theory is rarely sufficiently revealed, rendering largely impossible a more holistic understanding of either. An unintended consequence of this is the lingering impression that only irreconcilable differences between competing environmental theories exist, that tacit parallels upon which a more comprehensive understanding of the relationship between *well-being* and VES consumption in the post–Great Recession period can be built, simply don't exist. However, as the review in chapter 5 illuminated, parallels do indeed exist between EM and EUE theory that may provide greater insight into a variety of research questions if their investigation is pursued. While not a novel recommendation, it appears that the pronouncements of others advocating this viewpoint (e.g., Jorgenson and Clark, 2012; Thombs, 2018) have fallen on deaf ears as the major proponents of EM move the school toward the reconceptualization of society based on international networks and transnational flows.

EM, EUE, AND THE POST–GREAT RECESSION PERIOD

A global economic recession can provide a business environment where either economic or ecological rationality can prevail. For example, accompanying the Great Recession of 2007–2009 was a lower demand for energy resources, resulting in lower energy prices and a disincentive to transform production structures to more energy-efficient technologies. Moreover, operating efficiencies with respect to material inputs may also experience a prolonged decline. As incomes become stagnant, or fall, so, too, do individual expenditures on more expensive goods. Barring a panoply of incentives to do otherwise, one would expect businesses to hunker down in their existent economic rationality. The OECD (2009) aptly states this potentiality with respect to what you might typically expect of business behavior during the Great Recession:

> Efforts to promote a greener economy can also be compromised by the current crisis. Lower oil prices have already reduced incentives to switch to alternative energy sources—and the declining prices of raw materials are reducing pressures to use these resources more efficiently. Environmental innovation is also affected as consumers buy less expensive goods. Firms are therefore reluctant to introduce innovations because it is more difficult to reap a price premium. Moreover, as banks have reduced credit, process innovations that could reduce costs (e.g., energy-saving equipment) are more difficult to implement, as they imply capital investments. New entrants are also limited by lack of venture capital and declining market prospects. (p. 10)

Alternatively, one can argue that the Great Recession provided a "natural" *turning point* by which changes in sync with *reflexive modernization* could be instituted by producers and governments alike, if desired. In essence, a downturn in economic output may allow one to reconsider whether expansion of the resource base (i.e., economic rationality) or optimization and adaptation of the existing resource base, via technological innovation/implementation (i.e., ecological rationality), should be pursued. Although Obani and Gupta (2013) conclude that ecological rationality is wishful thinking, the OECD (2009) stood clear in its belief that the Great Recession provided the necessary impetus for ecological rationality to prevail:

> On the other hand, the prospect of industrial restructuring creates opportunities for new and greener businesses, whereas the depreciation of currently installed equipment (due to business downsizing or closure) offers opportunities for the promotion of environmentally friendly investments. (p. 10)

Moreover, the OECD (2009) went on to advocate that

> the current economic crisis should be used to strengthen efforts to achieve low-carbon economic growth. Recent OECD analysis shows that ambitious policy action to address climate change makes economic sense, and that delaying action could be costly. Providing that governments send a clear policy signal now about their medium and long-term climate change objectives, OECD analysis suggests that the actual cost of climate policy measures could be quite low in the initial few years, while countries are still struggling to move out of the

> crisis, notably in enhancing energy efficiency. The crisis offers an opportunity and an incentive to improve efficiency in the use of energy and materials, to move towards more sustainable manufacturing, and to develop new green businesses and industries. Dealing effectively with many environmental challenges will require investment in innovative energy-efficient buildings and transport systems, alternative energy supplies and "smart" electricity grids, pollution control, as well as investments in environmental infrastructures, such as sea walls to protect coastlines. Investing in the environment is thus an important element of many of the stimulus packages being put in place by governments in OECD and emerging economies. (p. 14)

The findings of the current study address the foregoing possibilities and reinforce the importance of the early EM emphasis on technology in transitioning to ecological rationality (save the LDC subset). However, the results also reflect the negative impact that a more capitalist orientation has on VES consumption (although insignificant for the OECD, LDC, and SIDS subsets). Given the latter, greater government intervention via targeted subsidies for environmental reform, as the OECD (2009) has recommended, would appear necessary to generate the ecological transition. The current findings also fail to provide evidence for the idea of reflexive modernization, let alone a lessening of environmental harms over time, as environmental economists argued in putting forward the EKC thesis. As such, the EM thesis pertaining to this happening in developed countries first, to be followed in developing countries, is entirely moot. There simply exists little to no evidence for the *decoupling* thesis, or a *stronger* ecological modernization in the immediate post-2009 period.

Similar to the findings for many EM arguments, the results regarding the utility of EUE in explaining the variation in VES consumption are reinforcing of many EUE theoretical propositions. Greater economic integration of non-CORE countries, regardless of the subset evaluated, results in significantly higher VES consumption (i.e., GSEIMPACT). More interesting, however, are the 2010–2017 temporal effects, as they indicate a certain level of support for the idea of a *recursive exploitative* relationship between the SEMI and PERI subsets. While the overall results for SEMI indicate a positive relationship between GEI and GSEIMPACT, the 2010–2017 temporal trend indicates that the impact of GEI on VES consumption is lessening over time. In marked contrast to this, however, is that the temporal trend for PERI is significantly increasing, reflecting a greater impact on VES consumption. This same disconnect is illustrated once more by the significant increases over the 2010–2017 period for both the LDC and LLDC subsets. However, this prima facie recursive relationship is not supported by the temporal trend exhibited by SIDS, as it parallels the temporal trend of the SEMI subset.

Given the relative mineral richness of many LLDCs, it is likely that its result is a rebound effect that supports the notion of economic rationality as the effects of the Great Recession begin to lessen over time.

While the present incorporation of monetary exchange value isn't necessarily the most intrusive measure, and certainly doesn't reflect specific types or amounts of material resource transfers, the results do indicate considerable support for that part of EUE theory pertaining to both the export intensity variable (i.e., GEI) above, the impact of CORE-PERI dependence and CORE-PERI primary export dependence as well. It is interesting that many developing country subsets reflect an increasingly significant disadvantage in VES consumption, vis-à-vis the CORE, when their export market is increasingly dependent on the CORE. While this result also applies with respect to CORE-PERI primary export reliance, albeit on a more limited basis, it is even more important to emphasize those results that run contrary to EUE expectations. The results for the SEMI, LDC, and SIDS subsets indicate that increasingly closer ties with the CORE facilitated lesser VES consumption in the post–Great Recession period. The importance of these results is that they leave open an entirely new area for EM/EUE exploration, especially with respect to the utility of each theory during significant global economic downturns.

WHAT IS TO BE DONE? SEVEN PATHS TO TRAVEL

There is indeed a goodly number of avenues for future research pertaining to the utility of EM and EUE theory in explaining VES consumption in postrecession periods. Perhaps most important among these roads is the emphasis on specific country subsets. Ciplet and Roberts (2017) have illustrated multiple "fissures" within the developing world when discussing environmental concerns and what is in the best interest of various subsets (i.e., LDCs, BASIC, OPEC, etc.) of developing countries. The results of the present study speak to the importance of country characteristics (i.e., splintering) that serve to identify critical commonalities. For example, the emphasis on the LIFDC subset is critical, given the EUE emphasis on the export of primary goods—where food transfers are a significant component of such exports. The resource-rich nature of many countries in the LLDC subset also speaks to the necessity of further developing country differentiation. Born out of Dunaway and Clelland (2017), there is also a need to further investigate the utility of EUE when considering the many regional semiperipheries, as they represent distinctive cultural peculiarities pertaining to many variables important to both EM and EUE theory.

Building on subset commonalities is the need to investigate and theorize about the present findings that run contrary to either EM and/or EUE expectations. With respect to EM theory, exempli gratia, why does greater well-being in LDCs consistently result in lower VES consumption over time? With respect to EUE theory, why does greater global economic integration result in lower VES consumption for LDCs? Moreover, what could explain why a greater democratic orientation results in significantly less VES consumption for the OECD subset, has no significant impact for LDC, SIDS, and LIFDC subsets, but results in a significantly strong *increase* in VES consumption for LLDCs?

Third, there is also a need to investigate more thoroughly specific aspects of each of these theories for various country subsets. For example, the current results indicate a prima facie case for the existence of a relatively strong recursive exploitative relationship between SEMI and the PERI, LDC, and LLDC subsets, respectively. However, there is virtually no evidence for recursive exploitation when evaluating both LIFDC and SIDS subsets. Moreover, why does greater primary export dependence on the CORE result in significantly larger VES consumption for PERI but significantly lesser VES consumption for the LDC and SIDS subsets while having no significant impact for the LLDC or LIFDC subsets? What is it about the nature of primary export dependence on the CORE that explains this? Given the present results for the capitalist orientation variable, is it conceivable that an interaction effect with primary export dependence on the CORE further explains the stark differences in VES consumption between different subsets of developing countries?

Beyond further subset investigation is the need to clarify the conceptual and measurable differences between such variables as well-being and affluence. Identifying the latter in relation to the traditional view of development (i.e., economic growth, economic development, consumption, etc.) foretells the unsurprising results of much research to date. Clarification of these concepts, for example, becomes even more critical when examining time periods that vary greatly on the continuum of global well-being, as affluence takes on a decidedly different orientation dependent on whether the global economy is significantly expanding or contracting.

Fifth, improving variable measures should continue to be a focus of both EM and EUE theory. While the reliability and validity of most measures associated with EM and EUE research is undoubtedly high, it is always possible to further refine measures to better reflect that which is being measured. For example, the current study has incorporated a measure of democratic orientation that includes both an electoral *and* participatory aspect to democracy. As was reviewed in chapter 6, a good deal of EM research surrounding the impact of democratic orientation on VES consumption only measures the extent to which "democracy" has been institutionalized, or the degree to which an outcome that is associated with democracy (i.e., civil liberties, political rights, etc.) is present. However, EM theory makes it quite clear that the existence of "civil society" needs to be accompanied by active citizen *participation* in placing demands on the relevant entities (e.g., governments, companies, etc.). One simply cannot assume the existence of citizen *participation* in a democratic polity, no matter how institutionalized "democracy" has become.

The measurement refinement of CORE-PERI export dependence, CORE-PERI primary export dependence, export intensity, and so forth in the EUE literature provides a magnificent example of the process of measurement refinement. Moreover, the early attempts (Giljum and Eisenmenger, 2004; Muradian et al., 2002; Rice, 2009) to move away from terms of trade to an environmental terms-of-trade measure, although victimized by a lack of quality data, also reflects this process. Perhaps the relatively new introduction of the Trade and Environment Database (TREND) by Morin et al. (2018) will be of benefit in this regard. Continuing to improve on existing measures, given the existence of reliable and valid datasets, can only result in enhanced policy prescriptions related to the GSE.

The main structural focus of much EUE research is with respect to the asymmetrical, power-based trade patterns between developing and developed countries. While trade characteristics are an important set of mechanisms to evaluate, many researchers have rightfully pointed to additional structured relationships, such as the presence of foreign direct investment (FDI) and military power asymmetries (Jorgenson, 2016b; Jorgenson and Clark, 2009). There is a need, however, to broaden the interpretation of these additional structural concerns and interpret them in association with EUE *and* EM theory. For example, investigation into the impact of FDI on VES consumption in developing countries has typically posited a positive relationship due to the tendency of host country governments to lessen environmental restrictions to entice greater development capital, an assumption that reflects the positive propositions of modernization theory as discussed in chapter 5. Indeed, Billet (1991) provides evidence of this with regard to mineral availability in different regions of the developing world.

Notwithstanding the foregoing, it is conceivable that FDI produces a net positive with respect to VES consumption via the dissemination of innovative, environmentally friendly technologies. Mert and Caglar (2020) provide a substantial review of the relevant literature while examining the case for Turkey and conclude that debate as to the relative merit of the *asymmetric pollution haven* and *asymmetric pollution halo hypotheses* continues with the results largely a function of the country chosen for analysis. Moreover, there is evidence suggesting that the pollution halo is more prominent in high-income countries, while the pollution haven hypothesis is more applicable to low-income countries (pp. 32935–32939).

Finally, future research assessing the utility of EM and EUE theory must further evaluate the specific role that international structural shocks, such as the Great Recession of 2007–2009, have on VES consumption. As the foregoing has made clear, relatively little literature exists on this matter (Huang, 2018, pp. 3–4). Known, however, is that national recessions don't automatically mean that a global recession will also happen. Moreover, global recessions don't impact all countries equally, and countries may choose different approaches for different periods of time to deal with the global economic downturn (Kose et al., 2020). For example, some governments may provide stimulus packages to business to facilitate recovery, perhaps even encouraging a shift to ecological rationality in the process. Government involvement in this respect would appear necessary given the reluctance of business to make new investments during recessionary periods, whether in the service of facilitating economic or ecological rationality. Moreover, the disruption in consumption and production patterns means that other structural considerations, including international trade and FDI, will also be impacted and that country responses will evince a wide variety of policies.

Ultimately, there are numerous research questions related to the importance of global recessions that have not been sufficiently investigated via the application of EM and EUE theory. A variety of these have been noted above, but a seemingly endless number still exist. For example, what is the impact of global recession on public opinion regarding the relative importance of the economic/environmental nexus? What is the role of "civil society," capitalism, and participatory democracy in facilitating government responses to global recession that are more conducive to ecological rationality? How does global recession impact VES consumption in different subsets of developing countries that represent different common denominators than those in the current study? Does SEMI recovery from global recession necessitate a recursive exploitative relationship vis-à-vis PERI countries? In sum, the utility of both EM and EUE theory is great in effectively answering these and related research questions regarding the impact of global recession on VES consumption. The objective reality of VES should move us to answer these in the quest for effective policies that are conducive to facilitating the health of the GSE.

Appendix A

Country Subsets (as of 2018)

These countries are counted in the data presented for vital environmental services in chapter 3. Due to data constraints, only those countries that are italicized are included in the chapter 7 analysis.

OECD (OECD n = 36/35)

http://www.oecd.org/about/membersandpartners/list-oecd-member-countries.htm

Australia
Austria
Belgium
Canada
Chile
Czechia
Denmark
Estonia
Finland
France
Germany
Greece
Hungary
Iceland
Ireland
Israel
Italy
Japan
Korea, South
Latvia
Lithuania
Luxembourg
Mexico
Netherlands
New Zealand
Norway
Poland
Portugal
Slovakia
Slovenia
Spain
Sweden
Switzerland
Turkey
United Kingdom
United States

CORE (CORE n = 10/10)

Belgium
Canada
France
Germany
Italy
Japan
Netherlands
Sweden
United Kingdom
United States

SEMIPERIPHERY (SEMI n = 21/21)

Argentina
Australia
Austria
Brazil
China
(including Hong Kong and Taiwan)
Denmark
Finland
India
Indonesia
Iran
Ireland
Israel
Korea, South
Mexico
New Zealand
Norway
Portugal
Singapore
South Africa
Spain
Switzerland

PERIPHERY (PERI n = 148/93)

Afghanistan
Albania
Algeria
Andorra
Angola
Antigua and Barbuda
Armenia
Azerbaijan
Bahamas
Bahrain
Bangladesh
Barbados
Belarus
Belize
Benin
Bermuda
Bhutan
Bolivia
Bosnia and Herzegovina
Botswana
Brunei
Bulgaria
Burkina Faso
Burundi
Cabo Verde
Cambodia
Cameroon
Central African Republic
Chad
Colombia
Comoros
Congo, DR
Congo, Republic
Costa Rica
Cote d'Ivoire
Croatia
Cuba
Cyprus
Djibouti
Dominica
Dominican Republic
Ecuador
Egypt
El Salvador
Equatorial Guinea
Eritrea
Eswatini
Ethiopia
Fiji
Gabon
Gambia
Georgia
Ghana
Grenada
Guatemala
Guinea
Guinea-Bissau
Guyana
Haiti
Honduras
Iraq
Jamaica
Jordan
Kazakhstan
Kenya
Kiribati
Kuwait
Kyrgyzstan
Laos
Lebanon
Lesotho
Liberia
Libya
Madagascar
Malawi
Malaysia
Maldives
Mali
Malta
Marshall Islands
Mauritania
Mauritius
Micronesia
Moldova

Monaco
Mongolia
Montenegro
Morocco
Mozambique
Myanmar
Namibia
Nauru
Nepal
Nicaragua
Niger
Nigeria
North Korea
North Macedonia
Oman
Pakistan
Palau
Panama
Papua New Guinea
Paraguay
Peru
Philippines
Qatar
Romania
Russia
Rwanda
Saint Kitts and Nevis
Saint Lucia
Saint Vincent and the Grenadines
Samoa
Sao Tome and Principe
Saudi Arabia
Senegal
Serbia
Seychelles
Sierra Leone
Solomon Islands
Somalia
South Sudan
Sri Lanka
Sudan
Suriname
Syria
Tajikistan
Tanzania
Thailand
Timor-Leste
Togo
Tonga
Trinidad and Tobago
Tunisia
Turkmenistan
Tuvalu
Uganda
Ukraine
United Arab Emirates
Uzbekistan
Uruguay
Vanuatu
Venezuela
Vietnam
Yemen
Zambia
Zimbabwe

LEAST DEVELOPED COUNTRIES (LDC n = 47/27)

https://www.un.org/ohrlls/content/list-ldcs

Afghanistan
Angola
Bangladesh
Benin
Bhutan
Burkina Faso
Burundi
Cambodia
Central African Republic
Chad
Comoros
Congo, DR
Djibouti
Eritrea
Ethiopia
Gambia
Guinea
Guinea-Bissau
Haiti
Kiribati
Laos
Lesotho
Liberia
Madagascar
Malawi
Mali
Mauritania
Mozambique
Myanmar
Nepal
Niger
Rwanda
Sao Tome and Principe
Senegal
Sierra Leone
Solomon Islands
Somalia
South Sudan
Sudan
Tanzania

Timor-Leste
Togo
Tuvalu
Uganda
Vanuatu
Yemen
Zambia

LANDLOCKED DEVELOPING COUNTRIES (LLDC n = 32/24)

https://www.un.org/ohrlls/content/list-lldcs

Afghanistan
Armenia
Azerbaijan
Bhutan
Bolivia
Botswana
Burkina Faso
Burundi
Central African Republic
Chad
Eswatini
Ethiopia
Kazakhstan
Kyrgyzstan
Laos
Lesotho
Malawi
Mali
Moldova
Mongolia
Nepal
Niger
North Macedonia
Paraguay
Rwanda
South Sudan
Tajikistan
Turkmenistan
Uganda
Uzbekistan
Zambia
Zimbabwe

SMALL ISLAND DEVELOPING STATES (SIDS n = 58/8)

https://www.un.org/ohrlls/content/list-sids

American Samoa
Anguilla
Antigua and Barbuda
Aruba
Bahamas
Bahrain
Barbados
Belize
Bermuda
British Virgin Islands
Cabo Verde
Cayman Islands
Comoros
Cook Islands
Cuba
Curacao
Dominica
Dominican Republic
Fiji
French Polynesia
Grenada
Guadeloupe
Guam
Guinea-Bissau
Guyana
Haiti
Jamaica
Kiribati
Maldives
Marshall Islands
Martinique
Mauritius
Micronesia
Montserrat
Nauru
New Caledonia
Niue
Northern Mariana Islands
Palau
Papua New Guinea
Puerto Rico
St. Kitts and Nevis
St. Lucia
St. Marten
St. Vincent and the Grenadines
Samoa
Sao Tome and Principe
Seychelles
Singapore
Solomon Islands
Suriname

Timor-Leste
Tonga
Trinidad and Tobago
Turks and Caicos Islands
Tuvalu
U.S. Virgin Islands
Vanuatu

LOW-INCOME FOOD-DEFICIT COUNTRIES (LIFDC n = 52/34) INFORMAL LIST BY UNFAO LATE 1970S

http://www.fao.org/countryprofiles/lifdc/en

Afghanistan
Bangladesh
Benin
Burkina Faso
Burundi
Cameroon
Central African Republic
Chad
Cote d'Ivoire
Comoros
Congo, DR
Djibouti
Eritrea
Ethiopia
Gambia
Ghana
Guinea
Guinea-Bissau
Haiti
India
Kenya
Korea, North
Kyrgyzstan
Lesotho
Liberia
Madagascar
Malawi
Mali
Mauritania
Mozambique
Nepal
Nicaragua
Niger
Nigeria
Pakistan
Papua New Guinea
Rwanda
Sao Tome and Principe
Senegal
Sierra Leone
Solomon Islands
Somalia
South Sudan
Sudan
Syria
Tajikistan
Tanzania
Togo
Uganda
Uzbekistan
Yemen
Zimbabwe

Appendix B

Variables, Measures, and Sources

Variable	*Measure*	*Source*
Dependent Variable		
GSE Impact	LN Ecological Footprint (constant global hectares per capita)	1
Independent Variables		
Well-Being	LN Human Development Index (0–1, low to high)	2
Relative Affluence	LN Percentage share of pretax national income of bottom 40 percent of adult income earners	7
Structure of Economic Activity	LN Services, value-added, as a percentage of GDP	3
Democratic Orientation	LN V-Dem Participatory Democracy Index (0–1, low to high)	4
Capitalist Orientation	LN Constructed Index of Six Dimensions of Economic Freedom (0–100, low to high)	5
Technological Sophistication	LN Percentage of Exports constituted by Manufactures with High Skill and Technology Intensity	3
Global Economic Integration	LN Total Exports as a percentage of GDP	3
Trade Inequality	LN Terms-of-Trade Index (Index pegged at 100 in 2010)	3
Core/Periphery Dependence	LN Total Trade with CORE countries as a percentage of Total Trade	3
Core/Periphery Primary Export Dependence	LN Total Primary Sector Exports to CORE countries as a percentage of Total Primary Sector Exports	3
Climate	LN Rounded Latitude	6

Sources:

1. Global Footprint Network. (2021). 2021 national footprint and biocapacity accounts. https://data.footprintnetwork.org/#

2. United Nations Development Programme. (2020). *Human development report, 2020: The next frontier: Human development and the anthropocene*. Palgrave Macmillan. (various issues)
3. UNCTADstat. (2021a). UNCTAD Data Center. https://unctadstat.unctad.org/EN/Index.html
4. V-Dem. (2021b). The V-Dem Project. https://v-dem.net/about/v-dem-project/
5. The Heritage Foundation. (2021). Index of Economic Freedom. http://www.heritage.org/index
6. CIA World Factbook (2021). Geographic-Coordinates. https://www.cia.gov/the-world-factbook/field/geographic-coordinates
7. World Inequality Database (2021). https://wid.world

References

Adcock, K. E., Reeves, C. E., Gooch, L. J., Leedham Elvidge, E. C., Ashfold, M. J., Brenninkmeijer, C. A. M., Chou, C., Fraser, P. J., Langenfelds, R. L., Mohd Hanif, N., O'Doherty, S., Oram, D. E., Ou-Yang, C.-F., Phang, S. M., Samah, A. A., Röckmann, T., Sturges, W. T., and Laube, J. C. (2018). Continued increase of CFC-113a (CCI3CF3) mixing ratios in the global atmosphere: Emissions, occurrence and potential sources. *Atmospheric Chemistry and Physics, 18,* 4737–4751.

Alkali Works Regulation Act. (1882, January). *The British Medical Journal, 1*(1097), 24.

Amin, S. (1970). International trade and international capital flows. *Man and Society* (18), 77–102.

———. (1974). *Accumulation of a world scale: A critique of the theory of underdevelopment.* Monthly Review Press.

———. (1976). *Unequal development: An essay on the social formations of peripheral capitalism*. Monthly Review Press.

Andreasson, S. (2017). Fossil-fuelled development and the legacy of post-development theory in twenty-first century Africa. *Third World Quarterly, 38*(12), 2634–2649.

Apter, D. (1965). *The politics of modernization*. University of Chicago Press.

Aristotle. (1908). *The Nichomachean Ethics* (W. D. Ross, Trans.). Clarendon Press. (Original work published 350 BCE)

Arndt, H. W. (1981). Economic development: A semantic history. *Economic Development and Cultural Change, 29*(3), 457–466.

Arrighi, G., and Drangel, J. (1986). The stratification of the world-economy: An exploration of the semiperipheral zone. *Review, 10*(1), 9–74.

Austin, K. F. (2017). Brewing unequal exchanges in coffee: A qualitative investigation into the consequences of the java trade in rural Uganda. *Journal of World-Systems Research, 23*(2), 326–352.

Babones, S. J. (2005). The country-level income structure of the world-economy. *Journal of World-Systems Research, 11*(1), 29–55.

———. (2015). What is world-systems analysis? Distinguishing theory from perspective. *Thesis Eleven, 127*(1), 3–20.

Bagliani, M., Bravo, G., and Dalmazzone, S. (2008). A consumption-based approach to Environmental Kuznets Curves using the Ecological Footprint indicator. *Ecological Economics, 65*(3), 650–661.

Baran, P. A. (1957). *The political economy of growth*. Monthly Review Press.

———, and Sweezy, P. M. (1966). *Monopoly capital: An essay on the American economic and social order*. Monthly Review Press.

Barder, O. (2012, August 16). *What is development?* https://www.cgdev.org/blog/what-development

Barrett, S., and Graddy, K. (2000). Freedom, growth, and the environment. *Environment and Development Economics, 5*(4), 433–456.

Beck, U. (1992). *Risk society: Towards a new modernity*. (Mark Ritter, Trans.). Sage Publications. (Original work published in German in 1986)

———, Giddens, A., and Lash, S. (1994). *Reflexive modernization: Politics, tradition and aesthetics in the modern social order*. Stanford University Press.

Bellu, L. G. (2011). Development and development paradigms: A (reasoned) review of prevailing visions (EASYPol Module 102). Food and Agricultural Organization of the United Nations. http://www.fao.org/docs/up/easypol/882/defining_development_paradigms_102en.pdf

Berna, F., Goldberg, P., Horwitz, L. K., Brink, J., Holt, S., Bamford, M., and Chazan, M. (2012). Microstratigraphic evidence of in situ fire in the Acheulean strata of Wonderwerk Cave, Northern Cape province, South Africa. *Proceeding of the National Academy of Sciences, 109*(20), E1215–1220. https://doi.org/10.1073/pnas.1117620109

Besharov, D. J. (2007). Measuring poverty in America: Hearing before the Subcommittee on Income Security and Family Support of the Committee on Ways and Means, 110 Congress. https://www.aei.org/wp-content/uploads/2011/12/-measuring-poverty-in-america_11320263975.pdf

Billet, B. L. (1991). *Investment behavior of multinational corporations in developing areas: Comparing the Development Assistance Committee, Japanese and American corporations.* Transaction Publishers.

———. (1993). *Modernization theory and economic development: Discontent in the developing world.* Praeger Publishers.

Blowers, A. (1997). Environmental policy: Ecological modernisation or the risk society? *Urban Studies, 34*(5–6), 845–871.

Borlu, Y., and Glenna, L. (2021). Environmental concern in a capitalist economy: Climate change perception among U.S. specialty-crop producers. *Organization & Environment, 34*(2), 198–218.

Borucke, M., Moore, D., Cranston, G, Gracey, K., Iha, K., Larson, J., Lazarus, E., Morales, J. C., Wackernagel, M., and Galli, A. (2013). Accounting for demand and supply of the biosphere's regenerative capacity: The National Footprints Accounts' underlying methodology and framework. *Ecological Indicators, 24*(1), 518–533.

Boughton, J. M. (2001). *Silent revolution: International Monetary Fund, 1979–1989.* International Monetary Fund.

Bradford, J. H., and Stoner, A. M. (2017). The Treadmill of Destruction in comparative perspective: A panel study of military spending and carbon emissions, 1960–2014. *Journal of World-Systems Research*, *23*(2), 298–325.

Bradlow, D. D. (2004). Development decision-making and the content of international development law. *Boston College International and Comparative Law Review*, *27*(2), 195–217.

Braudel, F. (1972). *The Mediterranean and the Mediterranean world in the age of Philip II: Volume I*. (Sian Reynolds, Trans.). Harper and Row, Publishers. (Original work published 1949)

———. (1973). *The Mediterranean and the Mediterranean world in the age of Philip II: Volume II*. (Sian Reynolds, Trans.). Harper and Row, Publishers. (Original work published 1949)

Brinkman, R. (1995). Economic growth vs. economic development: Toward a conceptual clarification. *Journal of Economic Issues*, *29*(4), 1171–1188.

Brohman, J. (1995). Universalism, eurocentrism, and ideological bias in development studies: From modernisation to neoliberalism. *Third World Quarterly*, *16*(1), 121–140.

Brolin, J. (2007). *The bias of the world: Theories of unequal exchange in history*. Human Ecology Division, Lund University.

Brulle, R. J., Carmichael, J., and Jenkins, J. C. (2012). Shifting public opinion on climate change: An empirical assessment of factors influencing concern over climate change in the US, 2002–2010. *Climatic Change*, *114*(2), 169–188.

Bunker, S. G. (1984). Modes of extraction, unequal exchange, and the progressive underdevelopment of an extreme periphery: The Brazilian Amazon, 1600–1980. *American Journal of Sociology*, *89*(5), 1017–1064.

———. (1985). *Underdeveloping the Amazon: Extraction, unequal exchange, and the failure of the modern state*. University of Chicago Press.

———, and Ciccantell, P. S. (2005). *Globalization and the race for resources*. The Johns Hopkins University Press.

Burns, T. J., Kick, E. L., and Davis, B. L. (2003). Theorizing and rethinking linkages between the natural environment and the modern world system: Deforestation in the late 20th century. *Journal of World-Systems Research*, *9*(2), 357–390.

Burns, T. R. (2013). Sustainable development. *Sociopedia.isa*. https://doi.org/10.1177/205684601392

Buttel, F. H. (2000). Ecological modernization as social theory. *Geoforum*, *31*(1), 57–65.

Cardoso, F. H., and Faletto, E. (1979). *Dependency and development in Latin America*. University of California Press.

Carolan, M. S. (2004). Ecological modernization theory: What about consumption? *Society and Natural Resources*, *17*(3), 247–260.

Catton, W. R., Jr., and Dunlap, R. E. (1978). Environmental sociology: A new paradigm. *The American Sociologist*, *13*(1), 41–49.

———. (1980). A new ecological paradigm for post-exuberant sociology. *American Behavioral Scientist*, *24*(1), 15–48.

Chase-Dunn, C. (1998). *Global formation: Structures of the World-Economy.* Basil Blackwell.

Chew, S. C. (1997). For nature: Deep greening world-systems analysis for the 21st century. *Journal of World-Systems Research, 3*(3), 381–402.

Chilcote, R. H. (1981). *Theories of comparative politics: The search for a paradigm.* Westview Press.

Chirot, D., and Hall, T. D. (1982). World-System theory. *Annual Review of Sociology, 8*(1), 81–106.

Christoff, P. (1996). Ecological modernisation, ecological modernities. In P. H. G. Stephens (Ed.), with J. Barry and A. Dobson, *Contemporary environmental politics: From margins to mainstream* (pp. 179–200). Routledge Publishing.

CIA World Factbook. (2021). Geographic-coordinates. https://www.cia.gov/the-world-factbook/references/definitions-and-notes

Ciplet, D., and Roberts, J. T. (2017). Splintering South: Ecologically unequal exchange theory in a fragmented global climate. *Journal of World-Systems Research, 23*(2), 372–398.

Clark, B., and York, R. (2005). Carbon metabolism: Global capitalism, climate change, and the biospheric rift. *Theory and Society, 34*(4), 391–428.

Clark, D. A. (2005). *The Capability Approach: Its development, critiques and recent advances.* Global Poverty Research Group. https://base.socioeco.org/docs/developments_critiques_advances.pdf

Clark, R., and Beckfield, J. (2009). A new trichotomous measure of world-system position using the international trade network. *International Journal of Comparative Sociology, 50*(1), 5–38.

Clelland, D. A. (2014). The core of the apple: Dark value and degrees of monopoly in global commodity chains. *Journal of World-Systems Research, 20*(1), 82–111.

Climate Research Board. (1979). *Carbon dioxide and climate: A scientific assessment*. National Research Council. National Academy of Sciences.

Cohen, M. J. (1998). Science and the environment: Assessing cultural capacity for ecological modernization. *Public Understanding of Science, 7*(2), 149–167.

Congleton, R. D. (1992). Political institutions and pollution control. *The Review of Economics and Statistics, 74*(3), 412–421.

Connell, R., and Dados, N. (2014). Where in the world does neoliberalism come from? The market agenda in southern perspective. *Theory and Society, 43*(2), 117–138.

Cooper, J. (1975). *Reason and human good in Aristotle*. Harvard University Press.

Cowen, M., and Shenton, R. W. (1996). *Doctrines of development*. Routledge Publishing.

Crafts, N. (2011). *The Marshall Plan: A reality check* (Working Papers Series 49). Centre for Competitive Advantage in the Global Economy. https://warwick.ac.uk/fac/soc/economics/research/centres/cage/manage/publications/49.2011_crafts.pdf

Currie-Alder, B. (2016). The state of development studies: Origins, evolution and prospects. *Canadian Journal of Development Studies, 37*(1), 5–26.

Dale, G. (2019). *Economic growth: A short history of a controversial idea.* openDemocracy. https://www.opendemocracy.net/en/oureconomy/economic-growth-short-history-controversial-idea

Daly, H. E., and Cobb, J. B. (1994). *For the common good: Redirecting the economy toward community, the environment, and a sustainable future.* Beacon Press.

Dean, J. M. (2002). Does trade liberalization harm the environment? *The Canadian Journal of Economics, 35*(4), 819–842.

Dietz, T., Rosa, E. A., and York, R. (2007). Driving the human ecological footprint. *Frontiers in Ecology and the Environment, 5*(1), 13–18.

Dos Santos, T. (1970). The structure of dependence. *The American Economic Review, 60*(2), 231–236.

Downs, A. (1972). Up and down with ecology: The "Issue-Attention Cycle." *The Public Interest, 28*(Summer), 38–50.

Dryzek, J. S. (1997). *The politics of the earth: Environmental discourses.* Oxford University Press.

Dunaway, W. A., and Clelland, D. A. (2017). Moving toward theory for the 21st century: The centrality of nonwestern semiperipheries to world ethnic/racial inequality. *Journal of World-Systems Research, 23*(2), 399–464.

Eckstein, H., and Gurr, T. R. (1975). *Patterns of authority: A structural basis for political inquiry.* Wiley & Sons, Inc.

Ehrhardt-Martinez, K., Crenshaw, E. M., and Jenkins, J. C. (2002). Deforestation and the Environmental Kuznets Curve: A cross-national investigation of intervening mechanisms. *Social Science Quarterly, 83*(1), 226–243.

Ehrlich, P. R. (1968). *The population bomb.* Ballantine Books.

———, and Holdren, J. P. (1971). Impact of population growth. *Science, 171*(3977), 1212–1217.

Emmanuel, A. (1972). *Unequal exchange: A study in the imperialism of trade.* Monthly Review Press.

Esteva, G. (1992). Development. In W. Sachs (Ed.), *The development dictionary: A guide to knowledge as power* (pp. 6–25). Zed Books.

Ewing, B., Reed, A., Galli, A., Kitzes, J., and Wackernagel, M. (2010). *Calculation methodology for the National Footprint Accounts, 2010 edition.* Global Footprint Network.

Ewing, J. A. (2017). Hollow ecology: Ecological modernization theory and the death of nature. *Journal of World-Systems Research, 23*(1), 126–155.

Feldman, M., Hadjimichael, T., Lanahan, L., and Kemeny, T. (2016). The logic of economic development: A definition and model for investment. *Environment and Planning C: Government and Policy, 34*(1), 5–21.

Fialho, D., and Van Bergeijk, P. A. G. (2017). The proliferation of developing country classifications. *The Journal of Development Studies, 53*(1), 99–115.

Fine, B. (2009). Development as zombieconomics in the age of neoliberalism. *Third World Quarterly, 30*(5), 885–904.

Fisher, D. R., and Freudenburg, W. R. (2001). Ecological modernization and its critics: Assessing the past and looking toward the future. *Society & Natural Resources, 14*(8), 701–709.

Flammang, R. A. (1979). Economic growth and economic development: Counterparts or competitors? *Economic Development and Cultural Change, 28*(1), 47–61.

Fomerand, J. (2004). Agent of change: The United Nations and development. In J. E. Krasno (Ed.), *The United Nations: Confronting the challenges of global security* (pp. 163–192). Lynne Rienner Publishers.

Foster, J. B. (1999). Marx's theory of metabolic rift: Classical foundations for environmental sociology. *American Journal of Sociology, 105*(2), 366–405.

———. (2012). The planetary rift and the new human exemptionalism: A political-economic critique of ecological modernization theory. *Organization & Environment, 25*(3), 211–237.

———, and Clark, B. (2012). The planetary emergency. *Monthly Review, 64*(7). https://monthlyreview.org/2012/12/01/the-planetary-emergency

———, and Holleman, H. (2014). The theory of unequal ecological exchange: A Marx-Odum dialectic. *The Journal of Peasant Studies, 41*(2), 199–233.

Frangie, S. (2011). Post-development, developmental state and genealogy: Condemned to develop? *Third World Quarterly, 32*(7), 1183–1198.

Frank, A. G. (n.d.). Changes in my view about dependence and capitalism. http://rrojasdatabank.info/agfrank/research.html#DEPENDENCE

———. (1966). The development of underdevelopment. *Monthly Review, 18*(4), 17–31.

———. (1967). *Capitalism and underdevelopment in Latin America: Historical studies of Chile and Brazil.* Monthly Review Press.

———. (1978). Development of underdevelopment or underdevelopment of development in China. *Modern China, 4*(3), 341–350.

Freedman, A. (2011, December 27). Top 5 extreme weather events of 2011 in the US from tornadoes to wildfires. *Washington Post*. https://www.washingtonpost.com/blogs/capital-weather-gang/post/top-5-extreme-weather-events-of-2011-in-the-us-from-tornadoes-to-wildfires/2011/12/26/gIQAA4gYKP_blog.html

Fudge, C., and Rowe, J. (2001). Ecological modernisation as a framework for sustainable development: A case study in Sweden. *Environment & Planning A: Economy and Space, 33*(9), 1527–1546.

Fukuyama, F. (1992). *The end of history and the last man*. Free Press.

Furtado, C. (1963). *The economic growth of Brazil: A survey from colonial to modern times*. University of California Press.

Gallup Organization. (2018). *Trend: Environment.* Gallup Organization. https://news.gallup.com/poll/1615/Environment.aspx

Galtung, J. (1971). A structural theory of imperialism. *Journal of Peace Research, 8*(2), 81–117.

Gastil, R. D. (1987). *Freedom in the world: Political rights and civil liberties, 1986–1987*. Greenwood Press.

Gellert, P. K. (2019). Bunker's Ecologically Unequal Exchange, Foster's Metabolic Rift, and Moore's World-Ecology: Distinctions with or without a difference? In R. S. Frey, P. K. Gellert, and H. F. Dahms (Eds.), *Ecological unequal exchange: Environmental injustice in comparative and historical perspective* (pp. 107–140). Palgrave Macmillan.

General Assembly resolution 35/56. (1980, December 5). *International Development Strategy for the Third United Nations Development Decade*. https://www.un.org/en/ga/search/view_doc.asp?symbol=A/RES/35/56

General Assembly resolution 45/199. (1990, December 21). *International Development Strategy for the Fourth United Nations Development Decade*. https://undocs.org/en/A/RES/45/199

General Assembly resolution 55/2. (2000, September 18). *Millennium Declaration*, A/RES/55/2. https://www.un.org/en/development/desa/population/migration/generalassembly/docs/globalcompact/A_RES_55_2.pdf

General Assembly resolution 1710/16. (1961, December 19). *United Nations Development Decade: A programme for international economic co-operation*. https://digitallibrary.un.org/record/204609?ln=en

General Assembly resolution 2626/25. (1970, October 24). *International Development Strategy for the Second United Nations Development Decade*. https://www.un.org/en/ga/search/view_doc.asp?symbol=A/RES/2626(XXV)

General Assembly resolution 3201/S-6. (1974, May 1). *Declaration for the Establishment of a New International Economic Order*, A/RES/3201/S-6. https://legal.un.org/avl/pdf/ha/ga_3201/ga_3201_ph_e.pdf

General Assembly resolution 3202/S-6. (1974, May 1). *Programme of Action on the Establishment of a New International Economic Order*, A/RES/3202/S-6. https://digitallibrary.un.org/record/218451?ln=en

Gibbs, D. (2006). Prospects for an environmental economic geography: Linking ecological modernization theory and regulationist approaches. *Economic Geography, 82*(2), 193–215.

Giddens, A. (1990). *The consequences of modernity*. Polity Press.

Giljum, S., and Eisenmenger, N. (2004). North-South trade and the distribution of environmental goods and burdens: A biophysical perspective. *Journal of Environment and Development, 13*(1), 73–100.

Gill, F. G. (1971). *Latin American-United States relations*. Harcourt Brace Jovanovich, Inc.

Givens, J. E., Huang, X., and Jorgenson, A. (2019). Ecological unequal exchange: A theory of global environmental injustice. *Sociology Compass, 13*(5), 1–30.

Global Footprint Network. (2021). 2021 national footprint and biocapacity accounts. https://data.footprintnetwork.org/#

Glynn, P. J., Cadman, T., and Maraseni, T. N. (2017). *Business, organized labour and climate policy: Forging a role at the negotiating table*. Edward Elgar Publishing.

Goldfrank, W. L. (2000). Paradigm regained? The rules of Wallerstein's World-System method. *Journal of World-Systems Research, 11*(2), 150–195.

Gore, C. (2010). The MDG paradigm, productive capacities and the future of poverty reduction. *IDS Bulletin, 41*(1), 70–79.

Goulet, D. (1971). *The cruel choice: A new concept in the theory of development*. Atheneum Press.

Grant, D., Jorgenson, A. K., and Longhofer, W. (2018). Pathways to carbon pollution: The interactive effects of global, political, and organizational factors on power plants' CO_2 emissions. *Sociological Science, 5*(4), 58–92.

Grell-Brisk, M. (2017). China and global economic stratification in an interdependent world. *Palgrave Communications, 3*(17087). https://doi.org/10.1057/palcomms.2017.87

Grove, R. (2002). Climatic fears: Colonialism and the history of environmentalism. *Harvard International Review, 23*(4), 50–55.

Gudynas, E. (2011). Buen vivir: Today's tomorrow. *Development 54*(4), 441–447.

Hajer, M. A. (1995). *The politics of environmental discourse: Ecological modernization and the policy process*. Oxford University Press.

———. (1996). Ecological modernization as cultural politics. In S. Lash, B. Szerszynski, and B. Wynne (Eds.), *Risk, environment & modernity: Toward a new ecology* (pp. 246–268). Sage Publications.

Hannigan, J. (2006). *Environmental sociology: A social constructionist perspective*. Routledge Publishing.

Hardin, G. J. (1968). The tragedy of the commons. *Science, 162*(3859), 1243–1248.

Hart, G. (2001). Development critiques in the 1990s: Culs de sac and promising paths. *Progress in Human Geography, 25*(4), 649–658.

Hartmann-Mahmud, L. (2009). Neoliberalism: A useful tool for teaching critical topics in political science. *PS: Political Science and Politics, 42*(4), 745–751.

Harvey, D. (2007). Neoliberalism as creative destruction. *The Annals of the American Academy of Political and Social Science, 610*(1), 22–44.

Heilbroner, R. L. (1963). *The great ascent: The struggle for economic development in our time*. Harper & Row Publishers.

The Heritage Foundation. (2012). Index of Economic Freedom. http://www.heritage.org/index

Herrera, R. (2006). The neoliberal "rebirth" of development economics. *Monthly Review, 58*(1). https://monthlyreview.org/2006/05/01/the-neoliberal-rebirth-of-development-economics

Hirschman, A. O. (1958). *The strategy of economic development*. Yale University Press.

Holmes, C., and Yarrow, D. (2016). *The politics of the post-GDP agenda: Progress beyond growth?* EMES Conferences Selected Papers Series, ECSP-P16-24. https://emes.net/publications/conference-papers/2nd-polanyi-emes-international-seminar/politics-post-gdp-agenda-progress-beyond-growth

Hornborg, A. (1998). Ecosystems and world systems: Accumulation as an ecological process. *Journal of World-Systems Research, 4*(2), 169–177.

———. (2003). Cornucopia or zero-sum game? The epistemology of sustainability. *Journal of World-Systems Research, 9*(2), 205–216.

———. (2009). Zero-sum world: Challenges in conceptualizing environmental load displacement and ecologically unequal exchange in the world-system. *International Journal of Comparative Sociology, 50*(3–4), 237–262.

———. (2013). *Global ecology and unequal exchange: Fetishism in a zero-sum world.* Routledge.

Howell, G. (2007). The North-South environmental crisis: An unequal ecological exchange analysis. *New School Economic Review, 2*(1), 77–99.

Howes, M., McKenzie, M., Gleeson, B., Gray, R., Byrne, J., and Daniels, P. (2010). Adapting ecological modernisation to the Australian context. *Journal of Integrative Environmental Sciences, 7*(1), 5–21.

Huang, X. (2018). Ecological unequal exchange, recessions, and climate change: A longitudinal study. *Social Science Research,* 73 (July), 1–12.

Huber, J. (1982). *Die verlorene Unschuld der Ökologie: Neue Technologien und Superindustrielle Entwicklung* (*The lost innocence of ecology: New technologies and super industrial development*). Fisher Verlag.

———. (1985). *Die Regenbogengesellschaft: Okologie und sozialpolitik* (*The Rainbow Society: Ecology and social policy*). Fisher Verlag.

———. (1989a). Social movements. *Technological Forecasting and Social Change 35*(4), 365–374.

———. (1989b). Eine sozialwissenschaftliche interpretation der humanökologie (A social science interpretation of human ecology). In B. Glaeser (Ed.), *Grundlagen Präventiver Umweltpolitik (Fundamentals of preventive environmental policy)* (pp. 57–75). West German Publisher.

Hume, D. (1906). *Hume's political discourses*. Walter Scott Publishing Company. (Original work published 1752)

Inglehart, R. (1990). *Culture shift in advanced industrial society*. Princeton University Press.

———. (1997). *Modernization and postmodernization: Cultural, economic, and political change in 43 societies*. Princeton University Press.

Intergovernmental Panel on Climate Change. (2021). Summary for policymakers. In V. Masson-Delmotte, P. Zhai, A. Pirani, S. L. Connors, C. Péan, S. Berger, N. Caud, Y. Chen, L. Goldfarb, M. I. Gomis, M. Huang, K. Leitzell, E. Lonnoy, J. B. R. Matthews, T. K. Maycock, T. Waterfield, O. Yelekçi, R. Yu, and B. Zhou (Eds.), *Climate change 2021: The physical science basis. Contribution of Working Group I to the Sixth Assessment Report of the Intergovernmental Panel on Climate Change*. Cambridge University Press.

Ish-Shalom, P. (2006). Theory gets real, and the case for a normative ethic: Rostow, Modernization Theory, and the Alliance for Progress. *International Studies Quarterly, 50*(2), 287–311.

Islam, M. S. (2017). Sustainability through the lens of environmental sociology: An introduction. *Sustainability, 9*(3), 1–11.

Jackson, P. (2007). A prehistory of the Millennium Development Goals: Four decades of struggle for development in the United Nations. *UN Chronicle: The Magazine of the United Nations, 44*(4). https://www.un.org/en/chronicle/article/prehistory-millennium-development-goals-four-decades-struggle-development-united-nations

Jänicke, M. (1985). *Preventive environmental policy as ecological modernisation and structural policy*. Internationales Institut für Umwelt und Gesellschaft (International Institute for Environment and Society) Discussion Papers. Wissenschaftszentrum Berlin für Sozialforschung (Science Center Berlin for Social Research).

———. (1988). Ökologische Modernisierung: Optionen und restriktionen präventiver umweltpolitik (Ecological modernization: Options and restrictions of

preventive environmental policy). In U. E. Simonis (Ed.), *Präventive Umweltpolitik (Preventive environmental policy)* (pp. 13–26). Fisher Verlag.
———. (2008). Ecological modernisation: New perspectives. *Journal of Cleaner Production, 16*(5), 557–565.
Jevons, W. S. (1866). *The coal question: An inquiry concerning the progress of the nation, and the probable exhaustion of our coal mines*. Macmillan and Company.
Jolly, R. (1976). The World Employment Conference: The enthronement of basic needs. *Development Policy Review, A9*(2), 31–44.
———, Emmerij, L., and Weiss, T. (2009). *UN ideas that changed the world.* Indiana University Press.
Jorgenson, A. K. (2009). The sociology of unequal exchange in ecological context: A panel study of lower-income countries, 1975–2000. *Sociological Forum, 24*(1), 22–46.
———. (2016a). Environment, development, and ecologically unequal exchange. *Sustainability, 8*(3), 1–15.
———. (2016b). The sociology of ecologically unequal exchange, foreign investment dependence and environmental load displacement: Summary of the literature and implications for sustainability. *Journal of Political Ecology, 23*(1), 334–349.
———, Austin, K., and Dick, C. (2009). Ecological Unequal Exchange and the resource consumption/environmental degradation paradox: A panel study of less-developed countries, 1970–2000. *International Journal of Comparative Sociology, 50*(3–4), 263–284.
———, and Clark, B. (2009). The economy, military, and ecologically unequal exchange relationships in comparative perspective: A panel study of the Ecological Footprints of Nations, 1975–2000. *Social Problems, 56*(4), 621–646.
———, and Clark, B. (2011). Societies consuming nature: A panel study of the ecological footprints of nations, 1960–2003. *Social Science Research, 40*(1), 226–244.
———, and Clark, B. (2012). Are the economy and the environment decoupling? A comparative international study, 1960–2005. *American Journal of Sociology, 118*(1), 1–44.
———, Clark, B., and Kentor, J. (2010). Militarization and the environment: A panel study of carbon dioxide emissions and the ecological footprints of nations, 1970–2000. *Global Environmental Politics, 10*(1), 7–29.
———, Dick, C., and Mahutga, M. C. (2007). Foreign investment dependence and the environment: An ecostructural approach. *Social Problems, 54*(3), 371–394.
Kennedy, J. F. (1961, March 13). *Address at a White House reception for members of Congress and for the diplomatic corps of the Latin American republics.* https://www.jfklibrary.org/archives/other-resources/john-f-kennedy-speeches/latin-american-diplomats-washington-dc-19610313
Key, V. O., Jr. (1961). *Public opinion and American democracy*. Alfred A. Knopf.
Kick, E. L., and McKinney, L. A. (2014). Global context, national interdependencies, and the ecological footprint: A structural equation analysis. *Sociological Perspectives, 57*(2), 259–279.
———, McKinney, L. A., McDonald, S., and Jorgenson, A. K. (2011). A multiple-network analysis of the world system of nations. In J. Scott and P.

Carrington (Eds.), *SAGE handbook of social network analysis* (pp. 311–328). Sage Publications.

Kirkwood, J. K., and Hubrecht, R. (2001). Animal consciousness, cognition, and welfare. *Animal Welfare, 10*(1), 5–17.

Koehler, G. (2015). Seven decades of "development" and now what? *Journal of International Development, 27*(6), 733–751.

Kose, M. A., Sugawara, N., and Terrones, M. E. (2020). Global recessions. Policy research working paper 9172. World Bank. https://elibrary.worldbank.org/doi/abs/10.1596/1813-9450-9172

Krasner, S. D. (1985). *Structural conflict: The Third World against global liberalism*. University of California Press.

Kraut, R. (1979). Two conceptions of happiness. *The Philosophical Review, 88*(2), 167–197.

Kuhn, P. M., and Bernauer, T. (2006). Does trade promote effective international environmental problem solving? http://www.cis.ethz.ch/publications/KuBeWater.pdf

Kumi, E., Arhin, A. A., and Yeboah, T. (2014). Can post-2015 sustainable development goals survive neoliberalism? A critical examination of the sustainable development–neoliberalism nexus in developing countries. *Environment, Development and Sustainability, 16*(3), 539–554.

Kuznets, S. (1973). Modern economic growth: Findings and reflections. *The American Economic Review, 63*(3), 247–258.

La Palombara, J., and Weiner, M. (Eds.) (1966). *Political parties and political development*. Princeton University Press.

Lambin, E. F., and Meyfroidt, P. (2011). Global land use change, economic globalization, and the looming land scarcity. *Proceedings of the National Academy of Science of the United States of America, 108*(9), 3465–3472.

Lawrence, L., and McConnell, J. (1999). *Earth Day: Past, present, and future.* http://www.wowzone.com/mc-lee.htm

Lengefeld, M. R., and Smith, C. L. (2013). Nuclear shadows: Weighing the environmental effects of militarism, capitalism, and modernization in a global context, 2001–2007. *Human Ecology Review, 20*(1), 11–15.

Lerner, D. (1958). *The passing of traditional society: Modernizing the Middle East*. Free Press.

Leroy, P., and van Tatenhove, J. (2000). Political modernization theory and environmental politics. In G. Spaargaren, A. P. J. Mol, and F. H. Buttel (Eds.), *Environment and global modernity* (pp. 187–208). Sage Publications.

Levinson, J., and De Onis, J. (1970). *The alliance that lost its way: A critical report on the Alliance for Progress*. Quadrangle Books.

Levy, M. J., Jr. (1966). *Modernization and the structure of societies: A setting for international affairs*. Princeton University Press.

Lewis, D. (2019). "Big D" and "little d": Two types of twenty-first century development? *Third World Quarterly, 40*(11), 1–19, https://doi.org/10.1080/01436597.2019.1630270

Lewis, W. A. (1955). *The theory of economic growth*. Allen and Unwin.

Liberman, N., and Trope, Y. (1998). The role of feasibility and desirability considerations in near and distant future decisions: A test of temporal construal theory. *Journal of Personality and Social Psychology, 75*(1), 5–18.

Lin, D., Hanscom, L., Murthy, A., Galli, A., Evans, M., Neill, E., Mancini, M. S., Martindill, J., Medouar, F. Z., Huang, S., and Wackernagel, M. (2018). Ecological Footprint Accounting for countries: Updates and results of the National Footprint Accounts, 2012–2018. *Resources, 7*(3), 58–64.

London, B. (1987). Structural determinants of Third World urban change: An ecological and political economic analysis. *American Sociological Review*, *52*(1), 28-43.

Lucas, R. E., Jr. (1988). On the mechanics of economic development. *Journal of Monetary Economics, 22*(1), 3–42.

Lv, Z. (2017). The effect of democracy on CO_2 emissions in emerging countries: Does the level of income matter? *Renewable and Sustainable Energy Reviews, 72*(May), 900–906.

MacLeod, R. M. (1968). Government and resource conservation: The Salmon Acts Administration, 1860–1886. *Journal of British Studies, 7*(2), 114–150.

Madeira. (2017). Portuguese Historical Museum. https://www.portuguesemuseum.org/?page_id=1808&category=4&exhibit=&event=137

Magid, J. (2012). The Marshall Plan. *Advances in Historical Studies, 1*(1), 1–7. http://dx.doi.org/10.4236/ahs.2012.11001

Mahutga, M. C. (2006). The persistence of structural inequality? A network analysis of international trade, 1965–2000. *Social Forces, 84*(4), 1863–1889.

———, and Smith, D. A. (2011). Globalization, the structure of the world economy and economic development. *Social Science Research, 40*(1), 257–272.

Marangos, J. (2009). The evolution of the term "Washington Consensus." *Journal of Economic Surveys, 23*(2), 350–384.

———, and Astroulakis, N. (2010). The Aristotelian contribution to development ethics. *Journal of Economic Issues, 44*(2), 551–558.

Marshall, M. G., Jaggers, K., and Gurr, T. R. (2011). *POLITY IV PROJECT: Political Regime characteristics and transitions, 1800–2010; Dataset user's manual.* Center for Systemic Peace.

McClelland, D. C. (1961). *The achieving society*. Van Nostrand.

McConnell, J. (2011). *Earth Day: Vision for peace, justice, and earth care: My life and thought at age 96*. Wipf and Stock Publishers.

McKinney, L. A., Fulkerson, G. M., and Kick, E. L. (2009). Investigating the correlates of biodiversity loss: A cross-national quantitative analysis of threatened bird species. *Human Ecology Review, 16*(1), 103–113.

McLaughlin, P. (2012). Ecological modernization in evolutionary perspective. *Organization & Environment, 25*(2), 178–196.

Meadows, D. H., Meadows, D. L., Randers, J., and Behrens, W. W., III. (1972). *The limits to growth: A report for the Club of Rome's project on the predicament of mankind.* Universe Books.

Mert, M., and Caglar, A. E. (2020). Testing pollution haven and pollution halo hypotheses for Turkey: A new perspective. *Environmental Science and Pollution Research International, 27*(26), 32933–32943.

Midlarsky, M. I. (1998). Democracy and the environment: An empirical assessment. *Journal of Peace Research, 35*(3), 341–361.

Mill, J. S. (2004). *Principles of political economy*. Prometheus Books. (Original work published 1848)

Millikan, M. F., and W. W. Rostow. (1957). *A proposal: Key to an effective foreign policy*. Harper & Brothers.

Minas Gerais. (2019). *Encyclopedia of Latin American history and culture*. https://www.encyclopedia.com/humanities/encyclopedias-almanacs-transcripts-and-maps/minas-gerais

Mol, A. P. J. (1995). *The refinement of production: Ecological Modernization Theory and the chemical industry*. Van Arkel Publishing.

———. (1997). Ecological modernization: Industrial transformations and environmental reform. In M. Redclift and G. Woodgate. (Eds.), *The International Handbook of Environmental Sociology* (pp. 138–149). Edward Elgar.

———. (1999). Ecological modernization and the environmental transition of Europe: Between national variations and common denominators. *Journal of Environmental Policy & Planning, 1*(2), 167–181.

———. (2002). Ecological modernization and the global economy. *Global Environmental Politics, 2*(2), 92–115.

———. (2003). *Globalization and environmental reform: The ecological modernization of the global economy*. MIT Press.

———. (2006a). Environment and modernity in transitional China: Frontiers of ecological modernization. *Development and Change, 37*(1), 29–56.

———. (2006b). From environmental sociologies to environmental sociology? A comparison of U.S. and European environmental sociology author(s). *Organization & Environment, 19*(1), 5–27.

———, and Sonnenfeld, D. A. (2000). Ecological modernization around the world: An introduction. *Environmental Politics, 9*(1), 3–16.

———, Sonnenfeld, D. A., and Spaargaren, G. (2009). Ecological modernization: Three decades of policy, practice, and theoretical reflection. In A. P. J. Mol, D. A. Sonnenfeld, and G. Spaargaren. (Eds.), *The ecological modernization reader: Environmental reform in theory and practice* (pp. 3–14). Routledge Publishers.

———, and Spaargaren, G. (2000). Ecological modernization theory in debate: A review. *Environmental Politics, 9*(1), 17–49.

———, and Spaargaren, G. (2004). Ecological modernization and consumption: A reply. *Society and Natural Resources, 17*(3), 261–265.

———, and Spaargaren, G. (2005). From additions and withdrawals to environmental flows: Reframing debates in the environmental social sciences. *Organization & Environment, 18*(1), 91–107.

———, Spaargaren, G., and Sonnenfeld, D. A. (2014). Ecological modernization theory: Taking stock, moving forward. In S. Lockie, D. A. Sonnenfeld, and D. R. Fisher. (Eds.), *Routledge International Handbook of Social and Environmental Change* (pp. 15–30). Routledge Publishers.

Moore, J. W. (2000). Environmental crises and the metabolic rift in world-historical perspective. *Organization & Environment, 13*(2), 123–157.

———. (2003). The modern world-system as environmental history? Ecology and the rise of capitalism. *Theory and Society, 32*(3), 307–377.
Morawetz, D. (1977). *Twenty-five years of economic development: 1950 to 1975*. The International Bank for Reconstruction and Development.
Morin, J. F., Dür, A., and Lechner, L. (2018). Mapping the trade and environment nexus: Insights from a new data set. *Global Environmental Politics, 18*(1), 122–139.
Morris, M. D. (1978). A physical quality of life index. *Urban Ecology, 3*(3), 225–240.
Muller, E. (1985). Income inequality, regime repressiveness, and political violence. *American Sociological Review, 50*(1), 47–61.
Muradian, R., O'Connor, M., and Martinez-Aler, J. (2002). Embodied pollution in trade: Estimating the "Environmental Load Displacement" of industrialized countries. *Ecological Economies, 41*(1), 51–67.
Myrdal, G. (1974). What is development? *Journal of Economic Issues, 8*(4), 729–736.
Nafziger, E. W. (2007). From Seers to Sen: The meaning of economic development. In G. Mavrotas and A. Shorrocks (Eds.), *Advancing development: Core themes in global economics* (pp. 50–62). Palgrave Macmillan.
Naim, M. (2000). Fads and fashion in economic reforms: Washington Consensus or Washington confusion? *Third World Quarterly, 21*(3), 505–528.
Nemeth, R. J., and Smith, D. A. (1985). International trade and World-System structure: A multiple network analysis. *Review*, *8*(4), 517–560.
Neumayer, E. (2002). Do democracies exhibit stronger international environmental commitment? A cross-country analysis. *Journal of Peace Research, 39*(2), 139–164.
Noble, M. D. (2017). Chocolate and the consumption of forests: A cross-national examination of ecologically unequally exchange in cocoa exports. *Journal of World-Systems Research, 23*(2), 236–268.
Nussbaum, M. C. (2011). The central capabilities. In M. C. Nussbaum (Ed.), *Creating capabilities: The human development approach* (pp. 17–45). Harvard University Press.
Obani, P. C., and Gupta, J. (2015). The impact of economic recession on climate change: Eight trends. *Climate and Development, 8*(3), 211–223.
Organisation for Economic Co-operation and Development. (2009). *Policy responses to the economic crisis: Investing in innovation for long-term growth*. OECD Publishing. https://www.oecd.org/sti/42983414.pdf
Ostry, J. D., Loungani, P., and Furceri, D. (2016). Neoliberalism: Oversold? *Finance and Development, 53*(2), 38–41.
O'Toole, G. (2007). *Politics Latin America.* Longman.
Oulu, M. (2016). Core tenets of the theory of ecological unequal exchange. *Journal of Political Ecology, 23*(1), 446–466.
Overseas Development Institute. (1978). Basic needs (Briefing paper No. 5). Overseas Development Institute. https://www.odi.org/sites/odi.org.uk/files/odi-assets/publications-opinion-files/6616.pdf
Paddock, W., and Paddock, P. (1967). *Famine 1975! America's decision: Who will survive?* Little, Brown.

Palma, G. (1978). Dependency: A formal theory of underdevelopment or a methodology for the analysis of concrete situations of underdevelopment. *World Development, 6*(7–8), 881–924.

Paris Agreement (2015). Opened for signature April 22, 2016. https://treaties.un.org/doc/Publication/UNTS/No%20Volume/54113/Part/I-54113-0800000280458f37.pdf

Peichl, A., and Pestel, N. (2011). *Multidimensional affluence: Theory and applications to Germany and the US.* Working Papers 218, ECINEQ. Society for the Study of Economic Inequality.

Petras, J. (1997). Alternative to neoliberalism in Latin America. *Latin American Perspectives, 24*(1), 80–91.

Pew Research Center. (2007). *Global Attitudes Project: Rising environmental concern in 47-Nation survey.* https://www.pewresearch.org/global/2007/06/27/global-unease-with-major-world-powers

———. (2008). *Global Attitudes Project: Some positive signs for US image.* https://www.pewresearch.org/wp-content/uploads/sites/2/2008/06/2008-Pew-Global-Attitudes-Report-1-June-12-2pm.pdf

———. (2009). *Global Attitudes Project: Most Muslims not so easily moved.* http://www.pewglobal.org/files/pdf/264.pdf

———. (2010). *Global Attitudes Project: Obama more popular abroad than at home, global image of US continues to benefit.* http://www.pewglobal.org/files/2010/06/Pew-Global-Attitudes-Spring-2010-Report.pdf

Pieterse, J. N. (2000). After post-development. *Third World Quarterly, 21*(2), 175–191.

Pillarisetti, J. R., and van der Bergh, J. C. J. M. (2010). Sustainable nations: What do aggregate indexes tell us? *Environment, Development, and Sustainability, 12*(1), 49–62.

Polanyi, K. (1944). *Origins of our time. The great transformation.* Farrar and Rinehart.

Prebisch, R. (1950). *The economic development of Latin America and its principal problems*. United Nations.

Pye, L. W. (1965). The concept of political development. *The Annals of the American Academy of Political and Social Science, 358*, 1–13.

Radice, H. (2008). The developmental state under global neoliberalism. *Third World Quarterly*, *29*(6), 1153–1174.

Reagan, R. (1981, October 22). Statement at the first plenary session of the International Meeting on Cooperation and Development. https://www.reaganlibrary.gov/research/speeches/102281a

Ricardo, D. (2015). *On the principles of political economy and taxation*. Cambridge University Press. (Original work published 1817)

Rice, J. (2007a). Ecological unequal exchange: International trade and uneven utilization of environmental space in the world system. *Social Forces, 85*(3), 1369–1392.

———. (2007b). Ecological unequal exchange: Consumption, equity, and unsustainable structural relationships within the global economy. *International Journal of Comparative Sociology, 48*(1), 43–72.

———. (2009). The transnational organization of production and uneven environmental degradation and change in the world economy. *International Journal of Comparative Sociology, 50*(3–4), 215–236.

Rifkin, J. (2014). *The zero marginal cost society: The internet of things, the collaborative commons, and the eclipse of capitalism*. Palgrave Macmillan.

Robbins, L. C. (1968). *The theory of economic development in the history of economic thought: Being the Chichele Lectures for 1966, revised and extended*. Macmillan and Company, Limited.

Roberts, J. T., and Grimes, P. E. (1997). Carbon intensity and economic development 1962–1991: A brief exploration of the Environmental Kuznets Curve. *World Development, 25*(2), 191–198.

Roebroeks, W., and Villa, P. (2011). On the earliest evidence for habitual use of fire in Europe. *Proceedings of the National Academy of Sciences, 108*(13), 5209–5214. https://doi.org/10.1073/pnas.1018116108

Rosa, E. A., York, R., and Dietz, T. (2004). Tracking the anthropogenic drivers of ecological impacts. *Ambio, 33*(8), 509–512.

Ross, S. R., Lukas, K. E., Lonsdorf, E. V., Stoinski, T. S., Hare, B., Shumaker, R., and Goodall, J. (2008). Inappropriate use and portrayal of chimpanzees. *Science, 319*(5869), 1487.

———, Vreeman, V. M., and Lonsdorf, E. V. (2011). Specific image characteristics influence attitudes about chimpanzee conservation and use as pets. *PLOS One, 6*(7), e22050.

Rostow, W. W. (1960). *The stages of economic growth: A non-communist manifesto*. Cambridge University Press.

———. (1971). *Politics and the stages of growth*. Cambridge University Press.

———. (1979). The key security tasks of the 1980s. *International Security, 4*(2), 180–188.

Rothman, D. S. (1998). Environmental Kuznets Curves—real progress or passing the buck? A case for consumption-based approaches. *Ecological Economics, 25*(2), 177–194.

Rowland, F. S. (2001). Climate change and its consequences: Issues for the new U.S. administration. *Environment: Science and Policy for Sustainable Development, 43*(2), 28–34.

Rudel, T. K., Schneider, L., Uriarte, M., Turner, B. L., II, DeFries, R., Lawrence, D., Geoghegan, J., Hecht, S., Ickowitz, A., Lambin, E. F., Birkenholtz, T., Baptista, S., and Grau, R. (2009). Agricultural intensification and changes in cultivated areas, 1970–2005. *Proceedings of the National Academy of Science of the United States of America, 106*(49), 20675–20680.

Ruvalcaba, D. M. (2020). The semiperipheral states in the twenty-first century: Measuring the structural position of regional powers and secondary regional states. *International Studies, 57*(1), 20–50.

Saat, S. A., and Ali, N. (2014). Analysing the sustainability of solid waste policy in Malaysia using the Ecological Modernization theory. *Malaysian Journal of Society and Space, 10*(6), 118–125.

Sachs, W. (1992). Introduction. In W. Sachs (Ed.), *The development dictionary: A guide to knowledge as power* (pp. 1–5). Zed Books.
Sahlins, M. (1972). *Stone age economics*. Aldine Atherton, Inc.
Sartori, G. (1970). Concept misformation in comparative politics. *American Political Science Review, 64*(4), 1033–1053.
Schumpeter, J. A. (1949). *The theory of economic development: An inquiry into profits, capital, credit, interest, and the business cycle* (R. Opie, Trans.). Harvard University Press. (Original work published 1911)
Seers, D. (1969). *The meaning of development*. Institute of Development Studies. https://www.ids.ac.uk/files/dmfile/themeaningofdevelopment.pdf
———. (1972). What are we trying to measure? *Journal of Development Studies, 8*(3), 21–36.
Sen, A. K. (1983). Development: Which way now? *The Economic Journal, 93*(372), 745–762.
———. (1987). The standard of living: Lecture 2, Lives and Capabilities. In G. Hawthorn (Ed.), *The standard of living: The Tanner lectures on human values* (pp. 20–38). Cambridge University Press.
———. (1988). The concept of development. In H. Chenery and T. N. Srinivasan (Eds.), *Handbook of development economics* (pp. 1:9–26). Elsevier Science Publishers.
———. (1992). *Inequality reexamined*. Oxford University Press.
Sezgin, Z. (2013). Ecological modernization at the intersection of environment and energy. *International Journal of Energy Economics and Policy, 3*(Special Issue), 93–101.
Shandra, J. M., Leckband, C., McKinney, L. A., and London, B. (2009). Ecologically unequal exchange, world polity and biodiversity loss: A cross-national analysis of threatened mammals. *International Journal of Comparative Sociology, 50*(3–4), 285–310.
———, London, B., Whooley, O. P., and Williamson, J. B. (2004). International non-governmental organizations and carbon dioxide emissions in the developing world: A quantitative, cross-national analysis. *Sociological Inquiry, 74*(4), 520–545.
———, Shor, E., and London, B. (2009). World polity, unequal exchange, and organic water pollution: A cross-national analysis of developing nations. *Human Ecology Review, 16*(1), 53–63.
Simonis, U. E. (1985). Preventative environmental policy: Prerequisites, trends, and prospects. *Ekistics: Reviews on the Problems and Science of Human Settlements, 52*(313), 369–372.
———. (1989). *Ecological modernization of industrial society: Three strategic elements*. Wissenschaftszentrum Berlin für Sozialforschung (Science Center Berlin for Social Research).
Singer, H. W. (1950). The distribution of gains between investing and borrowing countries. *The American Economic Review, 40*(2), 473–485.
———. (1989). The 1980s: A lost decade—development in reverse? In H. W. Singer and S. Sharma (Eds.), *Growth and external debt management* (pp. 46–56). Palgrave Macmillan Publishers.

Singer, S. F., and Avery, D. T. (2007). *Unstoppable global warming: Every 1,500 years.* Rowman & Littlefield.

Smith, A. (2007). *An inquiry into the nature and causes of the wealth of nations*. (S. M. Soares, Ed.). MetaLibri Digital Library. (Original work published 1776)

Smith, D. A., and White, D. R. (1992). Structure and dynamics of the global economy: Network analysis of international trade 1965–1980. *Social Forces, 70*(4), 857–893.

Snyder, D., and Kick, E. L. (1979). Structural position in the world system and economic growth, 1955–1970: A multiple-network analysis of transnational interactions. *American Journal of Sociology, 84*(5), 1096–1126.

Sommer, J. M., Shandra, J. M., and Coburn, C. (2019 ebook). Mining exports flows, repression, and forest loss: A cross-national test of Ecologically Unequal Exchange. In R. S. Frey, P. K. Gellert, and H. F. Dahms (Eds.), *Ecologically Unequal Exchange: Environmental Injustice in Comparative and Historical Perspective* (pp. 167–194). Springer International Publishing. https://doi.org/10.1007/978-3-319-89740-0_6

Soubbotina, T. P. (2004). *Beyond economic growth: An introduction to sustainable development.* The World Bank.

Spaargaren, G. (1997). Ecological modernization theory and the changing discourse on environment and modernity. In G. Spaargaren (Ed.), *The ecological modernization of production and consumption: Essays in environmental sociology* (pp. 1–42). Wageningen Agricultural University.

———, and Mol, A. P. J. (1992). Sociology, environment, and modernity: Ecological modernization as a theory of social change. *Society and Natural Resources, 5*(4), 323–344.

———, Mol, A. P. J., and Buttel, F. H. (Eds.). (2006). *Governing environmental flows: Global challenges to social theory.* MIT Press.

Stewart, F. (1985). *Planning to meet basic needs*. Palgrave Macmillan Publishers.

Streeten, P. (1981). The distinctive features of a Basic-Needs approach to development. In P. Streeten (Ed.), *Development perspectives* (pp. 334–365). The MacMillan Press, Ltd.

Streeten, P. P., and Burki, S. J. (1978). Basic needs: Some issues. *World Development, 6*(3), 411–421.

———., Burki, S. J., ul-Haq, M., Hicks, N., and Stewart, F. (1981). *First things first: Meeting basic human needs in developing countries.* Oxford University Press.

Swamy, R. (2017). Humanitarianism and unequal exchange. *Journal of World-Systems Research, 23*(2), 353–371.

Tarnoff, C. (2018). *The Marshall Plan: Design, accomplishments, and significance* (CRS Report 7–5700). Congressional Research Service. https://fas.org/sgp/crs/row/R45079.pdf

Thomas, C. (2001). Global governance, development and human security: Exploring the links. *Third World Quarterly, 22*(2), 159–175.

Thombs, R. P. (2018). The transnational tilt of the treadmill and the role of trade openness on carbon emissions: A comparative international study, 1965–2010. *Sociological Forum, 33*(2), 1–21.

Tikhomirov, E. (1999). Epidemiology and distribution of plague. In D. T. Dennis, K. L. Gage, N. Gratz, J. D. Poland, and E. Tikhomirov (Eds.), *Plague manual: Epidemiology, distribution, surveillance, and control* (pp. 11–41). World Health Organization.

Toke, D. (2011). *Ecological modernisation and renewable energy*. Palgrave Macmillan.

Trope, Y., and Liberman, N. (2010). Construal-level theory of psychological distance. *Psychological Review, 117*(2), 440–463.

Truman, H. (1949, January 20). *Inaugural address*. https://www.presidency.ucsb.edu/documents/inaugural-address-4

UNCTADstat. (2021a). UNCTAD Data Center. https://unctadstat.unctad.org/EN/Index.html

———. (2021b). UNCTAD Data Center. https://unctadstat.unctad.org/EN/Classifications/DimSitcRev3Products_Tdr_Hierarchy.pdf

———. (2021c). UNCTAD Data Center. https://unctadstat.unctad.org/EN/Classifications/DimSitcRev3Products_DsibSpecialGroupings_Hierarchy.pdf

Ungar, S. (1992). The rise and (relative) decline of global warming as a social problem. *Sociological Quarterly 33*(4), 483–501.

United Nations. (2019). *World population prospects 2019*. https://www.un.org/en/development/desa/population/publications/database/index.asp

United Nations Development Programme. (2003). *Human development report, 2003: Millennium development goals: A compact among nations to end human poverty.* Palgrave Macmillan.

———. (2011). *Human development report, 2011: Sustainability and equity: A better future for all.* Palgrave Macmillan.

———. (2015). Training material for producing national human development reports. United Nations Development Programme. http://hdr.undp.org/sites/default/files/hdi_training.pdf

———. (2019). *Human Development Index*. United Nations Development Programme. http://hdr.undp.org/en/content/human-development-index-hdi

———. (2020). *Human development report, 2020: The next frontier: Human development and the Anthropocene.* Palgrave Macmillan.

United Nations Environment Programme. (2011). *Keeping track of our changing environment: From Rio to Rio+20 (1992–2012).* United Nations Environment Programme.

United Nations Food and Agriculture Organization. (2010). *The state of world fisheries and aquaculture, 2010.* United Nations Food and Agriculture Organization.

———. (2012). *FAOStat.* http://faostat.fao.org/site/291/default.aspx

———. (2017). *The future of food and agriculture: Trends and challenges.* United Nations Food and Agriculture Organization.

———. (2017). *The Global Carbon Project*. https://www.icos-cp.eu/science-and-impact/global-carbon-budget/2017

———. (2018a). *Land use, irrigation, and agricultural practices—definitions.* http://www.fao.org/fileadmin/templates/ess/ess_test_folder/Definitions/Land_Use_Definitions_FAOSTAT.xlsx

———. (2018b). *The state of the world fisheries and aquaculture: Meeting the Sustainable Development Goals*. United Nations Food and Agriculture Organization.

———. (2021). Global Capture Production 1950–2019. FIGIS. https://www.fao.org/fishery/en/topic/166235?lang=en

United States Bureau of the Census. (1949). *Statistical abstract of the United States* (seventieth ed.). US Government Printing Office.

———. (1962). *Statistical abstract of the United States* (eighty-third ed.). US Government Printing Office.

Urry, J. (2000). *Sociology beyond societies: Mobilities for the twenty-first century*. Routledge Publishers.

V-Dem (2021a). V-Dem: Codebook, version 11.1. https://www.v-dem.net/en/data/reference-material-v11

———. (2021b). The V-Dem Project. https://v-dem.net/about/v-dem-project/

Vitousek, P. M., Ehrlich, P. R., Ehrlich, A. H., and Matson, P. A. (1986). Human appropriation of the products of photosynthesis: Nearly 40% of potential terrestrial net primary productivity is used directly, co-opted, or foregone because of human activities. *BioScience, 36*(6), 368–373.

Vlachou, A. (2004). Capitalism and ecological sustainability: The shaping of environmental policies. *International Review of Political Economy, 11*(5), 926–952.

Wallerstein, I. M. (1974a). *The modern world system: Capitalist agriculture and the origins of the European world-economy in the sixteenth century.* Academic Press.

———. (1974b). The rise and future demise of the world capitalist system: Concepts for comparative analysis. *Comparative Studies in Society and History, 16*(4), 387–415.

———. (1976). Semi-peripheral countries and the contemporary world crisis. *Theory and Society, 3*(4), 461–483.

———. (1979). *The capitalist world-economy*. Cambridge University Press.

———. (2002). The itinerary of World-Systems Analysis: Or, how to resist becoming a theory. In J. Berger and M. Zelditch, Jr. (Eds.), *New directions in contemporary sociological theory* (pp. 358–376). Rowman & Littlefield.

———. (2004). *World -systems analysis: An introduction.* Duke University Press.

Wallis, V. (2010). Beyond "Green Capitalism." *Monthly Review, 61*(9), 32–48. https://monthlyreview.org/2010/02/01/beyond-green-capitalism

Wang, Y., Zhou, T., Chen, H., and Rong, Z. (2019). Environmental homogenization or heterogenization? The effects of globalization on carbon dioxide emissions, 1970–2014. *Sustainability, 11*(10), 2752.

Weisskopf, T. (1972). The impact of foreign capital inflow on domestic savings in underdeveloped countries. *Journal of International Economics, 2*(1), 25–38.

Whitford, A. B., and Wong, K. (2009). Political and social foundations for environmental sustainability. *Political Research Quarterly, 62*(1), 190–204.

Wiedmann, T., Lenzen, M., Keyßer, L. T., and Steinberger, J. K. (2020). Scientists' warning on affluence. *Nature Communications, 11*(3107), 1–10.

Williams, G. P. (2013). Special contribution: Interview with Immanuel Wallerstein: Retrospective on the origins of world-systems analysis, *Journal of World-Systems Research, 19*(2), 202–210.

Williamson, J. B. (1990). What Washington means by policy reform. In J. B. Williamson (Ed.), *Latin American adjustment: How much has happened?* (pp. 7–40). Peterson Institute for International Economics.

———. (2005). The strange history of the Washington Consensus. *Journal of Post Keynesian Economics, 27*(2), 195–206.

Willis, K. (2013, February). *Development theory*. Oxford Bibliographies. https://www.oxfordbibliographies.com/display/document/obo-9780199874002/obo-9780199874002-0007.xml

Wong, M. L. (2012). The developmental state in ecological modernization and the politics of environmental framings: The case of Singapore and implications for East Asia. *Nature and Culture, 7*(1), 95–119.

Wooldridge, J. M. (2010). *Econometric analysis of cross section and panel data*. MIT Press.

World Commission on Environment and Development. (1987). *Our common future*. Oxford University Press.

York, R. (2009). The challenges of measuring environmental sustainability: Comment on "Political and social foundations for environmental sustainability." *Political Research Quarterly, 62*(1), 205–208.

———, Rosa, E. A., and Dietz, T. (2003). Footprints on the earth: The environmental consequences of modernity. *American Sociological Review, 68*(2), 279–300.

———. (2010). Ecological modernization theory: Theoretical and empirical challenges. In M. R. Redclift and G. Woodgate (Eds.), *The international handbook of environmental sociology* (pp. 77–90). Edward Elgar Publishing.

Zahran, S., Kim, E., Chen, X., and Lubell, M. (2007). Ecological development and global climate change: A cross-national study of Kyoto Protocol ratification. *Society and Natural Resources, 20*(1), 37–55.

Index

About the Author

Bret L. Billet is professor of political science and co-coordinator of the International Relations and Environmental Science and Studies programs at Wartburg College, in Waverly, Iowa. He has also taught at Dar Al-Hekma University in Saudi Arabia, the University of Cincinnati, and Miami University. He is the author of several books, including *Cultural Relativism in the Face of the West*, *Modernization Theory and Economic Development*, and *Direct Foreign Investment Behavior of Multinational Corporations in Developing Areas*, and he coauthored *America's National Pastime*. He has authored several articles dealing with development and democracy in the developing world.

www.ingramcontent.com/pod-product-compliance
Ingram Content Group UK Ltd.
Pitfield, Milton Keynes, MK11 3LW, UK
UKHW041452071026
15587UKWH00010B/771

9 781498 579575